Words That Bind

WORDS THAT BIND

Judicial Review and the Grounds of Modern Constitutional Theory

JOHN ARTHUR

WESTVIEW PRESS

Boulder • San Francisco • Oxford

Published in 1995 in the United States of America by Westview Press, Inc., 5500 Central Avenue, Boulder, Colorado 80301-2877, and in the United Kingdom by Westview Press, 36 Lonsdale Road, Summertown, Oxford OX2 7EW

Library of Congress Cataloging-in-Publication Data
Arthur, John, 1946–
  Words that bind : judicial review and the grounds of modern constitutional theory / John Arthur.
      p.   cm.
  Includes bibliographical references and index.
  ISBN 0-8133-2348-7 (hc). — ISBN 0-8133-2349-5 (pbk.)
  1. Judicial review—United States.   2. United States—Constitutional law—Interpretation and construction.   I. Title.
KF4575.A97   1995
347.73'12—DC20
[347.30712]
                                                                    94-29699
                                                                         CIP

Printed and bound in the United States of America

10   9   8   7   6   5   4   3   2   1

For Bob Gleason:
fly fisherman, teacher, uncle, friend—
and a man of great courage

Contents

Preface

This book is about the philosophical grounding of modern constitutional theory; more particularly, it is an extended discussion of the theory behind judicial review. Why, I will ask, should today's elected officials be bound by words of a document written more than two centuries ago as interpreted by nine unelected judges? Each of the five theories I discuss—original intent, democratic proceduralism, utilitarianism, Critical Legal Studies, and democratic contractualism—is described and evaluated in terms of its philosophical commitments as well as its (sometimes only implicit) vision of the justification of judicial review and the nature of constitutional interpretation. Although three of the interpretive theories—original intent, democratic proceduralism, and Critical Legal Studies—are familiar, at least in broad outline, to legal theorists, less attention has been paid to the philosophical assumptions and arguments on which each rests. Utilitarianism and contractualism, on the other hand, are well-developed and familiar political theories, but their implications for our understanding of judicial review and constitutional interpretation have heretofore not been fully explored. The book's central purpose, then, is to weave together political philosophy and legal theory by showing how disagreements among various theories of constitutional interpretation depend on deeper, philosophical disputes about the purposes of judicial review and the justification of democratic government itself.

Many individuals and institutions have provided valuable help to me in writing this book. I first became interested in questions of constitutional interpretation while attending a National Endowment for the Humanities (NEH) seminar directed by Walter Murphy in 1983 at Princeton University. I later was lucky enough to get a Law and Liberal Arts Fellowship at Harvard Law School, where I first began working seriously on the manuscript. Most recently I attended another NEH seminar, this one directed by Robert Audi at the University of Nebraska, where I completed the project. Many people have therefore contributed to its development—some wittingly and some not. I especially want to thank Lew Sargentich, director of Harvard Law School's Law and Liberal Arts Program, for extending my stay at the law school for a second year. Lew's considerable philosophical and legal abilities were also a real benefit to me in the early stages of the book. Others to whom I wish to express special thanks are Robert Audi, Paul Finkelman, Mel Leffler, Frank Michelman, Jim Montmarquet, Richard Nunan, Richard Parker,

Martin Perlmutter, John Rawls, and Cass Sunstein. Ron Fiscus, who has since tragically died, was a personal inspiration as well as a thoughtful critic. I have also had the benefit of comments by various students at Binghamton, including especially the participants in my seminars on constitutional democracy. But most importantly I wish to thank my wife, Amy Shapiro, for taking time from her busy law practice to read and comment on the book as well as for her unfailing encouragement.

John Arthur
Binghamton, New York

Introduction

One of the interesting aspects of American political and intellectual history is the bitter disagreement that often surrounds the U.S. Constitution.[1] The disputes began early; an opponent of the Constitution's adoption, William Manning, wrote in 1798 that he had "little doubt that the Convention who made [the Constitution] intended to destroy our free governments by it, or else they would never have spent four Months in making such an inexplicit thing."[2] Debate continued in the nineteenth century, as the country argued and eventually went to war over slavery.[3] In 1854 abolitionist William Lloyd Garrison famously described the Constitution as a "Covenant with Death and an Agreement with Hell." Burning a copy of the Constitution, he proclaimed, "So perish all compromises with tyranny."[4]

At other times Americans have treated their constitution with respect and even reverence, often turning it into a secular, democratic icon. Former Supreme Court Justice William O. Douglas expressed that sentiment in 1972: "The Supreme Court is really the keeper of the conscience. And the conscience is the Constitution."[5] Even Frederick Douglass, who as a former slave had as much reason to despise the Constitution as anybody could have, wrote of it admiringly. Where the Constitution is susceptible of two meanings, he said

> the one making it accomplish an innocent purpose, and the other a wicked purpose, we must in all cases adopt that which makes it accomplish an innocent purpose. Again, the details of a law are to be interpreted in light of the declared objects sought by the law. ... I only ask you to look at the American Constitution in the light of [these principles], and you will see with me that no man is guaranteed a right of property in man, under the provisions of that instrument.[6]

Among the explanations for these conflicting attitudes, besides the Constitution's early approval of slavery, is the well-known and intractable philosophical dilemma of democratic rule versus individual rights—ideals that have been central themes of American political culture since before there even *was* a U.S. Constitution. In the Declaration of Independence, Thomas Jefferson attacked Britain's rule over the colonies with a ringing endorsement of the "self-evident" truth that governments derive their just powers from the "consent of the governed." In the same document, however, he also spoke of the "inalienable rights" of individuals to life, liberty, and the pursuit of happiness. The Constitution's Preamble reflects similar commitments, promising both to "promote the general welfare" as well as to "secure the blessings of liberty" even for those, presumably, whose actions are believed to oppose the common good.

Contributing still more to this dispute about the purposes of government is the difficult task, faced since the beginning of the Republic, of governing diversity. Facing religious persecution in their homelands, many colonial settlers had come to North America hoping to find if not acceptance, then at least tolerance. Today that process is accelerating; there are now over two hundred religions represented in the United States, and some predict that early in the next century the descendants of the European settlers will themselves become a minority as Irish-, English-, German-, French-, Russian-, Italian-, and Jewish-Americans are joined by growing numbers of people whose roots extend from China and Viet Nam to Africa, the Islamic Middle East, and Latin America. These people bring with them to the United States an extraordinary array of values, religions, and political ideals—a fact that has been a source of strength and vitality.

Democratic processes in which representative assemblies are chosen by all the people in competitive and open elections have seemed to many the natural solution to the problem of governing people with conflicting moral and political views that are often made more intense by differences of race, religion, culture, and gender. Tolerance and open debate, followed by a binding vote in which all are allowed to participate as equals, often seem the only real possibilities. So given democratic traditions emphasizing popular consent combined with the practical need to find a common constitution acceptable to a widely diverse population, it would appear that the natural solution is a majoritarian system in which the people's representatives are sovereign.

But that vision of majority rule is not the U.S. system. Besides making it difficult for an electoral majority to work its will by dividing power among three different, independently chosen branches at the national level as well as between the national government and the states, the Constitution also includes a Bill of Rights and other explicit limits on what lawmakers may do, enforced by the practice of judicial review. Viewed in terms of the traditional commitment to democratic institutions, the practice of judicial review thus seems especially anomalous, which explains in part why the *methods* of constitutional interpretation themselves are often hotly disputed. Unelected Supreme Court justices, appointed for life, are empowered to invalidate laws passed by representatives of every state and district, and to do so in the name of a two-hundred-year-old constitution. Except for its familiarity, and the agreeableness that creates, judicial review seems contrary to the fundamental principle that government must be based on popular consent.

American ambivalence about democratic rule is mirrored in attitudes toward individual rights. Despite the Declaration's rhetoric, it was not until well into the twentieth century that the Supreme Court aggressively began to enforce the Bill of Rights on behalf of unpopular political and religious minorities in the face of popular pressure and restrictive laws. Nor, as we will see, has the philosophical grounding of individual rights been either clearly articulated or widely accepted—especially in light of contemporary society's rejection of the religious foundation of natural law as the source of such rights.

In light of these twin commitments to popular rule and individual rights, it is not surprising that controversy has surrounded both the purposes and methods of judicial review.[7] Discussion of these issues often centers on two catch phrases: "judicial restraint" and "judicial activism." Defenders of judicial restraint claim that controversial political decisions should be left to elected representatives. Judges, it is often said, should limit themselves to interpreting the law and resist the temptation to allow personal values to infect their legal decisions. Interpretive "neutrality" is thus thought to be the hallmark of any legitimate exercise of judicial review. Others, however, reject judicial restraint and neutrality in favor of judicial activism, arguing that judges should interpret the Constitution in accord with its spirit, as a "living" document, and aggressively defend individual rights against the tyranny of the majority. As will become apparent, however, there is far more richness and complexity to the debate than these popular slogans suggest.

The first of the five interpretive theories I will consider, original intent, insists judges must set aside their personal values and moral ideals, deferring instead to the elected branches. Judicial review is legitimate only in cases where history clearly shows the framers intended to limit the people's representatives. Originalism thus claims that the meaning of vague phrases such as "freedom of speech," "free exercise of religion," and "equal protection of the laws" are fixed by the specific, historical meanings intended by those who wrote or adopted the document and its amendments. Unless the framers had in mind to limit Congress in a specific way, according to originalism, the Constitution is silent and representatives are free to legislate as they see fit.

Other theories propose very different accounts of the role of judicial review in a constitutional democracy. Democratic proceduralism shares the originalist's commitment to judicial neutrality, though its appeal is to the political virtues of democratic procedures themselves, not to the framers' intentions. Judicial review, according to the proceduralist, serves primarily as a check on the tendency of governmental officials to pass laws that protect their own political positions at the expense of fair and open democratic processes. The right to vote and freedom of speech are therefore placed at center stage by proceduralists committed to using judicial review to protect and promote democracy. Underlying this proceduralist account of judicial review, I argue, is a conception of the democratic process as a self-legitimizing political decision procedure—a position that I will consider in detail.

Defenders of Critical Legal Studies (CLS) reject the claim, advanced by both original intent and democratic proceduralism, that constitutional interpretation must be insulated from a judge's political and moral goals. But because law and politics cannot be distinguished, argues CLS, the law is indeterminate and judges are free to exercise wide discretion. That leads CLS, I argue, to legal pragmatism.

Judges have no alternative except to focus on the future, reflecting pragmatically about how they can best serve whatever political ideals they feel are worthy. Because neither legal nor moral rights "exist," concludes Critical Legal Studies, judicial precedents relying on such rights do not constrain judicial power.

The last two theories, utilitarianism and democratic contractualism, reject both the wide discretion defended by Critical Legal Studies and the demands of originalism and proceduralism that constitutional interpreters eschew their own moral views in favor of either history or democratic processes. Utilitarians argue that judicial review is best understood in the context of a larger commitment by government to promote the general welfare. My discussion of utilitarianism includes the nature of welfare, the motivation behind the utilitarian's commitment to maximizing it, the relationship between economic wealth and welfare, the nature of rights, and the role judicial review would play in the utilitarian theory.

Despite its power and attractiveness, however, I argue that utilitarianism ultimately fails, and I defend instead a contractualist understanding of judicial review and constitutional interpretation. Rather than thinking of judges as enforcing the original terms of the social contract, perfecting democratic processes, acting pragmatically to make a better future, or working to increase the general welfare, democratic contractualism argues that judicial review should be understood as part of a larger commitment to enforce the fair terms of the social contract that, hypothetically, would be adopted by free and equal persons deliberating in what Madison termed a "temperate moment." Drawing on the writings of James Madison and Immanuel Kant as well as more recent work in the social contract tradition, I first describe the philosophical grounding of democratic contractualism. I then outline the terms such a contract would contain, turning finally to the role judicial review should play in such a system and the implications of the theory for constitutional interpretation. In that way, I argue, democratic contractualism offers a workable and attractive account of judicial review and constitutional interpretation—a view that is not, I conclude, vulnerable to feminist charges that it ignores issues of gender or reflects a distinctively male vision of government and politics.

The first three approaches, original intent, democratic proceduralism, and Critical Legal Studies, have grown mainly in legal soil. Since they were developed for the most part by judges and lawyers, my major task here is to explore their philosophical and theoretical commitments, including especially their vision of the justification of democratic government. Utilitarianism and contractualism, on the other hand, were developed in a largely philosophical context, so here the focus is legal, requiring an account of each theory's conception of the purposes of judicial review and the nature of constitutional interpretation. These efforts are largely constructive, since it is rare for defenders of legal theories to delve deeply into their political and moral assumptions, just as political philosophers often pay scant attention to constitutional and interpretive issues. Then, having filled out the philosophical and legal commitments inherent in each theory, I assess each one. Is the philosophical picture of judicial review in a democratic regime that I have constructed the best that can be done for the theory? Are its specific interpretive recommendations coherent and workable? Is this theory successful in weaving together an attractive vision of constitutional interpretation, judicial review, and democratic government? Focusing the debate in this way, I will argue, extends and deepens our understanding of disputes about judicial activism and constitutional interpretation while at the same time shedding new light on familiar political theories such as utilitarianism and contractualism.

Contractualism has many defenders these days, and much of what I say about it will be familiar to political philosophers working in the area. So although I do suggest important revisions of contractualist theory in light of the philosophical and political discussion of democratic processes, the book's most important original contributions lie elsewhere.[8] Although it is common for legal scholars to write about constitutional interpretation, it is rare for them to think in great depth about the philosophical assumptions on which their theories rest; and though abstract, philosophical conceptions of justice are familiar, and their theoretical implications for judicial review are also rarely explored in the sort of depth that is normally expected from philosophers. Yet, I will argue, we can learn much about originalism and other interpretive theories as we construct and then assess their political assumptions, just as our understanding of political theories, including utilitarianism and social contract theory, is extended and deepened by weighing their implications for judicial review and constitutional law. Indeed, a complete assessment of both interpretive and political theories must depend, in part, on the results of inquiries into their philosophical and legal implications. Before turning to the book's main themes, however, it is important to look briefly at the historical origins of judicial review. Although not clearly called for in the Constitution, judicial review was brilliantly defended by Chief Justice John Marshall; yet it remained controversial for years. That history, which includes discussions of the purposes of judicial review, provides important background for subsequent investigations into the philosophical and political grounds of constitutional theory.

1

Enforcing the Social Contract: Original Intent

Members of the Constitutional Convention met in Philadelphia in secret, fearful that word of their proposals would escape and the public outcry would doom the new government from the start. When work was finally completed and the proposed constitution published, it spawned widespread, heated controversy. Debate about the new constitution uncovered deep divisions—over the purposes of government, the dangers of majority rule, and the need to respect minority rights.

Many felt the new government was anti-democratic. Of its three branches, it provided for direct election of only one part of one of them, the House of Representatives. The proposed constitution also created vast powers for the new national government, powers that many felt would be exercised at the expense of the more democratic, less remote state and local governments. How were these new powers to be defined and exercised, many wondered. And what, exactly, would be the relationship between the national government and the states?

Answers were not to be found within the four corners of the document itself; the proposed constitution did little to specify the powers it conferred or the relationships among the branches it created. That vagueness occasioned especially sharp criticism and contributed to the demand that a Bill of Rights be adopted by the first Congress, which would set limits on the powers of the national government.

I begin this chapter with an account of how Chief Justice Marshall undertook to establish and justify the Supreme Court's power of judicial review over Congress.[1] Then I turn to the first theory of interpretation to be considered, original intent, and to two prominent defenders of originalism—Robert Bork and William Rehnquist. In defending original intent, I argue, these judges assume a contractualist account of government that, when spelled out, is implausible on its own terms and unable to offer an attractive, workable conception of judicial review and constitutional interpretation.

The Origins of Judicial Review

The role of the judiciary is the least well-defined of the three branches of government: Article III, which establishes the courts, speaks of "judicial power" that is "vested in one supreme court" and of the power of the Court to hear cases "arising under" the Constitution of the United States. The nature and limits of judicial power are not delineated, nor is it explained which cases "arise under" the Constitution.[2] Indeed, the Constitution neither explicitly gives the federal courts authority to overturn statutes passed by Congress and state legislatures nor states that judicial review is *not* among the Court's functions.

Yet despite the lack of a clear mandate for judicial review, the Supreme Court, exercising that power, has left a large mark on American history.[3] Within the past half-century the Court has overturned state laws criminalizing abortions and contraceptives, prevented prosecutors from using illegally acquired evidence, and prevented states from requiring school prayers or maintaining segregated educational facilities and structuring electoral procedures in favor of majority racial groups. At the same time, the Court has refused to prevent executions or the criminal prosecution of people for private, consensual sexual acts thought unnatural by a state's majority. The power to invalidate legislative enactments on grounds of unconstitutionality has often put the Supreme Court at the center of this nation's most divisive and intractable political issues. Disagreement over the Supreme Court's power is as old as the Constitution itself; indeed it was among the important disputes between those who supported adoption of the new constitution and their anti-federalist opponents.

It was anything but a foregone conclusion that the Constitution produced in the hot Philadelphia summer of 1787 would be adopted at the various conventions called for that purpose in the states. Besides *The Federalist Papers*,[4] a series of articles written by James Madison, Alexander Hamilton, and John Jay for New York newspapers encouraging adoption of the Constitution, many others opposed ratification. Often these anti-federalists took aim at Article III and the wide powers it proposed for the judiciary.[5] The new courts, they claimed, were but one more example of the centralization of power at the national level.

Writing in 1788 to the people of New York state, an anti-federalist named Robert Yates, who wrote under the name of "Brutus," explained his reservations about the powers that would be placed in all branches of the new national government, including federal judges. Such judges, he said, would be rendered "totally independent, both of the people and the legislature, both with respect to their offices and salaries. No errors they commit can be corrected by any power above them, if any such power there be, nor can they be removed from office for making ever so many erroneous adjudications."[6] But Brutus's worries were not limited to the lack of accountability of these new judges; he also believed that the Constitution gave them far too much power. Judges, he wrote, "are authorized to determine all questions that may arise upon the meaning of the constitution in law ... (and) also equity. ... The judicial power will operate to effect, in the most certain, yet silent and imperceptible manner, what is evidently the tendency of the constitution:—I mean, the entire subversion of the legislative, executive and judicial powers of the individual states."[7] These comments have a strikingly contemporary ring: Judges were to be unelected, they would serve for lifetime terms, and their salaries were beyond the control of the Congress. And what's more, the Constitution suggests they also have the power not only to interpret laws passed by Congress but, more ominously, the Constitution itself—all without review by other branches.

There were two alternatives available to those who rejected judicial review but nonetheless wanted laws to be subject to the Constitution. One, which might be termed legislative review, would give a legislative body final authority over questions regarding the meaning of the Constitution. It would then be up to the people to reject or accept the legislature's judgment about the constitutionality of laws at the ballot box. Such legislative review was advocated by James Madison and other supporters of the Virginia Plan. That plan, presented as a proposed draft constitution to the convention, recommended that the U.S. Congress be given the power not only to decide on the constitutionality of its own laws but also be allowed to negate state laws it considered unconstitutional.[8]

Besides calling for Congress to decide the constitutionality of laws, the Virginia Plan also offered a second proposal that could serve as an alternative to judicial review. It recommended that a "Council of Revision" be created with the power to negate acts of both Congress and state legislatures that in its view were unconstitutional. The full Virginia Plan thus would have allowed two bodies, Congress and the Council of Revision, to declare laws unconstitutional. Should the Congress and the Council of Revision disagree about the constitutionality of a state law, then presumably the electoral process would decide which view would prevail.

How the alternatives to judicial review might have worked, we do not know, but what does seem clear from the early disagreements is that judicial review was deeply controversial. Indeed, Madison himself felt that some other method of regulating states would work better. After the convention failed to adopt the Virginia Plan's proposal, Madison wrote a letter to Jefferson describing why he thought this failure was a fundamental defect in the new document. The convention's refusal to give Congress power to veto state laws meant, he said, that an indispensable element was lost in the battle to protect federal power against the states and to protect "individuals agst. (state) encroachments on their rights."[9] So although he strongly believed the power to interpret the Constitution and overturn invalid state laws should be built into the structure, Madison did not believe the judiciary was the best repository of that power. This was partly because such "parchment barriers" had not proved effective in the states[10] and partly because he did not think the judicial branch should be "paramount in fact to the Legislature, which was never intended and can never be proper."[11]

The classic federalist statement supporting judicial review is found in "Federalist Number 78," written by Alexander Hamilton. The interpretation of laws, he says, is "the proper and peculiar province of the courts. A constitution is, in fact, and must be regarded by judges as fundamental law. It therefore belongs to them to ascertain its meaning, as well as the meaning of any particular act proceeding from the legislative body."[12] But *why* should the Constitution be regarded as fundamental law? The answer, says Hamilton, is that the Constitution, which represents the will of the people, takes precedence over any law enacted by representatives. "If there should happen to be any irreconcilable variance between the two, that which has the superior obligation and validity ought, of course, to be preferred to the statute, the intention of the people to the intention of their agents."[13] It is a premise of constitutional government, says Hamilton, that Congress should be bound by the will of the people as expressed in the Constitution, and judicial review is thus inherent in the very idea of a written constitution adopted by the people. These ideas, we will see, were extended by Chief Justice Marshall in his successful defense of judicial review.

Besides Hamilton, judicial review also had strong support among others, including (according to Madison's notes at the convention) Luther Martin and Eldridge Gerry.[14] Noted constitutional law scholar Edwin Corwin perhaps summarized the situation best when testifying before Congress in 1937: "The people who say the framers intended [judicial review] are talking nonsense, and the people who say they did not intend it are [also] talking nonsense."[15]

Despite these controversies, the Supreme Court won the power of judicial review of Congress under the guidance of the first great chief justice, John Marshall, and in the process provided what is widely regarded as the classical defense of the practice. But besides being a brilliant legal scholar, Marshall was also a clever politician—a skill that proved of great value in the early, politically formative days of the national government.

Marbury v. Madison was decided in 1803, more than a decade after the Constitution was adopted. The case arose after Congress created a number of new judicial positions[16] and President Adams chose, with the advice and consent of the Senate, a man named William Marbury to receive one of them. President Adams signed Marbury's commission before leaving office, but the document was not physically delivered to Marbury before Adams's term expired.[17] Then, when he took over from Adams, President Jefferson withheld the commission, refusing to allow Marbury to take his position. Marbury later sued James Madison, now Jefferson's secretary of state, asking that the Supreme Court issue a "writ of mandamus" requiring Madison (and Jefferson) to deliver the commission.

The central issue in the case was whether Congress had exceeded its constitutional authority by passing the Judiciary Act of 1789, giving the Supreme Court the right to issue such writs of mandamus. If Congress did exceed its constitutional authority, then the Supreme Court's hands were tied and it could not issue the writ. Behind this question, of course, is the deeper one of the power of the Court to determine if an act of Congress is unconstitutional, in this case a segment of the Judiciary Act of 1789.

Marshall's opinion in *Marbury* is organized around three questions. First, Marshall asks if William Marbury has a right to the commission. If so, then the second question arises: Does he also have a legal remedy that will vindicate the right? Then, third: Is Marbury entitled to the remedy he has requested from the Supreme Court, that is, does the Court have the power to issue the writ of mandamus?

Marshall's first conclusion, that William Marbury indeed has a right to the commission, rests on the fact that the president and the Senate had already deliberated on the nomination and the commission had been signed. The appointment, says Marshall, had been made valid when the seal of the United States was affixed to the commission. In answer to the second question, whether the law provides a remedy for this violation of Marbury's right, Marshall writes: "The very essence of civil liberty certainly consists in the right of every individual to claim the protection of the laws, whenever he receives an injury. ... The government of the United States has been emphatically termed a government of laws, and not of men. It will certainly cease to deserve this high appellation, if the laws furnish no remedy for the violation of a vested legal right."[18] For a government to fail to provide a remedy when it has found a right to be violated would mean, says Marshall, that the government does not respect the ideal of the rule of law; law would become arbitrary power, protecting some but not all of its citizens' rights.

The key step in Marshall's argument is the third. Having established Marbury's right, and the legitimacy of his claim that government must provide a remedy, Marshall then turns to the question of whether Marbury is entitled to the particular remedy he requested: a writ issued by the Supreme Court based on the authority given it by Congress. Marshall's answer is that despite Marbury's strong claim on the merits, the Supreme Court does not have power under the Constitution to issue a writ of mandamus. Such a writ exceeds the power of the Court because, says Marshall, it does not fall within the jurisdiction established for the Court by the Constitution.

Under Article III, the Constitution gives the Court power to exercise original jurisdiction in cases affecting ambassadors and other consuls or where a state is a party. Otherwise, however, the Supreme Court is to exercise appellate jurisdiction. The problem, then, is that this case does not involve ambassadors or consuls, but neither does it involve an appeal from a lower court. The Supreme Court is being asked, pursuant to powers granted it by Congress under the Judiciary Act of 1789, to issue a writ of mandamus in a case where the Constitution forbids it to do so.[19] Congress lacks the power, Marshall concludes, to give the Court blanket power to issue such writs of mandamus except in those areas where the Court is given explicit jurisdiction under Article III. Put another way, what Marshall says is that although Marbury has a right and thus must have a remedy, he came to the wrong court; he should first have gone to a lower court and then, had he lost, appealed to the Supreme Court. Congress lacks constitutional authority to extend the Supreme Court's original jurisdiction beyond the narrow categories in Article III. Only in the last part of the opinion does Marshall consider why the *Court* rather than another branch should have the power to pass on the constitutionality of congressional enactments, as he had just done.

Before turning to Marshall's defense of the Court's authority to enforce its interpretation of the Constitution on an unwilling Congress, it is worth pausing to note his political shrewdness. He does not mention the question of judicial review until after establishing that Marbury has a right to the commission and that government should somehow afford him a remedy. He has thereby shown that the Court *wants* to issue the writ. Then by holding that the Court lacks the power to issue the writ, he claims for the Court the power of judicial review. So although Marshall is claiming vast judicial power with one hand, he is limiting the power of the Court with the other (by denying it the power to issue a writ of mandamus as provided for by the Judiciary Act). In that way, Marshall minimized the feeling that the decision in *Marbury v. Madison* was a grab for power by the judiciary.

The opinion is politically shrewd in another way. Unlike other instances where the Court might have asserted judicial review, this opinion does not require the cooperation of another branch: The Court simply found that it lacked the power Congress tried to give it and refused to issue the writ. This left those in the other branches who opposed judicial review, and they were many, without a means to resist. Had Marshall ordered the Congress, for example, not to exercise a certain power on constitutional grounds, then Congress would have had the option simply to ignore the Supreme Court's opinion, claiming that the Court was overstepping its authority. Here, however, it was unnecessary for either of the other branches to do anything in order for the decision to stand, just as there was little they could do to block it.[20]

Political strategies aside, we still have to weigh the legal and political arguments Marshall makes in support of his claim that the federal courts can exercise judicial review over acts of Congress.[21] He introduces the subject with the following observation: "The question, whether an act, repugnant to the constitution, can become the law of the land, is a question deeply interesting to the United States; but, happily, not of an intricacy proportioned to its interest. It seems only necessary to recognize certain principles, supposed to have been long and well established, to decide it."[22] What are these "certain principles ... long and well established" that make the argument so easy? He begins by observing that the people have established the Constitution and that this "original and supreme will organizes the government, and assigns to different departments their respective powers." Those powers, he stresses, are defined and limited, and it is a proposition "too plain to be contested, that the constitution controls any legislative act repugnant to it."[23]

But supposing this is true, why is it the responsibility of the *Supreme Court* to make the final decision when Congress has acted in a manner inconsistent with the Constitution? One answer, says Marshall,

> is that those who would take the opposite view, holding that the legislature may pass on constitutional questions, take a position incompatible with the principles underlying a written constitution. Those, then, who controvert the principle that the con-

stitution is to be considered, in court, as a paramount law, are reduced to the necessity of maintaining that courts must close their eyes on the constitution, and see only the law. This doctrine would subvert the very foundation of all written constitutions. ... [I]t reduces to nothing what we have deemed the greatest improvement on political institutions, a written constitution.[24]

But is this correct? Does the fact of a written constitution, rather than an unwritten one, require judicial review? It seems clear it does not. An unwritten constitution, existing merely in the form of widely accepted practices that limit legislative authority, might also require judicial review; whether the constitution is written or not does not matter. Similarly, if a system without a written constitution moved to write such limits down, that change would not in itself mandate judicial review.

Nor, second, does the fact that judges take an oath to uphold the Constitution require they be given the power of judicial review, as Marshall also suggested.[25] Presidents, members of Congress, and many others as well also take such an oath, so members of Congress could make the same argument to prove that *they* should have final say about the constitutionality of legislation. The fact that judges take an oath is useless as an argument in favor of judicial review.

That leads to the third and most important argument Marshall offered on behalf of judicial review. Besides suggesting that it follows from the fact of a written constitution or the requirement that judges take an oath to defend the Constitution, Marshall gave another argument, based on Article III, Section 2, of the Constitution. As we have seen, Article III states: "The judicial Power shall extend to all Cases in Law and Equity, arising under this Constitution."[26] Based on this, Marshall concludes, "It is emphatically the province and duty of the judicial department to say what the law is."[27] But Marshall's claim may seem to beg the question. The Constitution does not clearly define "judicial power," nor does it specify which cases "arise under" the Constitution. So what is the basis of the claim that the determination of a law's constitutionality properly belongs in the courts rather than before the electorate, for example?

For the argument to have much plausibility, Marshall must assume the Constitution is law in much the same way as statutes, so the courts should interpret its meaning just as they do ordinary legal enactments passed by Congress under its constitutionally granted powers. But a constitutional rule is obviously more fundamental or basic than an ordinary law enacted in accord with it: Constitutional rules form the basic structure of government, including establishment of the legislature, which is thereby empowered to enact law. The fact that a rule was passed in accord with the procedures outlined in the Constitution (i.e., by Congress rather than, say, the Joint Chiefs of Staff or the president's Cabinet) and does not exceed congressional powers is the U.S. criterion for its legal status. In that sense, constitutional rules are the foundation on which other law rests; constitutional principles and rules exist at a different level than statutes in that they enable us to recognize what is for us valid law.[28] Ought we to conclude, then, that the constitutionality of a properly enacted law is not itself a legal question "arising under" the Constitution but is a different, perhaps political, question?

Marshall rejects that suggestion, explicitly, in his *Marbury* opinion. The Constitution, he points out, is not silent on its own legal status; Article VI, Section 2, states: "This Constitution ... shall be the supreme law of the land." So there is some textual evidence that the Constitution may reasonably be thought of as "law." Does that mean, then, that Marshall's position is secure? Not necessarily, for even if we grant that the Constitution is law, it does not follow that the Supreme Court's exercise of judicial power, understood to include all cases of law arising under the Constitution, must include power to invalidate legislative enactments. For it could be argued that although it is a legal question, the question of whether an act violates the Constitution is *not* a legal question "arising under" the Constitution. How then would that argument go?

Pennsylvania Supreme Court Justice John Gibson wrote a dissenting opinion in 1825 directly attacking Marshall's decision in *Marbury*.[29] Gibson begins with a historical point. "Our judiciary is constructed on the principles of the common law, which enters so essentially into the composition of our social institutions as to be inseparable from them. ... Now what are the powers of the judiciary at the common law? They are those that necessarily arise out of its immediate business; and they are therefore commensurate only with the judicial execution of municipal law ... without extending to anything of a political case whatever."[30] Though of some relevance, the fact that common law judges were not empowered to pass on the constitutionality of Parliamentary enactments is not, in itself, persuasive. The U.S. Constitution differed from the British system in important respects, and so Marshall would surely respond that although much of the common law was adopted in the colonies and eventually by the United States, it was not received in its entirety. Indeed, Marshall has taken care to distinguish the U.S. Constitution, which the people adopted, from the common law system.

Justice Gibson does not rest with history, however. Elsewhere in his opinion he makes a more substantive, political argument against judicial review. "That the judiciary is of superior rank [to the other two branches] has never been pretended, although it has been said to be coordinate. ... It may be said, the power of the legislature, also, is limited by prescribed rules. It is so. But it is, nevertheless, the power of the people, and sovereign as far as it extends. It cannot be said that the judiciary is coordinate merely because it is established by the constitution ... [T]he legislative organ is superior to every other, inasmuch as the power to will and to command, is essentially superior to the power to act and to obey."[31] Justice Gibson suggests a political argument: That we do better, all things considered, if we understand the Constitution to establish the legislative branch as superior. His reason is familiar: Unlike judges, legislators are elected by the people, and since the people are the "sovereign power" their representatives should not be made accountable to anybody but them. That claim is political, rather than textual, since nowhere in the Constitution does it say that the legislative branch, because it represents the people, is superior; but neither, of course, does the Constitution contradict his position. Gibson's argument that Congress is superior, and that judicial review is therefore illegitimate, rests on the premise that it would make good sense philosophically to understand the Constitution in those explicitly democratic terms.[32]

One way to respond to Gibson's claim, though it is not one Marshall himself explicitly made, rests on another political ideal—the rule of law.[33] Inherent in that ideal, it might be claimed, is the notion that nobody should be a judge in her own case. Courts enforce the rule of law by requiring that a neutral judge and unbiased jurors sit in judgment; when either fails to be neutral the legal procedure is compromised.

This ideal is relevant not just when citizens have disputes among themselves or are charged with crimes; it also strengthens Marshall's defense of judicial review against Gibson's claim that judicial review actually undermines the Constitution's claim to political legitimacy. Suppose that Congress has passed a law, the constitutionality of which has been challenged, either as violating a constitutional right of a minority or as exceeding Congress's enumerated powers. Now if Congress rather than the Supreme Court is empowered to pass on the constitutionality of its proposed law, then the members of Congress would in effect be sitting in judgment of themselves, a situation incompatible with the ideal of the rule of law. Congress would be both a party to the dispute, since it enacted the law, and also empowered (assuming no judicial review) to decide whether it did the constitutionally correct thing.

Gibson's point, that Congress represents the people, does not save his argument. When the people enact a law, the constitutionality of which is in dispute, the rule of law requires that a neutral third party decide the dispute. But that means that neither Congress nor the people, as parties to the dispute, should decide the case, any more than the citizen who challenges the law's constitutionality should do it. The Supreme Court, Marshall might then argue, is the natural body to make such decisions since that would preserve the neutrality inherent in the ideal of the rule of law.

It could be responded, of course, that Congress is *not* sitting as a final, arbitrary power deciding the constitutionality of its own laws. Should the majority of voters disagree with Congress's interpretation of the Constitution, they can simply elect others to their seats, and so it is not quite true that members of Congress would act as judges in their own case: In the last analysis it is the electorate, not Congress, that controls Congress. Still, however, though not acting as ultimate authority, Congress is *initially* sitting in judgment of the constitutionality of its own enactment, and that offends the rule of law. Furthermore, if the question of a law's constitutionality is seen as a dispute between the majority of voters (that wants the law enacted and believes it is constitutional) and a minority that regards the law as unconstitutional, then allowing the majority to decide the question (whether directly or through its elected representatives) is just as incompatible with the rule of law as the suggestion that Congress can decide an issue to which *it* is a party.

So although Gibson's argument against judicial review may seem to have considerable merit, the democratic ideals on which it relies must be weighed against the competing ideal of the rule of law. It is open to Marshall and other defenders of judicial review to claim either that Gibson has overstated the importance of the ideal of democratic rule or that when democratic principles conflict with the rule of law the latter takes precedence.

Having said that, however, there is one further point worth noting about Marshall's decision in *Marbury v. Madison* and the rule of law. *Marbury*, of course, addresses the question of judicial review itself, which means that in this case (though not in others) the rule of law argument I offered to defend judicial review actually *cuts against* Marshall's conclusion. Since *Marbury* decides the extent of the Supreme Court's power vis-à-vis other branches, the Court can hardly be thought an uninterested, neutral party. So, although the rule of law argues for the general conclusion reached in *Marbury*, that the judicial branch should pass on a law's constitutionality, it also argues against the Court making that ruling. If, as I have suggested, the principle of the rule of law is crucial for Marshall's argument on behalf of judicial review, then in *Marbury*, at least, the Court ideally should have referred the question of judicial review to a neutral forum rather than deciding the issue itself.

But whatever the legal and philosophical merits of Marshall's *Marbury* opinion, judicial review of Congress (as well as, of course, of state laws) is no longer seriously questioned; relying on it, courts have gone on to strike down a vast array of laws as unconstitutional. Yet even if we grant the legal and philosophical justification I have described and agree that courts are better suited than legislatures to interpret the constitutional limits on legislative power, we still have not found in these discussions the answers to the political and interpretive questions that are our focus. How should responsible judges exercise their power of judicial review? How ought the Constitution be interpreted? In the remainder of this chapter and the chapters that follow, I will pursue these issues by testing the idea that we can deepen our understanding of interpretation and judicial review by constructing and then assessing the normative assumptions lying behind different interpretive theories. The first theory, original intent, rests, I will argue, on a familiar idea that Marshall appealed to in his *Marbury* opinion—that the limits imposed by the Constitution on elected officials are justified because they express the people's will.[34] In assessing it, I begin by identifying the philosophical foundation on which it relies, asking how, exactly, it understands the role of judicial review. That question leads, in turn, to an inquiry into the originalist's understanding of the justification of democratic government in general. Then, finally, I will weigh originalism's specific recommendations regarding constitutional interpretation along with the normative political assumptions about the purposes of judicial review that I have identified and on which originalism rests.

The Constitution as Contract

Constitutional interpretation's focus, of course, is on the words of the text. In *Marbury,* for example, the language whose meaning was in dispute is found in Article III's description of judicial power. Does the statement that the Court is to hear all cases in law and equity "arising under" the Constitution include judicial review, Marshall asks. Originalism's central claim, then, is that where there is dispute about its meaning, the Constitution's language should be interpreted as the framers originally intended: If the framers did not regard executions as "cruel and unusual punishment," for example, then the Eighth Amendment does not prevent states or Congress from imposing them.

We can usefully begin our discussion of originalism where its defenders often start: Why, they ask, have judicial review at all? The idea that an unelected group of judges can overturn laws passed by the people's representatives seems to run counter to one of this nation's most basic ideals—that law should reflect the consent of the governed. Where there is wide diversity of opinion, as there has always been in the United States, why should decisions not be left to the free and open democratic political process? The author of "Federalist Number 39," James Madison, testifies to the importance attached to this Republican ideal: "It is evident that no other form would be reconcilable with the genius of the people of America; with the fundamental principles of the Revolution; or with that honorable determination which animates every votary of freedom to rest all our political experiments on the capacity of mankind for self-government. If the plan of the convention, therefore, be found to depart from the republican character, its advocates must abandon it as no longer defensible."[35] Self-government, says Madison, is the "foundation" of the U.S. republic. Yet if that is true, why should the people's representatives, who far more accurately reflect the diversity of religious and moral ideas found in the nation, be encumbered by the dictates of a written constitution and its nine unrepresentative interpreters? The task of governing over a divided, diverse population seems far better suited to a representative, elected body than to a small group of fortunately situated judges.

These questions have been given new life in the writing of two influential judges: Supreme Court Chief Justice William Rehnquist and former federal appeals court judge and Supreme Court nominee Robert Bork.[36] They have argued that judges must remain morally neutral both out of respect for democratic political processes and on grounds of moral skepticism. Anybody who replaces the framers' understanding of "equal protection," "free exercise of religion," or other fundamental rights with her own simply expresses a personal value or preference. Judges who interfere with the majority's will under the guise of protecting a minority's rights act illegitimately, imposing their own values on the majority. Robert Bork, focusing on the wide diversity of opinion about fundamental issues of religion and morality, explains the reasoning behind these conclusions this way: "Unless we can distinguish forms of gratification, the only course for a principled court is to let the majority have its way ... There is no way of deciding these matters other than by reference to some system of moral or ethical values that has no objective or intrinsic validity of its own and about which men can and do differ … That, by definition, is an inadequate basis for judicial review."[37] Rehnquist expresses a similar view of the wide diversity of values found in the United States and the impossibility of reaching consensus about them: "There is no conceivable way," he writes, "in which I can logically demonstrate to you that the judgments of my conscience are superior to the judgments of your conscience, and vice versa."[38] Constitutional limits on legislatures win social acceptance and legitimacy, according to Rehnquist "neither because of any intrinsic worth nor because of any unique origins in someone's idea of natural justice but instead simply because they have been incorporated in a constitution by the people. … Beyond the Constitution and the laws of our society, there simply is no basis other than the individual conscience of the citizen that may serve as a platform for launching of moral judgments."[39] If logic and ideas of justice cannot be relied on to guide our moral judgments, where do values come from? Rehnquist quotes Oliver Wendell Holmes: "I love granite rocks and barberry bushes, no doubt because with them were my earliest joys that reach back through the past eternity of my life. But while one's experience thus makes certain preferences dogmatic for oneself, recognition of how they came to be so leaves one able to see that others, poor souls, may be equally dogmatic about something else. And this again means skepticism."[40] So given a diverse society whose people have widely divergent beliefs about values and rights, reflecting fundamentally different tastes and attitudes, it is essential that judges avoid reading into the Constitution their own values and preferences. To govern effectively and fairly a diverse population, the Constitution must rely instead on the electoral process, for it provides the best method for resolving issues of public policy in accord with the people's will. When the legislature has expressed its desires in law, it is not up to unelected judges to substitute their own. Judges who do so, he says, "impose by law their value judgments upon fellow citizens who may disagree with those judgments."[41]

But then how can this apparent incompatibility between judicial review and the Constitution's underlying commitment to allowing the legislatures to resolve value conflicts among a diverse and often divided people be resolved? One influential idea, expressed originally by Hamilton and Marshall, rests on the role of the people in forming the Constitution.[42] Describing the principles on which the power of judicial review rests, Marshall notes in *Marbury v. Madison* that it is *the people's will* that established the Constitution, a fact that he then uses to explain why the Constitution controls the legislature. That view echoes Alexander Hamilton's discussion of judicial review in "Federalist Number 78," quoted earlier, which many regard as the classic defense of judicial review. Hamilton sought to answer those who questioned whether the Constitution should be regarded as fundamental law: "If there should happen to be any irreconcilable variance between the two, that which has the superior obligation and validity ought, of course, to be preferred; or, in other words, the constitution ought to be preferred to the statute, the intention of the people to the intention of their agents."[43] The critical point, says Hamilton, is that the Constitution takes precedence over legislative enactments because it represents the intention or will of the people themselves, whereas laws passed by Congress are merely the product of the people's agents. Like other agents, legislators may sometimes fail to act in accord with the will of the people. The English model of *parliamentary* sovereignty has now been replaced with *popular* sovereignty, and the Constitution's power to bind all officials, including the people's elected representatives, expresses that important new idea. It is therefore natural that the proposed Constitution should be referred to the people, as called for in Article VII. Each state was to call a convention for the specific purpose of considering ratification.

This account of constitutional legitimacy has been a powerful one in U.S. history, finding expression in early state court cases as well as the theoretical writings of the federalists. Since the Constitution could not be "adjudged void," said one judge, the Courts were required to declare any act that was "inconsistent with it ... *no law*."[44] It was not for the courts, however, to consider the merits of legislative enactments; their responsibility was simply to compare "the legislative act with the constitution."[45] What this means, said one commentator at the time, is not that the judicial power is superior to the legislature but rather that "the power of the people is superior to both."[46]

The most influential nineteenth-century discussion of judicial review also saw the Constitution in those terms. Its origins, James Bradley Thayer argued, were with the political experience of the colonies before the War of Independence. During that period colonialists became accustomed to being governed by written charters from the Crown, enforced by parliament and judicial proceedings. But with the revolution came the elimination of the sovereign power of Great Britain. That power was replaced, however, with the people's. "Our conception," wrote Thayer in 1893, "now was that 'the people' took his place; that is to say, our own home population in the several states were now their own sovereign."[47] That meant written state and national constitutions were no longer seen as orders from outside—like those from the British Crown—but rather were thought of as "precepts from the people themselves who were to be governed, addressed to each of their own number, and especially to those who were charged with the duty of conducting the government."[48]

This familiar characterization of the U.S. constitutional system continues to exert powerful influence. Rehnquist and Bork both use it to answer those who claim judicial review is anti-democratic. Bork writes that the "anomaly" of judicial supremacy in a democratic society can be "dissipated by the model of government embodied in the structure of the Constitution, a model upon which popular consent to limited government by the Supreme Court also rests."[49] The key to resolving the conflict between democratic principles and judicial review, he continues, lies in the fact that the society "*consents* to be ruled undemocratically within defined areas by certain enduring principles believed to be stated in, and placed beyond the reach of majorities by, the Constitution."[50]

Mirroring this suggestion that consent of the people is the only sound footing for judicial review, Rehnquist writes that the people "are the ultimate source of authority; they have parceled out the authority that originally resided entirely with them by adopting the original Constitution and by later amending it."[51] But, he continues, if judges "abandon the idea that the authority of the courts to declare laws unconstitutional is somehow tied to the language of the constitution the people adopted then judges are no longer the *keepers of the covenant*."[52] So both Bork and Rehnquist understand judicial review as a means to assure that society's original "covenant" is maintained. For that reason, judges must avoid substituting their own values in interpreting the Constitution's various provisions. Bork puts the point this way: "We are driven to the conclusion that a legitimate Court must be controlled by principles exterior to the will of the Justices. ... It follows that the choice of 'fundamental values' by the Court cannot be justified. Where constitutional materials do not clearly specify the value to be preferred, there is no principled way to prefer any claimed human value to another. The judge must stick close to the text and the history, and their fair implications, and not construct new rights."[53] So while refusing to invent new rights, judges must instead rely on history and other "constitutional materials." So long as judges tie their decisions to history and to what the people have incorporated into their constitution and laws, they act consistently with the ideals of democratic government. The idea of the Constitution as a contract among the people makes judicial review compatible with the underlying majoritarian ideals.

But why would the people place such limits on themselves? Wouldn't a government based on consent and majority rule want no limits placed on decisions of the people? To answer this, we should first distinguish two types of rules: Those that are *constituitive* of a practice and those that *regulate* an already existing one.[54] Rules of a game ("three strikes and you're out" and "bishops move on the diagonal") are constituitive in the sense that they make possible the practice; without them there could be no game. Rules of order governing who is to speak at a meeting are another example, since nobody would be able to speak if everybody tried to do so at once.

The U.S. Constitution is dominated by this type of rule. Its various articles establish the three branches of government, define the powers of each, and prescribe the procedures by which officials are chosen as well as the qualifications and terms of office for the occupants of the positions. No government would be possible without constituitive rules, any more than baseball could be played without rules governing how runs are scored and umpires (or somebody else) given the power to apply them. Governments cannot exist, much less proceed in a democratic fashion, without constituitive rules defining the roles and responsibilities attached to official positions.

But what of regulative rules, which, rather than creating institutions and roles, limit what the government can do after it is established? Why would people interested in creating a democratic government based on the consent of the majority limit themselves in any way? To see why, take an individual case: Suppose you know that if you have ice cream around the house you will probably eat it every day, something you do not want to do. So you establish for yourself the rule that you will not buy it at the store. Or suppose that, like me, you tend to turn off the alarm clock in the morning and go back to sleep, so you put it across the room. Such situations can also involve other people. Imagine you believe you should exercise every day, but know that you will find an excuse unless you can somehow make yourself do it. So you agree to meet a friend every morning at 6:00 A.M. for a jog, knowing you will not want to admit to the friend you are not coming.

What these illustrations have in common is that we are deciding, in what we think are our more thoughtful moments, to do things that will make it more likely we will not fall victim to our own weaknesses in the future. Ulysses knew he would be tempted by the sirens, so he ordered his men to tie him to the mast and ignore his orders to turn the ship; you know you will be tempted to stay in bed so you promise to run with a friend, making it more difficult for you to change your mind.[55]

Regulative constitutional rules can be justified in the same way. People might worry that in the heat of the moment they may do something incompatible with their own settled "value preferences," for example, by taking advantage of a racial minority, and so they put roadblocks in their own way. Or perhaps they worry that they might be tempted to act out of religious prejudice, so they limit the legislature's power to favor one religion as the First Amendment does. Or they may worry that under certain circumstances they would not treat people accused or convicted of crimes in what they, in calm reflective moments, believe to be an acceptable way, so they put in place constitutional limits on police searches, trial practices, punishment, and so on. Each of these illustrates a different form of what might be termed "self-incapacitation": people choosing to limit their freedom of action in the future, in these cases because they fear they may not live up to their own ideals.

A second reason to choose the course of democratic self-incapacitation is that no one can ever be sure of being in a majority on all issues. People in a majority should know that neither they nor society will remain unchanged. Rules promising to limit the power of the majority in certain areas, for instance religion, protect not only current minorities but also all who may find themselves in the minority in the future. Furthermore, today's minority religious beliefs or other ideas may become attractive to the children of the majority or even to the majority themselves. In either case, self-incapacitation can provide (limited) assurance that such changes would not be too costly.

Regulative rules designed to achieve a degree of self-incapacitation would seem especially sensible to people worried about the dangers of majority rule, and few were more worried at that prospect than the people who wrote the U.S. Constitution. Alexander Hamilton, for example, asked in "Federalist Number 6" whether it has not "invariably been found that momentary passions, and immediate interests, have a more active and imperious control over human conduct than general or remote considerations of policy, utility, or justice? Have republics in practice been less addicted to war than monarchies? ... Are not popular assemblies frequently subject to the impulses of rage, resentment, jealousy, avarice and the other irregular and violent propensities?"[56] We thus have what seem perfectly good reasons why people interested in establishing a democratic government would write a constitution that includes both constituitive and regulative rules. The former are necessary to establish and maintain a government at all, while the latter reflect the people's doubts that in the future they will always act in accord with their most important values or their fear that they may someday find themselves in the minority. In that way, original intent claims to provide an attractive account of judicial review and of constitutional democracy—one that is able to present the Constitution as a reasonable effort to achieve *worthy* ends.

Self-incapacitation also seems to explain why the amendment process outlined in Article V makes it so difficult to change the Constitution: The required two-thirds and three-fourths majorities help assure that self-incapacitation is effective. Limited by its (previously made) regulative rules and unable to amend the Constitution without two super-majorities, electoral politics and interest group bargaining can then proceed with less fear that it may go awry and violate the deeper principles to which the people, at the constitutional convention, committed themselves.

Although constitutional amendment is possible, most amendments have involved constituitive rules, extending the vote to new groups, revising procedures for electing officials, or providing for the transfer of power during emergencies. Times when substantive matters of basic constitutional principle limiting the majority are widely and intensely discussed and then acted on by the society at large are, in fact, relatively rare. The adoption of the Bill of Rights by the first Congress is the most obvious example of a time when basic regulative rules and principles were chosen; the Civil War and the amendments that followed it is another. The framing period, including the debates surrounding adoption and the insistence on the Bill of Rights, obviously constituted a fundamental change in the relationship between the individual, local government, and (new) national government, while the Civil War amendments expressed a deepened commitment to the ideal of equality for all citizens. Ordinary politics, however, operates against a backdrop of settled constitutional principles that limit the powers of elected officials in ways the people have previously chosen.[57]

This picture also squares nicely with the fact that the Constitution called on "the people" for its ratification. The new document was not to be seen as an agreement between the people and their rulers but rather as a contract among the people themselves to constitute a government, establish the process by which their governors would be chosen, and define the limits of the powers elected officials would be allowed to exercise. Unlike the Magna Charta, which was created after the people's representatives to parliament bargained with the king and agreed to terms that would define the powers of each, the U.S. Constitution envisions no king or other officials from whom power was being taken. Thus, the Preamble begins: "*We the People* ... do ordain and establish this Constitution"—a clear indication of the Constitution's origins as a social contract made among the people themselves.[58]

Judicial Review and Original Intent

Let's assume for the sake of argument, then, that the Constitution's legitimacy is grounded in its status as a contract among the people—a contract that sets the constitutive and regulative rules and thereby provides the basic framework of government. What would that mean for how we understand judicial review and constitutional interpretation? The natural answer, already suggested, is that in exercising judicial review the Supreme Court is simply enforcing the terms of that agreement on behalf of the people. Judicial review assures that the regulative and constitutive rules, including various forms of self-incapacitation, are strictly enforced and, therefore, that the original contract is kept. But how are judges to know when the social contract has been broken? What method of constitutional interpretation would be compatible with this conception of constitutional legitimacy?

Both Bork and Rehnquist suggested an answer: Judges should enforce the terms of social contract to which the people who framed the Constitution and those who later amended it *actually consented*. Thus, Rehnquist noted, it must be interpreted in a way that is "tied to the language of the constitution that the people adopted."[59] Judges should be "neutral," as Bork said, and in no case should they replace the values of the people, expressed through the legislature or in the original document, with their own. They must "stick closely to the text and the history ... and not construct new rights."[60]

Interpretation therefore depends on history: The question to be asked in interpreting vague constitutional language is how those who originally wrote the words understood them; the limits imposed on elected officials by the Constitution are exactly the limits that the framers had in mind to impose. So, for example, if the original understanding of the ban on "cruel and unusual punishment" referred to the rack and thumb screws but not executions, then that is how judges should interpret the language today, and executions are therefore not incompatible with the Eighth Amendment.

Viewed from this perspective, constitutional law resembles contract law. Suppose, for example, that a group of lawyers signed a partnership agreement and that a dispute has now arisen among them regarding whether the majority can force one of the other partners out of the firm. Suppose further that the partner has committed a minor crime and that the relevant provision in the agreement states that people can be forced out only for "conduct unbecoming a member of the bar." The question, therefore, is how to interpret that vague phrase, and according to original intent the answer depends on the original understanding of the partners who wrote the agreement and formed the partnership. Did they, as a matter of historical fact, believe that petty crimes constitute "conduct unbecoming a member of the bar?" If so, then the evil-doer may be fired; if not, he may not be. He can be fired, in other words, only if he violated the terms of the contract he actually signed. That question, however, is different from whether what he did is *now* regarded by the partners as "unbecoming." The original agreement envisioned a specific definition, and that was what the partners adopted when they joined the firm. To reinterpret it now would be tantamount to changing their agreement.

On this view of the law of contracts, a contract is like a promise in which there has been a "meeting of the minds" between the parties, signifying their mutual understanding of the terms of their agreement.[61] Judges are then charged with deciding the case in accord with the original terms; for a judge to replace the understanding of the original parties with her own ideas about what they *should* have agreed to is beyond the scope of the judge's power. Whatever she may think of the agreement—however one-sided or ill-advised it may seem—the judge is to *enforce* the contract, not to replace it with one she thinks is more just. Neutrality, which Rehnquist and Bork both stressed, is therefore the ideal; judges must not inject their personal opinion into matters that have already been decided by the parties to the contract.

Consent and the Social Contract

We have seen that both *The Federalist Papers* and early opinions by John Marshall and others rely on the idea that in overturning laws, the Supreme Court was enforcing the people's will against the will of the people's agents, the legislature. The people's will, expressed in the Constitution, is superior to the legislature's, and the Supreme Court acts legitimately only when it enforces the Constitution's exact limits. Laws enacted by elected officials can be thought to have the consent of the people because the majority can reject those officials through the ballot; but the limits placed on the legislature by the Constitution, enforced through judicial review, are also consented to. They are forms of self-incapacitation imposed by the people on the legislators and, indirectly, on themselves. In that way, the Constitution is superior; it is a more exacting statement of the people's will in certain narrowly specified areas. In this section I will weigh these ideas by discussing how a defender of originalism might argue that, in fact, judicial review serves to protect the terms of the social contract to which the people have consented.

Contractual obligations obviously differ from other types, such as the duty not to kill and steal or to help others in need, because they grow out of agreements. But a person who is a child or mentally impaired and so cannot understand what he is doing cannot obligate himself by making a contract. The power to contract is a power people have to knowingly and voluntarily create obligations for themselves; and since children and the mentally incompetent lack the requisite capaci-ties to bind themselves in that way, they are not able to create contractual obligations.

Even competent adults, however, are not always held to the terms of their contracts. Besides being able to understand the terms of the contract, parties must also perform the act of making the agreement voluntarily. If Smith signed a contract to purchase a house with a gun at her head, then she will not be required to meet its terms. However, people can acquire contractual obligations when others act as their agents as well as through their own explicit agreements. Smith may assign power of attorney to a lawyer with the understanding that the lawyer will buy a house whenever one of a certain design and price comes on the market. When the lawyer does that, acting as Smith's agent, the lawyer has created a contractual obligation that Smith must now meet: The house is now Smith's and she is required to assume the payments on it as though she had signed the purchase agreement herself.

But of course there is a difference between these typical examples of contracts and the social contract: People do not explicitly agree to abide by a constitution the way they sign a paper promising to purchase a house. Arguably, perhaps, a judge who relied on original intent immediately after ratification was heeding the "will of the people" to limit the legislature, but we who are alive in the late twentieth century were not consulted about its adoption, much less did we *freely join* the new government and accept its original terms. We might prefer, if asked, not to have any limits placed on what the majority may do. Or maybe we would accept some of the forms of self-incapacitation found in the Constitution but reject others. So it seems that whatever limits the framing generation set on its legislators, nobody living today consented to them. Thus the notion that the Constitution's legitimacy flows from consent of the governed and the Court's legitimacy from its role as "keeper of the covenant" seems deeply confused on a remarkably simple point.

Indeed, Thomas Jefferson himself stressed this point about social contract theory. "The earth," he wrote to Madison "belongs to the living . . . the dead have neither powers nor rights over it." No man, he continued, "can by natural right oblige the lands he occupied or the persons who succeed him in that occupation, to the payment of debts contracted by him. ... What is true of every member of society individually, is true of them all collectively, since the rights of the whole can be no more than the sum of the rights of individuals."[62] In order to assure that each generation genuinely consents to the government, Jefferson suggested that "every constitution, then, and every law, naturally expires at the end of 19 years. If it be enforced longer, it is an act of force, and not of right."[63] His suggestion was not followed, of course, which makes the problem all the more acute: In what sense, if any, do the people consent to constitutional limits enforced by judicial review of the legislature when those limits were selected by generations long dead? Is there any sense in which *we* consent to that constitutional contract and thereby bind ourselves to its terms?

Tacit Consent

The most familiar solution, appealed to by Madison[64] and defended by John Locke, distinguishes two forms of consent: While later generations do not *explicitly* consent, they do consent *tacitly* to be governed by the legal regime. Applying this to the originalist's understanding of judicial review, we might then say that although members of the present generation have never explicitly accepted the original terms of the Constitution, they "tacitly" accept them. In order to weigh this conclusion, however, we must first understand how, exactly, current generations "tacitly" consent to the original terms of the social contract.

Put simply, the point of the distinction is that while explicit consent involves an actual statement of agreement or, perhaps, some other clear sign that the terms are accepted (a nod of the head, for example), "tacit" consent is given in a more indirect way. So, for instance, Jones might explicitly consent to Smith using his private road by signing a contract or perhaps by simply telling Smith that it would be all right. But Jones might also give his consent in a less explicit way. Suppose Jones knows that Smith has been using the road and simply continues to allow her to do so, without raising any objection. Assuming nothing unusual about the situation (such as that Jones would find it difficult for some reason to stop her), then in this case we can reasonably say Jones "tacitly" consented. Or, to take another example, imagine a meeting in which the chairwoman asks anybody seated at the table who has an objection to changing the meeting time next week to say so, and seeing no sign from anybody, she concludes they have all consented to the change.[65] It again seems natural to say they did, indeed, consent and that it was "tacit" rather than explicit. Each indicated agreement to the delay, though nobody actually did anything except sit silently.

A legal analogue to tacit consent is estoppel, understood as the "preclusion of a person by his act or conduct or silence from asserting rights which might otherwise have existed."[66] The basic idea is that a person is prevented ("estopped") by virtue of his own behavior from making a claim that otherwise could be made, even though the claim is, in fact, true. Thus, in the example mentioned above, if one of the members were to demand after the meeting that the time not be changed, then assuming he had no good reason for waiting to make his objection, he would be "estopped" from raising it and the date would be changed. In law, it is generally true that estoppel occurs only when the other person (e.g.,the chairwoman) has relied to her disadvantage on the earlier act or silence.[67]

On what grounds, then, might it be claimed that people living under today's legal regime have tacitly consented to the terms of the original social contract? One answer appeals to the fact that the Constitution can be amended: Since under Article V the Constitution can be changed, by choosing not to exercise that option, it could be claimed, the people tacitly accept the Constitution's self-incapacitating limits on their power. It would be another story, of course, if amending were impossible; but the fact that it has now been changed twenty-seven times and could obviously be amended again constitutes a solid basis on which to rest consent.

There are, however, two important objections to this easy solution. The claim that "the people" have consented by not amending cannot mean that *everybody* has consented; no one person has such power. Therefore the argument must be understood as claiming that the people consent because the *majority* have chosen not to exercise their right to amend. Thus, while it must be admitted that some might wish to make changes, the majority do not and in that sense the "people" consent to the Constitution.

One problem with equating tacit consent with the majority's failure to amend, however, is that Article V requires super-majorities of two-thirds to propose and three-fourths to adopt any proposed amendment.[68] That means, of course, that it is possible for a substantial majority to want an amendment yet not be able to win passage and, therefore, that an amendment's failure does not even justify the claim that a majority of the people consent to the (current) Constitution.

Another problem with equating tacit consent and failure to amend focuses on the question of what it is, exactly, that is being consented *to*. In order to be of use to originalism, the argument must link tacit consent not just with the Constitution and laws in general but with the specific interpretation of the self-incapacitating constitutional limits envisioned by the framers. Why think, however, that by not amending, the people have tacitly consented to *that*? Certainly there is no general understanding among people that originalism is the best interpretive approach; nor can we assume that the majority even understand, let alone accept, the interpretive position of the framers on specific questions. So even if we set aside the first problem and grant that failure to amend constitutes tacit consent to the Constitution's limits on the majority, the argument would lead to the conclusion that people consent to the *current* interpretation of the Court—whatever that might be—and not to the one the framers intended, which, after all, may be at odds with current law and practice. If failure to amend suggests anything, it is that people accept the law as it is, not the law as it would be if the Court consistently followed the originalist's recommendation. We need, therefore, to look beyond the failure to amend as a basis on which to defend originalism's account of judicial review and constitutional government.

John Locke offers an alternative conception of tacit consent with the following, oft-quoted comment. "The difficulty," he says, "is, what ought to be look'd upon as a *tacit Consent* and how far it binds, i.e. how far any one shall be looked on to have consented, and thereby submitted to all government where he has made no Expressions of it at all. And to this I say, that every Man, that hath any Possession, or Enjoyment, or any part of the Dominions of any Government, doth thereby give his *tacit Consent*, and is as far forth obliged to Obedience to the Laws of that Government. … whether this his Possession be of Land, to him and his Heirs for ever, or a Lodging only for a Week; or whether it be barely travelling freely on the Highway."[69] Locke's suggestion is that anybody who enjoys the benefits of society (its protection of property and freedom to live and travel) has tacitly consented to the social contract or, to use legal terminology, is "estopped" from claiming not to have consented to the social contract and is under the legal authority of the state.

Originalists then add to this the claim that those living in society are obligated to accept the terms of the social contract as defined by the original intent of the framers. This argument, as we will see, raises a variety of questions and problems about tacit consent itself as well as its connection to original intent, and we will consider them in turn.

It is important to note first that there is some ambiguity in Locke's famous passage. On one reading, the responsibility to abide by the contract rests entirely on a person's having *accepted benefits*. But another interpretation, which I will also consider, focuses not on the idea that a person accepts benefits but instead on the fact the person did things that imply she consents, whether she actually intended to abide by the agreement or not.

We begin with the first interpretation: that people are bound to the social contract merely by accepting various benefits from society. To fill in the details somewhat, Locke seems to assume that society is a cooperative undertaking in which each person benefits. But, he claims, in order to realize those benefits (primarily protection of life, property, and liberty) the vast majority of people must willingly accept the burdens of membership. But since it is possible for a person to continue to enjoy the fruits of others' acceptance of the burdens (their obedience to law) without himself accepting the burdens, he concludes that anybody who accepts the benefits of the political regime without fulfilling his responsibilities to meet its burdens has not abided by the terms of the social contract. Such a person acts unfairly with respect to others in the society who have accepted their share of the burdens.[70]

Put that way, however, the argument is not really about consent at all, and so is of little use to the originalist. The point of the argument is that political authority rests on the *unfairness* of accepting benefits of others abiding by the law without shouldering those burdens oneself. That is not, however, a contractualist argument. For even if we agree that citizens who disobey laws are unfairly accepting the benefits of society without shouldering their share of the burdens, this is different from the claim that citizens have, in fact, *consented* to the terms of the social contract, as originalism requires. The fairness or unfairness of accepting benefits should not be confused with the claim that accepting benefits is a form of tacit consent. We need, then, to look beyond accepting burdens and ask what, if anything, could constitute tacit consent to the Constitution.

I will begin with an example of explicit consent, outside the context of law. Suppose Smith agrees to let Jones use a tool next week but unbeknown to Jones plans to break the promise when the request finally comes. Has Smith then "consented" to loaning the tool even though he secretly plans not to loan it? It seems that in one sense he has consented. Jones believes, reasonably, that she can borrow it, and Smith knows that Jones has taken him to agree. Let's call that "objective" consent. Notice, however, that in another, subjective sense it might be said Smith has only appeared to give consent since he privately plans not to loan the tool.[71] Now when Locke speaks of tacit consent he cannot mean subjective consent, that is, that people always have the subjective intention to abide by the laws. What he must mean is captured by the other, objective sense. People consent, he was suggesting, regardless of their actual intentions to refuse later.

But how then might it be argued that citizens bind themselves, objectively, to the state regardless of subjective intentions? Suppose a newcomer shows up at a card game already in progress and after watching for a while sits down to play. Sometimes she wins, other times she loses. She does nothing to suggest she is unwilling to accept the rules, paying off when she loses and taking her winnings when she is successful. When disagreements arise, people appeal to a rule book—a practice to which she does not raise any objection. But now imagine there is a misdeal of the cards, which the group notices only after the newcomer has collected her winnings on that hand. The group consults the rule book and finds a rule stating that a misdealt hand must be played again. Can the newcomer then keep the winnings from that hand, pointing out that she never explicitly consented to abide the rules and, in fact, intended all along to follow the rule book only when it was to her advantage?

It seems clear that although she did not subjectively consent to abide by the rules, she nonetheless did consent in the objective sense and therefore has an obligation to follow the rules. Nobody forced her to play, and she happily continued to participate in the game knowing that others reasonably took her to be intending to follow the rules. She thus *led others to believe, reasonably, that she would follow them* even when she didn't like the result, and so she continues to be bound by them.[72]

The key question, then, is whether this (revised) understanding of tacit consent can be extended to the political arena, thereby grounding the originalist's claim that judicial review functions to enforce the original, self-incapacitating rules adopted by the people. Suppose, then, that after campaigning in a fair election, the losing candidate refuses to abide by the outcome, saying she never actually promised she would accept the results and never in fact planned to go along if she lost. In a sense this is like the silent assent to delay the meeting and the refusal to allow the hand to be re-dealt. The candidate has at least arguably also given tacit consent to abide by the rules if she should lose, even though she neither subjectively intended to abide by them and never explicitly promised to follow them. She did so by knowingly leading others reasonably to believe she consented.

But now the question is whether these arguments can be stretched as far as Locke would like, to include all members of society and not just candidates for office. It is important to note, first, that Locke's examples of traveling and living in society do not signify tacit consent to abide by the terms of the social contract (though, as I indicated, they *may* provide a different ground for obligation based on fairness). The question, then, is whether there are other occasions when people knowingly do what *will* reasonably lead others to believe they subjectively consent and thereby give tacit consent. It is arguable, I think, that we do. Besides running for office, citizens participate in society's legal institutions in innumerable ways: We follow traffic signals, vote, pay our taxes and debts, demand that others pay debts to us, exercise a variety of rights, including freedom of speech and religion, and demand that society enforce the law when others violate them or when they have harmed us through their negligence. It seems, then, that if those actions are added up, the originalist may have at least a plausible claim that the average citizen is in a similar position to players in the game who knowingly and reasonably lead others to think they consent. In demanding that others obey laws, pay their debts to us, and so on, citizens suggest to others their willingness to abide by the rules. Like the card player who appealed to the rules when it was to her advantage, others can reasonably infer that fellow citizens who appeal to laws and rights, demand others will follow, participate in the political discussion and voting process, and so on will themselves obey when their turn comes.

There remains, however, another obstacle to be overcome by defenders of tacit consent: As I have noted, contractual agreements (whether explicitly or tacitly made) must be *voluntary* as well as informed if they are to be binding. Yet as David Hume famously pointed out in 1777, there is serious doubt that a resident's decision to remain in society and live under its legal protection is genuinely voluntary. "Can we seriously say," he asks, "that a poor peasant or partizan has a free choice to leave his country, when he knows no foreign language or manners, and lives from day to day, by the small wages which he acquires? We may as well assert that a man, by remaining in a vessel, freely consents to the domain of the master; though he was carried on board while asleep, and must leap into the ocean and perish, the moment he leaves her."[73] Hume poses a well-known problem for anybody who wishes to understand political obligation on the basis of consent. Choosing to perform an action, he is pointing out, is insufficient to establish that it is done voluntarily, as victims who turn over their money to a robber, for example, clearly illustrate. Nor do people who remain on a ship consent to the master in virtue of their choice not to jump overboard. Yet the argument based on tacit consent must show not just that people have done things that convey their agreement but also that they did so *voluntarily*.

These are large and complex issues, and I will not deal with them in detail here. It is important to note, however, how this dispute bears on the discussion of original intent. Hume's slave ship example might be relevant if the originalist were arguing that merely living in society and accepting benefits constitutes tacit consent. But that, I have suggested, cannot be the ground of tacit consent. What, then, of the argument I *did* envision the originalist making—that people who participate in politics, insist on their legal rights, and so on tacitly give consent? It is less clear, it seems to me, that these actions are open to Hume's objection since it may be easier for people to refuse to participate than it would be to leave society altogether. Still, however, one may wonder if it is really *that* easy for people to avoid doing the things I described that would lead others to conclude they tacitly consent.

The case of the robber suggests a different way of understanding coercion, however, since here the coercion seems to result not only from the psychological pressure the victim is under but also the fact that the gunman wrongs her.[74] That "moralized" understanding of coercion and voluntariness may seem better than the psychological one when we focus on examples where rights are not violated. Consider, for instance, a doctor who refuses to perform a needed operation unless the patient pays a reasonable fee. This refusal does not seem to be "coercive"—however much psychological pressure the patient is under to agree to pay for the services—since, unlike the robber, the doctor is entitled to request the fee and does nothing wrong in refusing to operate.

Looking at voluntariness and coercion in that second, moralized way would not seem to raise any problems for the originalist, however. Citizens who find themselves at a political or economic disadvantage because of their refusal to participate in the political process have not had their rights violated. They are not like the person facing the gunman, even if both feel great psychological pressure to act. On that second, moralized view the case against tacit consent seems even weaker.

My aim here is not to join these disputes about the nature of coercion and voluntary consent, however, since the originalist has much more serious problems that must be confronted. So let's assume, for the sake of argument, that originalism's picture of judicial review and democratic government is correct: Judicial review is to be understood as an effort by the people at self-incapacitation, and tacit consent provides a defensible ground for political obligation. Still, however, originalists face two further hurdles, both related to their legal and interpretive program. One involves the connection between tacit consent and original intent; the other, to be discussed in the next section, centers on the interpretive theory itself and the contention that judges should defer to history.

Originalists need to show not just that people tacitly consent to the self-incapacitating rules expressed in the Constitution; they also need somehow to connect that consent to the specific meaning of those rules as reflected in the historical intent of the framers. But that inference—from tacit consent to original intent—is far from obvious. Indeed, I will argue, originalism cannot successfully link tacit consent with its conception of constitutional interpretation. There is no plausible defense of the claim that the people, today, consent to the specific, historical limits on elected officials envisioned by the framers.

To begin, it is clear that modern-day citizens are not generally aware of the actual, historical meanings historians might tell us were in the minds of the framers at the time the Constitution was ratified. Indeed, historians are themselves often at odds about such questions. But how, then, can citizens today be said to have tacitly consented to *those specific* meanings, if they cannot and do not understand them?

Suppose, for instance, that historical research showed that the widely accepted, settled meaning given by the current generation of judges to a constitutional provision was not the one shared by the framers. Would originalists then argue that the Constitution has been wrongly understood because the people had consented to those original limits on their legislature instead of the limits the Courts have settled on? That seems completely implausible. How can it be that although judges used to think that people had consented to one meaning of "equality," we now know, *based on historical evidence,* that they actually consented to a very different meaning? History cannot change the terms of what people, today, agree to; and to suggest that it can seems to confuse what the living generation consents to with another question entirely: namely, what historical evidence tells us was the framers' understanding of the document.

Perhaps, then, the originalist needs to take another approach. As I noted earlier when describing tacit consent, it is possible for people to delegate powers to others that they have the right to exercise, such as purchasing a house, without knowing ahead of time just how the power will eventually be used. Relying on this, originalists might then argue that the people have delegated to the courts the responsibility to enforce the original terms of the social contract *whatever they might turn out to be.* For that reason, originalists might conclude, it is not necessary for people to know before the fact just what interpretations of the Constitution judges will settle on. Though ignorant of the specific terms of the social contract to which they consented (they may not know if the framers thought executions were cruel and unusual punishment, for example), the people do commit, according to this view, to the more abstract interpretive theory of originalism.

This attempt to link the social contract and tacit consent with original intent also fails, however. It says, in effect, that people actually consent, in the abstract, to *whatever* historians might conclude were the framers' intentions. The problem, however, is that this seems wrong on the face of it; it is *not* widely agreed among the people that the Constitution should be read in accord with the historical intention of the framers, and to say that "the people" tacitly consent to those specific limits on their elected officials, and no others, is simply false. This is especially clear when we focus on the possibility that the framers' interpretation, for example of "equal protection of the laws" or "freedom of speech," may be neither the *most reasonable* interpretation nor the one the people would actually support. To say that there is wide agreement among the people that the Court should choose the interpretation favored by the framers over the most reasonable one is incompatible with the commonplace that the Constitution is a "living document" and must be interpreted in accord with changing times and values.

So even if it were accepted that people *tacitly* consent to the Constitution by actions such as demanding that others abide by the law and by participating in the political process, it is far from clear that they have thereby consented to the specific, historically defined terms of that original agreement among the people. Why not say instead that the people tacitly consent to the best interpretation of the document rather than to a less sound one that was envisioned by the framers? Even assuming the current generation has voluntarily consented, tacitly, to abide by the Constitution, the terms of that agreement are not necessarily those envisioned by the framers.

Originalism in Practice

Besides the theoretical problems I have outlined, originalism also faces another set of problems. Assuming, then, that the originalist could rely on tacit consent as a basis of the original contract and, contrary to what I have been arguing, then be able to link tacit consent with the framers' intentions, how would its specific interpretive recommendations actually work? Can originalism, in other words, offer a workable, coherent interpretive program to judges? I will argue that it does not.[75]

Suppose a judge wishes to decide a case, based on original intent, that hinged on whether a wiretap on a public telephone is a "search," in which case the police must first get a warrant as required by the Fourth Amendment.[76] Plainly, the framers never heard of a telephone, much less a wiretap on a public one. What should the judge conclude, following original intent, regarding the question whether it constitutes a search? One possibility would be that the framers *had no intention* on this issue and therefore the Constitution is indeterminate. That, however, is of no help to our judge.

A second possibility may be more hopeful. We may think, assuming the facts as stated, that because the framers did not explicitly have in mind to rule out wiretaps, the Constitution does not prevent police from using them, and so the judge should accept the evidence because there was no "search." This is a narrow view of constitutional rights. It says, in effect, that unless a specific limit on the government was explicitly contemplated by the framers, it is not part of the Constitution. But why make that assumption rather than one that provides a more generous conception of the meaning of "search"? Do we know that the framers intended for judges to adopt such a narrow view of citizens' rights, protecting them only when the framers specifically envisioned the exact violation?

Suppose we ask, instead, if the framers would have wanted to limit wiretaps, given the objectives they sought to achieve by the warrant requirement. That suggests a third path defenders of original intent might follow: to ask, hypothetically, what the framers *would have decided* in this case, given their values, if they were alive today. The question in our example would then become whether they would have regarded bugging a public telephone as a "search" had they known what we know about telephones, their role in modern society, the importance of privacy in an age of electronic communication, and so on. But herein lies another troubling problem.

Defenders of original intent stress that judges should ignore their own values in favor of the values of the framers, so presumably in this case we would need to ask what the framers would do, given their values, if they understood our world as we do. But it is by no means clear that the "values" people hold can be sharply separated from their beliefs about the "facts." The value the framers (or anybody else) place on privacy and the importance of a warrant will be influenced by their beliefs about the dangers posed by modern technology as well as the risks posed by police intrusions on privacy. But if (as this suggests) the framers' values would change as they learned what we know, then what is left of the original claim that judges should rule in accord with the framers' values but not their (now outdated) understanding of the world? How are judges to know what *the framers'* values were?

The temptation, of course, will always be for judges to attribute their values and beliefs to the framers, thinking that if the framers were here they would see the world as we do. Put that way, however, it is no longer clear that we are talking about "the framers" as much as about ourselves. Since any judge would presumably think the framers would take a reasonable position on these issues, there will no longer be a sharp distinction between our own ideas about what the Fourth Amendment requires and what the framers understood it to require.

These are only the start of the practical problems confronting an originalist interpreter, however. We have yet to explain who, exactly, the framers were and whose intentions or values we are trying to discover. Are the framers the people who actually drafted the wording and presented it to the convention, or do they include everyone in attendance? If we keep in mind the theory behind originalism—the idea of a self-incapacitating covenant among the people—there is still another possibility: Since the constitutional limits are placed by *the people* on themselves, it would seem that the framers include a far larger group. One defender of originalism, Richard S. Kay, suggested in this vein that since it is the people as a whole whose "judgments and approval gave the Constitution authority," the focus of originalism should be on the intentions of the various "ratifying bodies who possessed the constituent authority."[77]

That quick answer cannot be right, however, since women, slaves, and sometimes white males without property were excluded from the adoption process. And even if we say (however implausibly) that women were "virtually represented" in the sense that their wishes were reflected in the votes of their husbands, fathers, and brothers, that cannot be said for other groups. Similar problems arise for constitutional amendments: They were originally drafted by members of Congress and then referred to state legislatures for adoption, often in an environment in which only a minority of adults were allowed to vote. If the framers were "the people," as Kay and other defenders of the theory suggest, then the intention of the "representative bodies" made up exclusively of white males, and sometimes *propertied* white males, would be a poor indicator of the intentions of the entire "people."

But even if we resolve that issue and agree on which group of people constitutes the "framers," other hurdles remain. The originalist judge must also confront the fact that however we define the group, it will often turn out that its members differed among themselves over what the Constitution's various provisions mean when applied to various cases—a problem that is made to seem less serious by the originalists' tendency to speak of "the people" when justifying originalism but only of the smaller and more homogeneous "ratifying bodies" when trying to figure out what the framers intended. In response, an originalist might try to develop a conception of a "group intention," allowing for the possibility that the group's intentions may be at odds with the intentions of (at least some) of the "framers" belonging to the group. But even assuming, implausibly, that we can focus only on the ratifying bodies, how is such a "group" intention to be identified when the language may have been a compromise between different individuals with different ideas about what the words mean?

The most likely answer to this would be that where there is disagreement about the meaning of a provision, the intent would be whatever the *majority* took it to be.[78] Minority intentions, an originalist might argue, can be safely ignored. But why assume that such a majority opinion would exist? If, as seems likely, there were only various plurality opinions about how a provision should be interpreted in hard cases, then there would be no original intention on which originalism could rely.

Another possibility is that at least some of the framers *expected* that a certain provision would be interpreted by later generations one way, though they regretted that fact *hoping* it would be interpreted differently.[79] What then would the "intent of the framers" consist in? An originalist judge would be forced to choose between following the meaning the framers *believed* they would be communicating to later judges and the meaning they *wanted* the phrase to convey to later interpreters. It is unclear which of these should be chosen by the originalist.

These, then, are some of the major difficulties that would need to be resolved before any originalist theory could lay claim to being a reasonable, practical theory of interpretation. It would have to give an account of how we are to define the framers whose intentions control the Constitution's meaning, how to square that definition with the fact that the ratifying bodies were far from representative of the entire people, how to identify a group intention given that the framers disagreed about what their document meant, and, finally, whether the Constitution's intended meaning is to be defined by their hoped-for interpretations or, where they diverged, by their beliefs about how later judges would interpret their words. Yet although these are major practical problems, there also exist even more fundamental challenges to originalism's claim to offer a coherent, workable interpretive strategy.

Consider, first, the possibility that the framers' intended meaning and the one we now believe, reasonably, to be the soundest may differ significantly.[80] It has been argued, for example, that the free speech clause was originally intended by its sponsors only to limit prior restraint by government and that its original proponents did not intend for the First Amendment to prevent government officials from attacking their critics *after* publication.[81] That position, of course, is sharply at odds with both current legal practice and widely accepted political principles; most would find the current interpretation of speech more reasonable than this one. Or, to take another example, consider the question of segregation and the Fourteenth Amendment. Assuming (as some have argued[82]) that members of Congress who adopted it believed that equality and segregation were not incompatible, then that interpretation would again be at odds with what almost everybody today believes equality requires. If the historical facts are as envisioned, and current views of speech or equality are also correct, then the framers of these amendments had inconsistent commitments: to freedom of speech and equality, on one hand, and to preventing only prior restraint and allowing segregation, on the other. Because they were wrong about what equality and free speech require, their general goals of respecting equal protection and free speech cannot be reconciled with their more specific understanding of what equality and freedom of speech require. Originalists must therefore consider which of the framers' "intentions" is the real one—protecting equality and free speech or allowing segregation and post-publication attacks on controversial speech—when the general and specific are incompatible.

One possibility, of course, would be to ask whether the framers would have given priority to the general goal or to their specific understanding of how to realize it. Put that way, however, it seems at least plausible to suppose the framers would *not* have wanted later generations to sacrifice the ideals of equality and free speech to their own (misconceived) visions of what those provisions require.[83] One reason for thinking this is that the framers (many of whom were very good lawyers) chose not to use specific terms but instead included vague words like "equal protection," "freedom of speech," "free exercise of religion," and "due process of law." Had they wished to, they could easily have inserted their specific understanding of these phrases, yet they rejected that in favor of general, undefined concepts.[84]

The second reason to think the framers often intended for later generations not to rely on their specific intentions is that they sometimes said as much.[85] In the debate over the national bank, for example, Hamilton observed: "Whatever the intention of the framers of a constitution or of a law, that intention is to be sought for in the instrument itself, according to the usual and established rules of construction. ... Arguments drawn from extrinsic circumstances regarding the intention of the Convention must be rejected. ... Nothing is more common than for laws to express and effect more or less than was intended."[86] James Madison expressed a similar view in 1821 when he wrote: "As a guide in expounding and applying the provisions of the Constitution, the debates and incidental decisions of the Convention can have no authoritative character."[87] In debating the constitutionality of a national bank, however, Madison appealed to the intentions of the framers. But others disagreed with Madison's use of an intentionalist argument, including at least one who had also been in attendance at the convention. Quoting Blackstone, Elbridge Gerry argued that the will of the legislator must be understood in terms of the "words, the context, the subject-matter, the effect and consequence, or the spirit and reason of the law" and not on the basis of events at the ratifying convention.[88] And, finally, the great defender of judicial review, John Marshall, wrote in *McCulloch v. Maryland* that the Constitution is different from a "legal code" and that "we must never forget that it is a constitution we are expounding."[89] Judges, he went on to say, must maintain the "right to judge of [the framers'] correctness."[90]

The authors of the Fourteenth Amendment expressed a similar view about how their language should be interpreted. Speaking of the privileges and immunities clause, Senator Howard, who authored the language, said as he presented the amendment to the Senate: "To the privileges and immunities, whatever they may be—for *they are not and cannot be fully defined in their entire extent and precise nature*—to these should be *added* the personal rights guaranteed and secured by the first eight amendments of the Constitution."[91] Here we have a person who by anybody's definition must be included among the framers of one of the Constitution's most important amendments, saying in unambiguous terms that the rights it secures "cannot be fully defined" in either their "extent" or "nature." He too rejected originalism, intending instead that later judges *not* follow blindly his or anybody else's definition but instead be left free to define for themselves the "extent" and "precise nature" of the terms.

Besides refusing to offer precise definitions and their own statements about interpretation, the framers signaled their rejection of original intent in still another way. Madison, Hamilton, and others later participated, as citizens, in debates about the Constitution's meaning. But they did not argue, as defenders of original intent would suppose, that their way of interpreting it was privileged because the meaning was what *they*, the framers, had intended when they wrote the document. Instead they joined the debate over the meaning of the Constitution as equals, with others who had not been at the convention. The question in these debates, as always, was how *best* to understand the meaning of the document, given the language, the structure of the government, and the Constitution's purposes.[92]

Additionally, the Constitution itself suggests rights should be protected that are not explicitly mentioned in the text. The Ninth Amendment reads: "The enumeration in the Constitution, of certain rights, shall not be construed to deny or disparage others retained by the people," suggesting that the fact some rights are "enumerated" should not be taken to mean the list is exhaustive.[93] It is sometimes suggested that this interpretation of the amendment is mistaken because the Ninth Amendment only limits what *Congress* can do by reiterating that *its* powers are limited to ones explicitly described in the Constitution. In other words, the Ninth Amendment only makes the point that the limits placed on the U.S. Congress by the Bill of Rights should not be taken to mean Congress can do *everything but* violate those explicit rights; despite the Bill of Rights, this is still a government of enumerated powers.

Doubtless, the possibility the Bill of Rights would be taken that way was a concern of many, including Madison, who expressed reservation about listing *any* rights for fear people would infer only those rights limit the government.[94] But the problem with that way of interpreting the amendment is that the Tenth Amendment says exactly what this interpretation has the Ninth saying: "The powers not delegated to the United States by the Constitution, nor prohibited by it to the States, are reserved to the States respectively, or to the people." If that were *all* the Ninth meant, why say it twice?[95]

Originalism is beset with serious problems and objections to its claim to offer a coherent or even usable account of constitutional interpretation: it is far from clear who the framers were, why the unrepresentative bodies like the original convention and Congress should be thought to express the original intent of the "people," and how a single "intention" could be inferred from their many inconsistent positions. Nor did many of the drafters even *want* later generations to follow the jurisprudence of original intent and restrict the document to the authors' original but mistaken understanding of its key provisions. They intentionally used broad, undefined terms in the Constitution; in later debates about the document's meaning they made no claims that their views should be privileged because they were framers, and some of them said, explicitly, that later generations should not follow the jurisprudence of original intent. None of these familiar problems with originalism's interpretive recommendations to judges should detract from the theory's other, more theoretical difficulties that I outlined in earlier sections. The suggestion, made by both Bork and Rehnquist, that we understand judicial review as a means to enforce the "covenant" among the people, does not succeed; nor can originalism provide a workable, coherent set of recommendations to judges in interpreting the Constitution.

Constitutional Interpretation and Constitutional Purpose

Before turning to the next interpretive theory, democratic proceduralism, I want to consider the lessons to be learned from originalism's failure. What, if anything, can be said about the nature of interpretation in general once we reject the originalist's claim that the meaning of the text is to be sought in the authors' original understanding? Besides suggesting an alternative vision of legal interpretation, this discussion will also underscore one of the central themes of this book: that each theory of constitutional interpretation rests on a distinctive conception of the role of judicial review and political legitimacy.

It is important to emphasize, as I noted earlier, that despite originalism's failure to establish the claim that judges must ignore their own values and defer to the framers, judges nonetheless do have different responsibilities from political philosophers. Even the most activist judges hold to the distinction between giving their *own view* of who ought, morally, to win a lawsuit and their responsibility as judges to determine who *the law* says has a right to win. Everybody agrees that the task of interpretation concerns how best to understand the meaning of words, and that context and precedent are both relevant to that task. But that point should not be confused with the claim by originalists that there must be a sharp *dichotomy* between the moral or political views of a judge and the best interpretation of the Constitution, and that judges should defer to the specific intentions of the law's authors. Neither of these extreme positions is a good characterization of legal interpretation. Responsible interpreters are neither legally unconstrained nor are they able to forsake their political or moral convictions. But if we reject the originalist's claim, what then *is* the connection between political convictions and legal interpretation?[96]

First, a comment about judicial activism, since the term "activist" has been used in different and sometimes confusing ways. Sometimes it indicates a willingness to see the judiciary exercise judicial review more often than others; at other times, it indicates a willingness to overturn precedents. An originalist might be "activist" in the second sense, overturning precedents that are incompatible with what she thinks is the intent of the framers. Whether originalism requires activism in the first sense would depend on how often legislators pass laws that contradict the framers' intentions. A third sense of "activism" cuts across these two: It holds that constitutional interpretation cannot and should not be attempted in a morally or politically neutral way, so that judges have no reasonable alternative but to invoke their own values. In one respect, of course, originalists reject activism in this third sense, since they ask judges to set aside their own moral ideas in favor of the framers' understanding of legal concepts. But in another sense, originalists (like all others who hold an interpretive theory) *are* activists in this third sense. As we have seen, the originalists' demand that judges ignore their own values and rely instead on the specific meanings envisioned by the framers is itself a political decision; it follows (they claim) from the theory of constitutional interpretation that they think (for political reasons) is the best theory.

More, however, needs to be said about this important claim, for it underlies much of what I have to say about constitutional interpretation. Consider, then, the following familiar example of constitutional argument. The First Amendment states that Congress shall make no law "abridging freedom of speech." But what, exactly, constitutes "speech"? Does it include only words, or should actions such as raising a fist or burning a flag also be thought of as constitutionally protected forms of speech? Deciding if an action is (constitutional) speech is only the beginning, however, for there must also be limits even on speech. But what then are those limits? Can government restrict speech based on its offensiveness? Does political speech have more protection than other forms, such as scientific, literary, or erotic? What if the speaker advocates violence or the elimination of the right to speak? Such interpretive questions are inevitably controversial, in large part just because answers cannot be separated from political judgments about the *purposes* of the free speech clause itself. Some interpreters have stressed the First Amendment's political purpose, since free speech is essential if the government is to function democratically. Others have seen the free speech clause as a way of protecting the basic right of each individual to develop his or her own ideas about how best to live[97] or as a way for society to assure it is able to gain truth through the "marketplace of ideas."[98]

That connection, between interpretation and the purposes of the specific constitutional provisions, has long been recognized. In "Federalist Number 40," James Madison wrote: "There are two rules of construction, dictated by plain reason, as well as founded on legal axioms. The one is, that every part of the expression ought, if possible be made to conspire to some common end. The other is, that where the several parts cannot be made to coincide, the less important should give way to the more important part."[99] Judges must look to general canons of construction. That means, said Madison, that the different provisions of the text should be understood as far as possible to serve a "common" or consistent end. But where that is impossible, Madison added, the less important purposes of the document should be sacrificed in favor of the more important. In other words, judges are responsible for making two independent judgments: They must first determine the purposes behind the text and then assess which is the "less important" should there be conflict among those different purposes.

Behind these points lies another, equally important one about the role of judges. Madison assumed here that something akin to a principle of charity (or, as Dworkin termed it, the dimension of justification) operates on those who interpret law. No judge, he said, should impute inconsistency to the law, nor should she allow a lesser purpose to take precedence over a greater one. But if that is true, then the interpreter's task *is* in part that of the political philosopher: to read the Constitution in a way that allows it to be both coherent and serve important purposes.

That point is well illustrated in Marshall's *McCulloch* opinion, mentioned earlier. As we saw, Marshall rejected original intent in that decision. But besides making that argument, he went on to describe an assumption judges should always make about the framers' purposes. In asking whether the "necessary and proper" clause gives Congress the power to establish a national bank, he wrote: "It *must have been* the intention of those [framers] who gave [Congress] these powers to insure, as far as human prudence could insure, their beneficial execution."[100] Judges are to *assume,* then, that it was the intention of the framers to be prudent and to take effective means to their ends. But this of course means that faced with an interpretive question such as the meaning of "necessary" or "freedom of speech," interpreters should seek to put the *best* construction on the Constitution that is available, one which the framers *can most reasonably be said to have meant.*

So Marshall relied, explicitly, on the interpretive assumption that those who created the document acted in a reasonable fashion. Its authors, he noted later in the opinion, would never have made an "unwise attempt to provide, by immutable rules, for exigencies which, if foreseen at all must have been seen dimly, and which can be best provided for as they occur."[101] He also asked, rhetorically, "Can we adopt that construction . . . which would impute to the framers of that instrument, when granting these powers for the public good, the intention of impeding their exercise by withholding a choice of means?"[102] So the clear effect of Marshall's interpretive assumptions—that the framers were "wise" and took reasonable means to their ends—is to require interpreters to put the best face on the document as they interpret it. Marshall's point, like Madison's before him, is that when reading the Constitution judges should attempt to understand it in a reasonable way, avoiding the imputation of inconsistency, faulty reasoning, and mistaken beliefs to its authors.

But Marshall did not leave it there. What happens, he next asked, when despite all a judge's efforts, the purpose the framers had for some legal provision is *not* the most reasonable one? The answer, which he gave near the end of the *McCulloch* opinion, and which I quoted earlier, is that "no tribute can be paid to them which exceeds their merit; but in applying their opinions to the cases which may arise in the progress of our government, *a right to judge of their correctness must be retained;* and to understand the argument, we must examine the proposition it maintains, and the objections against which it is made."[103] Though the framers deserve great tribute, said Marshall, we must always seek to interpret the document in a reasonable light; this means judges must reserve the right to "examine" the framers' understanding of the Constitution. In interpreting the document's various provisions, judges should seek always to ascribe *reasonable* purposes to the document. The judge's task, of necessity, is dependent on the text, precedents, and the institutional practices within which judges function; so while they are not to conduct themselves as philosophers, unconstrained except by the tools of free moral reasoning, neither can interpreters discharge their responsibilities in a political vacuum, ignoring the purposes of the document and their own judgments of the relative weight of the purposes. Their interpretive responsibility, in short, is to make the text, insofar as it is possible, into a reasonable effort to achieve worthy goals.

Behind this picture of legal interpretation lies a second important assumption about the nature of law and its progress. Another of the leaders at the ratifying convention, James Wilson, put the point this way: "This [common law] system has stood the test of numerous ages: to every age it has disclosed new beauties and new truths. In improvement, it is yet progressive ... It acquires strength in its progress. From this system, we derive our dearest birthright and highest inheritance."[104] The common law system (in which both Madison and Marshall were also trained) requires judges to apply established legal precedents to new circumstances, yet at the same time reevaluate prior decisions as well as the purposes and principles that they serve. No prior opinion or decision is beyond criticism, which means that precedents may either be explicitly overturned or reinterpreted to stand for a different, sounder legal rule or principle. In that way, said Wilson, the law acquires "strength in its progress" as judges constantly reevaluate and reinterpret past decisions. Law represents the collective experience of generations of interpreters and their critics; it has withstood "the test of numerous ages" not because it is unchanging but because it provides the means for its own "improvement." That requires judges to seek ways of understanding legal materials (whether precedents or a constitutional text) that show the law to be a reasonable attempt to achieve worthy goals.

So taken together, Madison, Marshall, and Wilson offer the following picture of interpretation. Legal interpretation rests on judgments about the purposes that the text in question serves. One cannot understand the meaning of the First

Amendment's free speech clause without relying, even if only implicitly, on an understanding of its role in the larger constitutional framework. Identification and then weighing of those purposes is part of the interpretive process, which means that interpretation is inevitably normative. In order that the legal system evolve and improve, judges make the assumption that the legal texts they are interpreting are reasonable; that is, that they are workable, consistent, and seek important purposes. If reading the text one way presents it as an effective attempt to achieve worthy goals, while interpreting it differently leaves it incoherent, ineffective, or unjust, then the former is to be preferred to the latter. Interpretations are constructed, not discovered as the originalists imagined.

That brings us, finally, to a point that I have emphasized from the beginning and that is one of this book's major themes. Not only do those charged with interpreting specific provisions of the text seek a reasonable balance among the various purposes that the provision might serve, but interpretive theories themselves also seek to understand the document's overall structure and especially judicial review in much the same way. In accord with that, we have tested original intent by asking whether its implicit assumptions about the purpose and justification of judicial review are sound. Would an interpreter, guided by original intent, succeed in presenting the Constitution as a reasonable effort by the framers to achieve truly worthy ends? In that way, the choice among interpretive theories resembles the issue confronting interpreters of specific textual provisions, who must often make judgments about the purposes served by a specific clause. Not only is interpretation itself normative but, not surprisingly, so is the choice among *theories* of interpretation that are offered as guides to interpretation. Neither can be undertaken independently of the requirement that the text be understood as a reasonable effort to achieve worthy ends; and so as a result, Wilson and the others would say, the Constitution is able to acquire "strength in its progress."

Originalism therefore fails on two levels—as both a theory of constitutional interpretation and a theory of legal interpretation in general. Interpreters do not do well to understand the Constitution as an agreement the terms of which are enforced by the Supreme Court, nor does interpretation in general demand that judges set aside their political views and rely solely on the intentions of the document's authors. Instead, interpreters of specific parts of the text, as well as interpretive theories themselves, seek to construct the meaning of the document in light of the best understanding of its underlying purposes. Interpretive theories seek legitimacy in that way, as do those who, guided by such theories, interpret specific words and phrases of the text. That vision of interpretation, while allowing judges to reject the historical intentions of the authors of the words, nonetheless acknowledges the important distinction between political theory and legal interpretation since it is always the *text* whose meaning and purposes are at issue in interpretation. In that way, interpretation walks the line between unconstrained political theory, on one hand, and politically neutral, historical excavation into the specific meanings envisioned by the authors of the law, on the other. Interpretation is not entirely normative, like political theory, but neither is it purely descriptive, as originalists envision.

Having rejected originalism, then, we now turn to the second theory of constitutional interpretation I will discuss—democratic proceduralism. Although resting on a very different conception of constitutional democracy and the role of judicial review, democratic proceduralism shares originalism's belief that judges should set aside their own values in interpreting the Constitution. For the proceduralist, however, judicial review rests not on the demand that the social contract be maintained but instead on the political and moral advantages of democratic processes.

2

Perfecting the Democratic Process

Robert Bork and William Rehnquist both put great stock in majority rule; Bork even compared an activist Supreme Court with a military coup, suggesting that the justices have no more basis on which to impose their values on the majority than the Joint Chiefs of Staff.[1] Since values are subjective, originalists argue, and there is a wide diversity of opinion about them, the best alternative is for the majority to decide. In that way, decisions are made by elected officials who are far more representative of society's moral, ethnic, and religious diversity than unelected judges.

As we have seen, however, it is in fact no more "undemocratic" for the Court to impose the values of long-dead framers on contemporary majorities than for military leaders to impose *their* values. The progression of this argument nicely illustrates how interpretive issues are tied to philosophical ones. Beginning with a question about the meaning of a specific provision limiting legislative power ("cruel and unusual punishment," for instance), the originalist's answer is that judges must rely on the intentions of the framers. But then, when asked *why* that is the right interpretive approach, originalists respond with the claim that judicial review serves to keep the constitutional "covenant"—a view of government that is at once deeply philosophical and, when explored in detail, completely unattractive.

Two broad alternatives to original intent are available. One is to acknowledge that judges cannot avoid giving expression to their own moral views in exercising judicial review—a position I will consider in later chapters. The other option, which is the subject of the present chapter, follows originalism in rejecting this form of activism while replacing originalism's interpretive and philosophical assumptions with an account of constitutional interpretation and judicial review based on the nature and value of democratic processes themselves. So, like originalism it takes seriously the claim that political legitimacy is best achieved through majoritarian procedures; but unlike originalism it does not envision judicial review as serving to enforce the terms of the social contract—a contract that proceduralism agrees the people cannot fairly be said to have accepted. But although it may seem that its democratic commitment is incompatible with judicial review, proceduralism rejects that conclusion, arguing instead that judicial review could still play a key role even in a government whose deepest commitments are to democratic procedures. To develop this argument, we must first consider carefully just what the democratic ideal actually involves; then we can go on to discuss the role of judicial review and the nature of constitutional interpretation in light of that understanding.

The Meaning of Democracy

It is sometimes thought that "democratic" governments are ones in which the people are sovereign. But what exactly might that mean? Both Hitler and Stalin claimed to be speaking for the people, and at times each had wide popular support. Neither, however, was the head of a democracy. Nor would it be right to understand democratic governments as ones whose officials are influenced or controlled by the governed, since most political institutions are in some sense influenced by the people—through riots and strikes if nothing else.

These reflections suggest we would do better, instead of focusing on vague notions like "popular sovereignty," to think of democracy in more procedural terms. With that in mind, we might define democratic government as a process in which the people choose the laws that will regulate their lives. If we use this definition, the purest form of democracy, modeled on the New England town meeting, takes place when people meet together to express their opinions and vote on each issue.

That definition of democracy came in for considerable criticism in the 1940s and 1950s by scholars who regarded widespread citizen participation and strong self-government as neither workable nor desirable.[2] According to these theorists, democratic governments are distinguished from others not by a process allowing the people themselves to determine the laws but by a process whereby those who make the laws are themselves chosen. Instead of leaders winning power through a military coup or kinship with a previous ruler, a democratic political regime was thought of by these critics as one where leaders are chosen through fair elections. Widespread, popular participation in the actual lawmaking process was viewed as a destabilizing, often irrational force.

But what, exactly, is meant by a democratic electoral process? Although perhaps tempting, it would again be wrong to say *simply* that democratic governments are ones where policies or leaders are elected. Brezhnev won landslide victories in the former Soviet Union, though I assume we agree the Soviet system was not a democratic one. So although elections are *in some sense* necessary, only certain electoral forms provide for truly democratic government. But what sort of elections? The answer is in three parts.

First, the leaders must be chosen in elections that are *regular;* elections once a century or even once a generation are not sufficient. Elections must also have two other characteristics: They must be both *open* and *fair,* though it is controversial just what each requires in practice.

Openness refers to the fact that a genuinely democratic government cannot un-reasonably forbid categories of people (for example, women or racial groups) from holding office and voting. Truly democratic regimes allow all qualified individuals an opportunity to participate in public life. Just what that means in practice, however, is sometimes controversial since there may be wide disagreement about what groups are truly "qualified." Prior to passage of the Twenty-sixth Amendment in 1971, the voting age in different states at different times ranged from eighteen to twenty-one. Others have felt, including many at the time of the framing, that only people who own property should be allowed to vote, and it is still sometimes suggested that school board elections should be limited to people with a stake in the outcome—parents and property owners.[3] Others have claimed there should be a minimum standard of education or literacy.[4] But whatever one thinks about these particular issues, the fact remains that a genuinely democratic government cannot deny the opportunity to vote and hold office to those who de-serve such rights. Openness, like regular elections, is at the core of democratic government; a system allowing only members of one political party to vote would not be democratic.

Besides regularity and openness, democracy also requires its elections be *fair* in the sense that the influence or power of the voters be correctly distributed, giving everybody an equal opportunity to participate. Here there arise, for instance, var-ious questions about weighted voting: Is it the ideal that all voters should have equal influence, or is it compatible with democracy that U.S. senators from Cali-fornia represent over twenty million people while those from Wyoming have less than a half million constituents? The Supreme Court requirement is that (except in the Senate) there be one person, one "equally weighted" vote,[5] though just what that requires in practice has been hotly disputed. Does a fair voting system require voting districts be drawn to assure that minority groups are represented in rough proportion to their numbers, for example?[6] And what about the possi-bility that the wealthy might exercise undue influence on the electoral process?[7] All of these questions, then, fall under the general heading of fairness.

The ideal that voting power is distributed fairly has another dimension. In or-der to secure genuinely competitive elections where each has an equal chance to participate, freedom of speech and the press must also be assured. No system is fully democratic unless candidates and citizens have the ability to defend one can-didate and criticize the policies and character of others. Without that right, no election can be genuinely fair and no system truly democratic; those in power and their supporters would enjoy a serious advantage, freed of the possibility that crit-ics would be able to hold them accountable by appealing to the electorate without fear of censorship or punishment.

This, then, is the "minimalist" understanding of democracy: Either people vote on the laws directly or leaders are chosen to make them under a regime of regular, open, and fair elections, including freedom of speech and the press. The nature of the relationship between the governed and the laws can therefore be either direct or indirect, that is, the laws may be chosen directly by the people or they may be the result of decisions made by democratically elected representatives. And although we may think of the former as "more democratic" than the latter, both clearly fall within the concept of democratic government. In what follows I will use this minimalist definition in discussing democratic legitimacy and the "proceduralist" theory of constitutional interpretation. We now turn to the substance of the theory, asking first how a court exercising judicial review and committed to democratic proceduralism might define its responsibility. Then in the next sections I consider whether democratic proceduralism succeeds in showing the Constitution to be a reasonable attempt to achieve worthy objectives. Along the way, I distinguish two versions of proceduralism, standard and strong, arguing that although the stronger version comes closer to providing an adequate account of judicial review and constitutional interpretation, neither version succeeds.

Democratic Proceduralism

Both Rehnquist and Bork claim that a natural antipathy exists between judicial review and democracy. Judges are not elected, nor are their decisions on a law's constitutionality subject to popular review (except through a very cumbersome amending process). What could then be more anti-democratic than giving these nine people authority to declare unconstitutional laws enacted through referendum or passed by elected legislators? This is an especially sharp question since, as we saw in the last chapter, the response that in exercising judicial review the Court is merely enforcing the original contract agreed on by the people is really no answer at all.

The position I now want to consider—democratic proceduralism—holds that justices must ignore their own opinions about the substantive merits of legislation whose constitutionality is challenged, focusing instead on making sure that the political process is genuinely democratic. Then, assured the process has worked correctly, judges are to ignore their own opinions of a law's merits and assume that because they emerged from a democratic process there is no constitutional reason to reject them.

We can begin with a point that was considered in the last chapter. All political processes, we noted, rely on constituitive rules to establish the institutions of government and then to set out the powers of each. Such rules must define the size of the representative assembly, its membership, and its authority. Beyond that, any regime, but especially one that includes different branches within the national government as well as state and local governments, must have an elaborate scheme of rules defining the powers of each branch. What happens when state and federal laws conflict? How much power can Congress delegate to executive agencies? When may a president refuse to comply with a request by Congress?

What are the limits on Congress's power to regulate commerce among the states? A supreme court is a natural institution to resolve such questions. Congress or some other branch is another possibility, though as we saw earlier, the ideal of the rule of law suggests that no branch should serve as judge in its own case, including cases in which the boundaries of its power are at stake. And although referring the issue to the people is a theoretical possibility, that would be cumbersome at best and perhaps even impossible in practice.

Here, then, is the first potential role for a procedurally oriented supreme court: to assure that the various governmental institutions function within their respective bounds, according to the constituitive rules found in the Constitution. But that is only the beginning of the role the court should play in a system committed to democratic ideals. Democratically elected officials cannot be counted on to see that the process remains democratic, especially when it is not in their interests. Nor can they be counted on to eliminate already well-entrenched, anti-democratic practices that might have helped legislators win their seats. Elected officials generally want to stay in office, and that goal is often furthered by political processes that are *not* fully democratic.

The earliest and most famous statement of this problem came in a footnote to *Carolene Products,*[8] a 1938 Supreme Court case upholding the constitutionality of a federal statute prohibiting interstate shipment of "filled" milk (i.e., skim milk with vegetable oils added to increase the fat content). In order to understand the significance of the footnote, it is important first to place *Carolene Products* in its historical context. During the recently concluded period in the Court's history known as the Lochner Era, the Court had sought, unsuccessfully, to stem the tide of economic regulation in the name of the free market, overturning a wide range of laws designed to benefit workers by limiting the hours they could be required to work,[9] providing minimum wages,[10] and assuring the right to organize a union.[11] All of this was carried out in the name of individual rights against state and national governments' efforts to regulate the market. Freedom of contract, said the Court, is a fundamental right that government cannot take away.

By 1938, the Lochner Era was in full retreat in the face of Franklin Roosevelt's overwhelming presidential victory in 1936 and his aggressive attack on the Court. Many Supreme Court justices no longer saw themselves as guarantors of citizens' natural rights to freedom of contract and private property, as they had during the Lochner Era. Indeed, the purposes and legitimacy of judicial review had become an open question, much debated among judges, politicians, and the public at large.

Though the particular case was relatively unimportant, Footnote 4 of the majority opinion suggested a new direction the Court might take in exercising its power to review the constitutionality of laws. The opinion stated that although the Court was willing to allow Congress wide latitude in regulating the economy, such as the regulation at issue in *Carolene Products,* it might in the future look more critically at a different type of case. Justice Stone went on to say that in the future the Court would recognize that "legislation which *restricts those political processes* which can ordinarily be expected to bring about repeal of undesirable legislation, is to be subjected to more exacting judicial scrutiny."[12] Footnote 4 thus suggested that although it was not the Court's primary responsibility to enforce rights like freedom of contract, at least ones not explicitly stated in the Constitution, it remained for the Supreme Court to insure that the political process functioned correctly, that is to say, democratically. And by limiting itself to *process* rather than substance the Court would not be usurping the prerogatives of democratically elected representatives. Indeed, the Court's new role was quite the opposite of the one it had assumed during the Lochner Era: It was now *on the side* of the democratic process rather than opposing it in the name of individual rights.[13] It seemed that the Court had found its legitimate role.

But how, exactly, was the Court to fulfill its new role as guarantor of democracy? What did Justice Stone mean when he said the political process itself could become "restricted" by legislation? The answer is found in the definition of democratic procedures discussed in the last section: Democratic governments select leaders through regular, open, and fair electoral processes. When such processes exist, the government is genuinely democratic. Viewed in that light, the defects or "restrictions" referred to by Justice Stone are really failures of the political process to meet the standards of a truly democratic government.

Even if provision is made for regular elections, as required by the Constitution, governments may nonetheless fail to see that procedures are either open or fair. The most obvious of these defects is restriction on voting. No government is genuinely democratic unless it protects the rights of all who are entitled to participate in the political process. Judicial review therefore becomes important because those enjoying the powers and other perquisites of office may resist opening up the process or may even work to close the process, since new voters and ideas may threaten their power and position. It is both natural and necessary, then, that an unelected body such as the Court should be charged with perfecting the democratic political process by overseeing the voting process.[14]

Concerns about voting procedures played a critical role in the Court's thinking during the tenure of Chief Justice Earl Warren. Beginning in the mid-1960s, the Warren Court decided numerous cases on these grounds, often to the great horror of elected officials. One example occurred in 1965 when the Court overturned a law preventing soldiers stationed in a state from voting in that state due to insufficient periods of residency.[15] Another decision invalidated a Tennessee law requiring everyone, including college students, to have resided in a state for at least a year before they could vote.[16] The Court also overturned a New York law requiring voters in certain school districts to either own property there or have children in public schools.[17] Justice Warren, in delivering the Court's opinion in that case, described the Court's rationale in these cases as follows: "The presumption of constitutionality ... [is] based on the assumption that the institutions of state government are structured so as to represent fairly all the people. However, when the challenge to the statute is in effect a challenge to this basic assumption, the assumption can no longer serve as the basis for presuming constitutionality."[18] This description of the Court's thinking comports well with Stone's footnote in *Carolene Products:* Although the Court should be wary of intervening when the political process has worked fairly, it should scrutinize laws carefully when that premise is challenged. The vote, Justice Warren stressed, is the foundation of representative government.

But openness in the sense of seeing that all those entitled to vote are allowed to vote is only part of the picture; democracy is also compromised when *fairness* is sacrificed and some people's votes count for less than others. And here again the Warren Court was in the forefront, overturning laws that diluted the influence of voters. In 1960 the justices invalidated a proposed redistricting plan on the basis that it had been drawn with the purpose of limiting the influence of blacks.[19] But a far more controversial and far-reaching case occurred a few years later.

In 1964 the Court held unconstitutional a Georgia districting plan that allowed a fifth of the state's population to elect only 10 percent of its members to Congress. Relying on the requirement under Article I, Section 2, that U.S. representatives must be chosen "by the people," Justice Black stated that "one man's vote ... is to be worth as much as another's."[20] "No right," he went on, "is more precious in a free country than that of having a choice in the election of those who make the laws under which, as good citizens, they must live. Other rights, even the most basic, are illusory if the right to vote is undermined."[21] Soon thereafter the Court went much further, attacking districting patterns for state and local offices as well as national ones. Alabama had not reapportioned its state legislature in over sixty years, during which time there had been significant shifts in the population from rural to urban areas. The result was that a minority of people elected a majority of the state legislators. Similar conditions existed in five other states, where migration from rural to urban areas gave rural voters disproportionate influence in their state legislatures. Relying on the Equal Protection Clause of the Fourteenth Amendment, the Court held in these cases that it is a violation of the Constitution whenever a citizen's vote is diluted as compared to others in the state. One person, one vote, it again said, was to be the constitutional standard by which the political process was to be judged.[22] Again the Supreme Court acted to assure that the ideals behind the democratic process, equality and fairness, were maintained. To give one citizen only half of the voting power of another, as many legislatures had done by refusing to reapportion themselves in light of population shifts, did not assure fairness or protect citizens' rights to equal concern and equal standing. In subsequent cases the Court applied the one person, one vote principle to a county school board,[23] to a city council,[24] and eventually to any governmental agency that exercises "general governmental powers" over a geographical area.[25]

Besides fair voting processes, freedom of speech and the press are also, I have argued, essential features of a fair democratic government. Citizens opposed to government policy cannot be said to have the opportunity to participate on equal terms unless they are able to make their views known to others, and a vote is not fair if some candidates for office are denied the opportunity to win supporters by criticizing those in power. If those in power were allowed to limit either type of speech—about issues or candidates—they would win a substantial advantage over those not yet in power and unknown to the electorate.

It can be expected, then, that a Court following principles of democratic proceduralism described in Footnote 4 would be led to reject laws limiting free speech. And just as the theory suggests, in the early part of this century the Court began a long process, culminating during the 1960s, that established wide constitutional protections for political speech. A leading case, *Brandenburg v. Ohio*, held that citizens are free to criticize government policies unless the speech is "directed to inciting or producing immanent lawless action and is likely to produce such action."[26] No longer could government prosecute people for criticizing the government or advocating its overthrow. To withstand constitutional scrutiny, the law must be limited to speech that is both aimed at producing lawlessness *and* is uttered in an environment likely to produce such illegal acts.

Besides protecting people who criticize governmental policies and structures, the post–*Carolene Products* Court also strengthened the right of citizens to criticize public *officials*. In another major case, *New York Times v. Sullivan*, the Court held that public officials could sue for libel only if statements made were both false and made with "actual malice," defined as either knowledge that the statement was false or else reckless disregard of whether it was false or not.[27]

Quite clearly, then, the Supreme Court in the previous generation made serious strides toward opening up the political process: It has promoted openness by extending the right to vote and fairness by both assuring that votes have the same weight and securing wide protections for political speech. Like original intent, proceduralism seeks to assure that the value judgments of judges are kept in check. It asks judges to focus entirely on the democratic process, not on substance, when exercising judicial review. If a law emerges from a genuinely democratic process, then from the constitutional standpoint the law must not be rejected. Judges should exercise judicial review only in order to assure that the democratic processes work properly.

Proceduralism thus rests on democracy's special claims of legitimacy, asserting that we *do well* to understand our political system as committed, at its deepest level, to democratic values; understood that way, says the proceduralist, the Constitution becomes a reasonable effort to achieve worthy objectives. Like original intent, proceduralism too has its own normative infrastructure. But rather than enforcing the terms of the original contract, proceduralism sees the Constitution as establishing a government whose deepest commitment is to democracy itself.[28] We must therefore consider the merits of this underlying political commitment: Do democratic processes provide a distinctive justification for constitutional government?

Democracy as Fair Compromise

For democratic proceduralism, the most natural way to picture the link between democratic processes and the effort to understand the Constitution as a reasonable effort to achieve *worthy* objectives, I will argue, is to assume democratic processes are self-legitimizing in the sense that *whatever* laws emerge will be legitimate, just because they are the outcome of a fair and open political process. This view of democracy invites us to think of democratic processes as an example of a certain type of justice, identified by John Rawls as pure procedural justice.[29]

To understand pure procedural justice and its significance for proceduralism, it should be contrasted with two other types, perfect and imperfect. Imperfect procedural justice is illustrated by a criminal trial. There, justice demands that all (but only) the guilty are punished; but the trial procedure itself is *imperfect* since the guilty are not always convicted and more infrequently (we hope), the innocent are sometimes found guilty. A system of *perfect* procedural justice, in contrast, *guarantees* that justice is reached (hence the term "perfect"). An example of this might be a rule designed to assure that two people receive equal shares of cake by providing that one person cuts the cake into pieces while the other selects his piece. If the procedure works in this idealized way, of course, it would not matter who divided and who chooses, or, if there are more than two, who chooses first. Justice (equal shares) is assured.

Though perfect and imperfect procedural justice differ in one respect—only perfect guarantees the process will give the just result—they are similar in that in both we know what justice requires independently of the procedure. A third form is *pure* procedural justice. Unlike the trial (imperfect) and the cake dividing (perfect), in gambling, for example, we do not have any such criterion by which to decide, independently of the process itself, if the outcome is just. We cannot say that it is just that Jones or Smith wins at poker; we can say only that if the rules are fair and the game is played by the rules, then justice will be served no matter who comes out ahead. With pure procedural justice, then, we cannot know ahead of time, before the procedure is completed, what justice requires. There is no independent criterion, and justice is guaranteed whatever result the process produces.

Now, justifications of democracy fall into the two categories of pure and imperfect procedural justice.[30] According to those who defend democratic procedures on the model of imperfect procedural justice, democratic government is an instrument, but only an instrument, by which to achieve important values. Defenders of this view differ widely, of course, about what those values are as well as over what specific procedures will most likely achieve them. John Stuart Mill stresses two goals of democracy: (1) it allows people to protect themselves and their rights and (2) it encourages free thinking and moral independence.[31] John Rawls says surprisingly little about the subject, though his basic assumption is that some form of majority rule is most likely to produce laws that are compatible with the two principles of justice.[32] Earlier disputes about the importance of po-

litical participation, for example in the work of Joseph Schumpeter[33] and Carole Pateman,[34] see democracy as an imperfect procedure. Critics of too much popular involvement, like Schumpeter, focus on the role elections play in maintaining stability, while Pateman, in contrast, stresses the value of participation in creating a rational and democratic populace. But in each case it is assumed we have on hand independent criteria for judging political procedures, and majority rule cannot guarantee they will be met.

Not surprisingly, those who view democratic procedures through the lens of imperfect procedural justice are sometimes anxious to limit majority rule. Indeed, despite his advocacy of representative government in general, John Stuart Mill famously defends plural voting—giving the better educated extra votes—as an effective way for democratic government to improve its chances of accomplishing the ends he thinks it is designed to serve.[35] Indeed, anybody who envisions democratic government on the model of imperfect procedural justice—that is, as an instrument useful only for achieving other ends—may on occasion wonder just how much democracy is a good thing. Mill and Schumpeter both illustrate this, claiming it is unreasonable *not* to limit it when that is more efficient.

It is unclear, then, that the deep commitment to democratic government found in the Warren Court and often expressed by proceduralist-oriented constitutional theorists can live comfortably with the model of imperfect procedural justice. If democratic procedures are *only* viewed as imperfect means to achieving ends, such as protection of basic rights, then there will always be a tendency to limit democratic government in order to realize such goals better.

In order to explore the merits of democratic proceduralism I will assume, then, that it seeks a firmer foundation for democracy on the model of pure procedural justice.[36] This is natural, however, given proceduralism's emphasis on democratic values, its insistence on moral and political neutrality of judges, and its skepticism about rights. Once the democratic process is functioning properly, says the proceduralist, judges must abide by its results and avoid injecting their own values into the law. Skeptical about natural rights, proceduralists also lack an independent criterion by which to judge the results of the political process. Those who envision democracy on the model of perfect or imperfect procedural justice, by contrast, would have to consider the possibility that more activistic judges should facilitate the (non-procedural) goals of the political system in other ways, for instance by protecting minority rights or helping secure the general welfare. But for democratic proceduralists committed to judicial neutrality, once they reject originalism there is little on which to base legitimacy other than democratic procedures themselves.

How then might a defense of democratic government on the model of pure procedural justice proceed? We can begin with the following example. Imagine a group of friends who decide to form an eating club for the purpose of visiting a different restaurant each month. While discussing their new club, the friends wonder how they will decide which restaurants to go to. As the discussion proceeds it becomes clear there is wide disagreement among the members: some prefer meat and potatoes, some Chinese food, some Italian.

Now imagine that one member, Claiborne, rises to propose a solution: *He* should be given the authority to decide for the group, since he is known to have especially good taste. Others, however, object. It is unfair, they say, that they should be excluded from the process. The best decision-making procedure, one that achieves the ideal of a fair compromise, is a democratic vote.[37] Nor would it matter if the club decides to elect a committee to make the decision rather than having everybody participate in the deliberation. As long as the representatives are chosen democratically, the outcome will still be a fair compromise: Nobody is excluded from voting, and nobody has extra votes.

A related point on behalf of voting, besides the fact it is a fair compromise, is connected with another ideal—equality. Even though citizens differ in natural talents and moral virtue, it is often claimed that nevertheless we are all still equal. But given the many ways we are *unequal*, what might equality mean? One answer, suggested by the example of the eating club, is that equality is a normative ideal that teaches how we should treat each other rather than a psychological or sociological one concerning our abilities or personalities. To say all persons are equal means we are entitled to equal standing in the political community.[38] But clearly one way government may deny equal standing is to deny the vote. Only if all are given a vote, equal to the votes of others, can we say the government assures equal standing. To allow only some to vote, or to weigh the votes of some more than others, says to citizens that they are not full members of the political community—they are outsiders who do not really "belong" or else they lack the moral or intellectual powers necessary to claim the title of equal citizen.[39]

So the case for claiming that democratic procedures are a form of pure procedural justice is based on two of the features unique to democratic government: the inherent fairness of the process and the fact that it expresses the ideal of equal citizenship. But besides fairness and equality, democratic processes have still another basis on which to stake a special claim to legitimacy.

As we have seen, the notion that governments derive their authority from the "consent of the governed" has been an especially powerful one in American political culture. In the last chapter we discussed one of the ways judicial review can be thought to rest on consent: in the fact that the people adopted the original contract (the Constitution) and judges are charged with enforcing its terms. That approach failed, but we should not conclude that consent is irrelevant—only that we must seek to understand it in different terms.

Now democratic processes can also be thought to give expression to the ideal of governmental power flowing from the consent of the governed, though in a different sense than originalism. John Locke elaborated on the idea this way. Once a government is initially established, which he said must be by *universal consent,*[40] it must then make decisions—"move one way," as he put it. But since it is not possible to get universal consent to each law, he said, it is "necessary the Body should move that way whither the greater force carries it ... [and that] is the *consent of the majority.*"[41] So in other words, given the fact a government must make some decision or other, yet cannot hope for unanimous agreement on every law, it can still reflect the consent of the people by relying on democratic procedures. In that sense, following democratic processes and acting in accord with the consent of the people are just two sides of the same coin. Although those who lose the vote have not had their way, and in that sense *they* did not consent, still the fact the decision was made in accord with majority rule gives at least some sense to the notion that laws are consensual. Indeed, perhaps that is the most we can hope for, or should expect, from the ideal of a government based on the consent of the governed.

This claim should not, however, be taken to establish more than it does. Majority rule is no guarantee that laws will reflect the "will of the people" in any stronger sense than that they were chosen by direct or indirect vote. If there are more than two alternatives available to voters, for example, then a mere plurality could determine the outcome while a majority would prefer another alternative. There is also the possibility of "cyclical majorities," that is, a (different) majority may prefer A to B, prefer B to C, and yet prefer C to A. In that case, it seems, there simply *is no* "will" of the people.[42] Yet although democratic procedures may not reflect the majority's "will" in any strong sense, they nonetheless do reflect popular consent, if only because the decision results from a fair and open election.

The case for understanding democratic process as an instance of pure procedural justice thus rests on three features of democracy to which a proceduralist may point: the assurance that everybody has the same opportunity to participate by casting one equally weighted vote and therefore that the outcome is a fair compromise; the expression of the ideal of political equality; and the fact that it provides a basis for the claim that the system reflects the consent of the governed. Indeed, we might ask, what more could be expected of a constitution seeking the mantle of legitimacy than that?

This is an important theory, worthy of careful consideration. Before turning to democratic proceduralism's account of the role of judicial review in constitutional interpretation, it is important to consider whether the Constitution actually corresponds to this proceduralist approach. To what extent, in other words, does the proceduralist's theory describe the language and doctrines that have been developed by courts? That question, as we will see, leads to an important issue involving the grounds on which different interpretive theories are to be chosen: Are they to be judged solely in normative terms, or is there another, descriptive dimension against which democratic proceduralism, original intent, other theories must also be tested? Then, in the next section we will weigh proceduralism's central claims: that judges should remain morally neutral by focusing only on procedural defects and that an open and fair democratic process is an instance of pure procedural justice. The chapter concludes with a discussion of a second type of democratic proceduralism, which I will term strong proceduralism, that attempts to meet the objections I raise against the more familiar version described in this section. First, however, I turn to the question of whether this proceduralist model accurately describes the various provisions of the U.S. Constitution and to the importance of that question for the overall assessment of this or any interpretive theory.

The U.S. Constitution in Democratic Perspective

To begin, we should note that democratic proceduralism is at odds with the views of many of the Constitution's authors. Far from being enthusiastic supporters of majority rule, Madison and other framers took great pains to restrain the influence of the majority—often out of fear of the threat to individual rights posed by electoral majorities. Limiting the vote to those who own property, Madison wrote, secures "the two cardinal objects of Government; the rights of persons, and the rights of property. ... It is well understood that interest leads to injustice as well where the opportunity is presented to an interested majority as to an interested minority. The time to guard against this danger is at the forming of the Constitution."[43] Madison believed attacks by the majority on individual rights, mainly to property and religious freedom, were the chief danger to sound government. He wrote a year after the Constitutional Convention in a letter to Thomas Jefferson: "The invasion of private rights is chiefly to be apprehended, not from acts of government to the sense of its constituents, but from acts in which the Government is the mere instrument of the major number of the Constituents. This is a truth of great importance."[44] In "Federalist Number 48" Madison had been even more explicit about the anti-democratic nature of the proposed Constitution. The concentration of all power, he wrote, "in the same hands is precisely the definition of despotic government. It will be no alleviation that these powers will be exercised by a plurality of hands. ... An *elective despotism* was not the government we fought for."[45] These were not idle worries, and when it came time to construct a government, the framers gave full expression to their concerns about the dangers of democracy. Following the approach Madison later elaborated in his famous "Federalist Number 10," in which he outlined the dangers of political "factions" including majorities that sacrifice rights and the common good to their own interests, the framers structured the government in such a way as to set one branch against another, with each having limited power and each being able to check the other.

Even more importantly, the Constitution employed a variety of tactics to insulate the levers of power from the will of the people. Madison indicated the importance of this in "Federalist Number 51," noting that "dependence on the people is, no doubt, the primary control on the government; but experience has taught mankind the necessity of auxiliary precautions."[46] Those "auxiliary precautions" were numerous. The original constitution not only called for a bicameral Congress but members of the Senate were appointed by state legislatures, not popularly elected. Similarly the president, rather than being directly elected was (and still is) chosen by an electoral college that, before the Twelfth Amendment, was in turn chosen by state legislatures. According to the original plan, the Electoral College was to sit as a deliberative body and exercise its own judgment in selecting the president. And the third branch, the judicial, was even more insulated from popular will. It is not an exaggeration to summarize the original Constitution this way: The president (not popularly elected) was to appoint judges with the "advice and consent" of the Senate (the legislative house that was neither proportionately representative nor directly elected). Judges were to serve for life terms, could not have their salaries reduced by elected officials or anybody else, and were removable only for "treason, or other high crimes and misdemeanors."[47]

The original Constitution was thus explicitly undemocratic, placing a variety of roadblocks between the majority and the law, though subsequent amendments have reduced this anti-democratic character. As we have already seen, the right to vote, originally left to states to determine, has been extended to women, former slaves, and persons as young as age 18; poll taxes have been eliminated; the rights of military personnel to vote in state elections secured; and the principle of one person, one equally weighted vote has been extended first to federal and then to state and local elections. Senators are also now popularly elected, and there have been numerous major Supreme Court opinions strengthening free speech and the rights of the press to criticize governmental policies and officials. In that way, it might be argued, the Constitution has evolved into one modeled on democratic contractualism.[48]

Nevertheless, the Constitution is still far from a straightforwardly majoritarian system. Perhaps most important in this regard are the many structural features that make it difficult for majorities to make their presence felt. An elaborate system of checks and balances that divides national power among the three branches and also splits authority between the national and state governments continues, it seems clear, to demonstrate distrust of democracy rather than faith in its capacity to assure the correct outcome. Why, we may ask, would a proceduralist constitution provide for an executive veto and bicameral legislature? Federalism also does not seem to fit comfortably with the proceduralist's understanding, yet the powers of Congress are specifically enumerated in the Constitution, while the remaining powers are, says the Tenth Amendment, "reserved to the States respectively, or to the people." There are other apparently anti-democratic features as well: the Electoral College, which insulates the selection of president from the people, and the Senate, which represents states of varying size rather than population; both seem incompatible with pure majoritarian democracy.

Besides these structural features there is also considerable constitutional language, doctrine, and precedent that do not square easily with democratic proceduralism. One notable example is the First Amendment's protection of freedom of religion. The free exercise clause and the anti-establishment clause both protect individual rights against the majority and have little to do with making the democratic process fair and open. Indeed, a government committed to the inherent worth of democratic processes and to the denial of natural rights would have little room for such protections.[49] Other features of the Bill of Rights also seem at odds with proceduralism, even broadly construed. Why, for example, should the Constitution forbid cruel and unusual punishment if it works on a model of pure procedural justice? And why limit the power of police by requiring search warrants, forbidding self-incrimination, and having all the other constitutional limits of the Fourth and Fifth Amendments?[50]

We have seen, however, that proceduralism is compatible with many of the free speech and voting rights opinions of the Warren Court. Yet if the Constitution were exclusively concerned with democratic processes, as proceduralism argues, then it is unclear why the First Amendment should be extended to protect non-political speech. Once it is clear the democratic process is working properly, proceduralist judges would have no grounds on which to overturn laws limiting other categories of speech that are not political. True, the First Amendment does not say *explicitly* that only speech that involves the political process is protected, but neither does it say the opposite—that artistic, scientific, literary, and other forms of speech cannot be censored by the Congress. The reason democratic proceduralists should tend to limit First Amendment protection to political speech is twofold. First, their vision of the Constitution as an essentially political document concerned only with assuring that the process is democratic clearly suggests that the Congress should be free to restrict all behavior, including speech, that is *not* of a political character. And, second, unless "speech" is limited in that way, constitutional interpreters will be forced to decide which categories are protected and which are not, a decision that almost surely would require judges to forsake the political and moral neutrality that is at the heart of proceduralism.[51]

But the fact is, of course, that the Court has rejected proceduralism's limited, political conception of "speech," holding instead that aside from a few specific categories, *all* speech deserves constitutional protection. These unprotected categories include libel, obscenity, words likely to incite immanent lawlessness, words endangering national defense, and speech uttered at a time, place, or manner that is unreasonable or disruptive. So according to this well-established constitutional practice, any speech falling outside these and a few other categories, whether political or not, is protected by the First Amendment—a fact that seems clearly incompatible with the most fundamental tenets of democratic proceduralism.

A defender of proceduralism might respond, however, that the concept of "political speech" is not as narrow as I have suggested. History, economics, and philosophy are important to political debate; and literature, music, and art also sometimes include important political ideas. Admitting this, however, it is still unclear if one could defend physics on these grounds, let alone mathematics; and although those other forms of speech may sometimes be of use to the electoral process, much of the time they are not and therefore would fall outside the Constitution's protection.

It seems clear, then, that the U.S. Constitution does not fit precisely the proceduralist's vision of government, either in terms of the government's structure, the plain language of the Bill of Rights, or well-established precedents; it often does not look like the proceduralist predicts it should. The question, however, is whether this tension between what the proceduralist's theory predicts and the actual constitutional structures, precedents, and practices constitutes a weakness in proceduralism's claim to offer the soundest conception of judicial review and constitutional interpretation. The proceduralist has two possible answers to this. The first is substantive; the other, more important point involves a methodological issue: What, precisely, are the grounds on which we are to choose among competing interpretive theories?

Constitutional Theory and the Problem of Fit

Substantively, the proceduralist might point out that although the Constitution did originally reflect a strong anti-democratic sentiment, the numerous amendments extending the franchise and restructuring the government have made the current Constitution (which is the focus of our concern) far more democratic than the original. The early document was thus flawed from the proceduralist perspective, but by now its basic nature has changed, so that today proceduralism fits the document fairly well, and justices should interpret it in accord with proceduralism's understanding of the role of judicial review in a constitutional democracy. And, finally, insofar as the Constitution is *not* as democratic proceduralism would predict, it is open to the theory's defenders to claim this constitutes not a criticism of the theory but rather an indication that more amendments may be warranted and earlier anti-democratic opinions challenged.

We might wonder, however, if the Constitution really has changed so radically from its origins. Its most fundamentally anti-democratic structures remain, particularly separation of powers among the three branches. But coming now to the second, methodological issue, it is also open to the proceduralist to argue that not much hinges on the question. The reason for this has to do with how we are to understand the choice we are to make among different conceptions of judicial review and their corresponding accounts of constitutional interpretation. What is needed, then, is a sharper understanding of constitutional theory itself. I will use Ronald Dworkin's view as a point of contrast.[52] First, I will say something about Dworkin's theory of interpretation; then I will ask whether he is correct in thinking the choice among competing interpretive *theories* is itself an interpretive decision, analogous to the choice among different, specific interpretations of a given law or constitutional provision.

According to Dworkin's well-known and influential theory, literary and legal interpretation takes place along two dimensions: fit and justification. Thus, he argues, in deciding if the Constitution protects the right to choose an abortion or to burn the flag, responsible interpreters should seek an equilibrium between these two dimensions, asking which principles of justice best fit and justify the constitutional language, precedent, doctrines, and other aspects of the "practice." Then, armed with those principles, interpreters should extend them to the current case.

This is relevant to the question we have been addressing regarding the choice among competing theories since, according to Dworkin, the twin dimensions of fit and justification apply at this level as well. If one constitutional theory, such as original intent, does not fit well, then that counts against it, just as its failure to justify the document by casting it in a reasonable light also counts against it. He believes that in this way theories such as original intent and democratic proceduralism are themselves interpretive and therefore that to the extent they do not accurately describe the Constitution, they are subject to criticism.

If that were true, and proceduralism is to be judged partly on the grounds of how well it fits constitutional law and practice, then the objection I have been considering would count against democratic proceduralism. The fact that proceduralism fits poorly some of the Constitution's most basic features constitutes a criticism of the proceduralist's account of interpretation.

But it is not clear the proceduralist must accept this conclusion since it is also possible to maintain, along the lines I have suggested, that the Constitution has not yet fully realized its ideal and so would be improved if it were made more democratic. Anti-democratic features of the document would then be viewed as structural weaknesses or even mistakes that, ideally, should be modified or eliminated. Assuming the proceduralist takes that position, the question then becomes why the mere fact the proceduralist would be led to criticize an important aspect of constitutional law or practice constitutes, *in itself*, a ground for rejecting the theory. Indeed, the proceduralist might point out that by assuming that "fit" is a virtue of a political and legal theory Dworkin introduces a conservative bias into the choice among such theories. There is no reason, absent convincing argument, to assume that one account of judicial review and its role in a constitutional democracy is better than another merely because it would require less significant revision of the document.

The proceduralist is not saying, of course, that theories of judicial review and constitutional interpretation are unconnected entirely to the language and history of the Constitution, for that would make such theories indistinguishable from the more general, abstract concerns of pure political philosophy. Put simply, constitutional theories must be about what they say they are about, namely how to interpret the U.S. Constitution, and that requires some minimal amount of "fit." But once it is clear that the Constitution is the subject rather than pure political philosophy, the dimension of fit drops out and no longer has any justificatory power. Beyond that minimum, however, the fact that original intent or proceduralism fits precedents, doctrine, and structure less well (or better) than its rival is not in itself a consideration in assessing the theory. Given that the theory fits sufficiently well that it can plausibly claim to be about *this Constitution*, then the question of fit disappears and the theory is judged on the basis of the normative, philosophical issues I have been discussing.

Whether this proceduralist response is finally convincing may perhaps be doubted, though I do think it has at least some merit. This means, then, that proceduralism cannot be dismissed simply on the grounds that it is more democratic than the Constitution, unless it misses the mark so badly that it cannot even be said to be a theory of the U.S. Constitution but is instead simply concerned with either legal theory in general or a different constitution. Assuming the theory is not misfocused as badly as that, the key proceduralist normative argument must therefore still be confronted. Is the claim that democracy is self-legitimizing a reasonable one, able to present an attractive account of judicial review and constitutional interpretation that thereby presents the Constitution as a reasonable effort to achieve worthy ends?

Is Democracy Self-Legitimizing?

In this section I consider the claim that democratic processes, if working correctly, are a form of pure procedural justice. We need to look closely at this claim, for it appears, at first glance, that such a defense of democracy is clearly inadequate since there is no assurance decisions reached on the basis of majority rule will protect the fundamental interests and rights of minorities. Suppose, for instance, that after genuinely democratic, free, and open elections, a majority in the new legislature passes laws mandating that a certain minority will no longer be allowed to hold prestigious jobs, practice their religion, live among the majority, or attend public schools with their fellow citizens. The new government remains staunchly democratic, however; *democratic processes,* it stresses, will not be disturbed. Members of the despised minority will still be allowed to participate in the political process as equals; they can run for office, vote, and exercise freedom of speech just as before. But the other basic rights they have enjoyed, including freedom of religion, equal protection against discrimination, and normal procedural guarantees securing a fair trial, will henceforth be denied them—all according to the will of the majority as expressed through a fair and open electoral process.

What is the democratic proceduralist to say about this? One possible response is that the proposed laws should be rejected because they are contrary to the plain language of the Bill of Rights and the Fifth and Fourteenth Amendment guarantees of equal protection of the laws. That proceduralist response is inadequate, however, since, to take just one example, the important cases involving discrimination against minorities were clearly *not* decided on the basis of the plain, uncontroversial meaning of "equal protection of the laws." Even the school desegregation cases were met with serious scholarly criticism on the grounds that the judges were using their own values rather than sticking to the plain language and "neutral principles" of the Constitution. Requiring desegregation infringed upon freedom of association, it was argued, and so required judges to impose their own value judgments that preventing legal segregation is more important than protecting freedom of association.[53] On what morally "neutral" basis can the democratic proceduralist override the majority's desire for segregation?

Nor, moreover, is it clear the law should be overturned even if a law is incompatible with the plain meaning of the Constitution. Why, we may ask, should there be *any* limits on elected officials beyond the demand that voting and speech be secured for everybody? Proceduralism thus owes us an account of the Constitution's evident commitment to minority rights, including rights against unfriendly, discriminatory laws that have won the support of an (admittedly prejudiced) democratic majority. The proceduralist must do this, of course, in a way that is compatible with both skepticism about natural rights and with the requirement that the Court concern itself with the political process, never with substantive values.

Footnote 4 suggests an answer. After describing how the Court should scrutinize laws that "restrict" the political process, Justice Stone goes on to state that the Court should also consider "whether similar considerations enter into the review of statutes directed at particular religious ... or national ... or racial minorities; whether prejudice against discrete and insular minorities may be a special consideration which tends seriously to curtail the operation of those political processes ordinarily to be relied upon to protect minorities."[54] Justice Stone thus proposes to expand the concept of a well-functioning democratic process. Besides unwarranted limits on democratic processes, he says, laws motivated by "prejudice" against "discrete and insular minorities" are also of special concern and may henceforth receive "more exacting judicial scrutiny." The suggestion, then, is that even a completely open and fair democratic political process can go wrong when the majority's representatives are *motivated* improperly. Beyond insuring fair and open elections, judicial review demands that courts also scrutinize the political process to assure that the motives of legislators are free of prejudice. So instead of opposing democratic process, judges who use judicial review to filter prejudice from the system can thereby help assure that it exemplifies pure procedural justice.

How might this work? When Stone wrote these words, the United States had still done little to make good on its promises to blacks made after the Civil War. Although the Fourteenth Amendment declares that no state shall deny its people "equal protection of the laws," the amendment had been given little attention by the Court. Indeed, in the infamous 1896 case, *Plessy v. Ferguson,* the Court interpreted equal protection to allow segregated public facilities.[55] If blacks feel that laws requiring them to sit in segregated railroad cars stamp them with a "badge of inferiority," said the Court, it is only because "the colored race chooses to put that construction on it." Prior to *Plessy,* the Court had also held that Congress lacked the power to pass laws prohibiting states from denying blacks the right to vote.[56]

A few years after Stone's *Carolene Products* opinion, however, the Court took its first, halting steps against segregation and other laws disadvantaging minorities. An early case, *Korematsu v. United States,* involved the U.S. military's World War II policy of interning Japanese-Americans living on the West Coast. Although the Court upheld the law on grounds of national security, it adopted what has now become the standard methodology used by the Court in equal protection cases. It held that laws directed at a racial group are "immediately suspect" and subject to "strict judicial scrutiny" by the Court.[57]

Equal protection analysis proceeds in two steps. First, judges identify groups that are in need of special judicial protection against the majority ("suspect classifications," in modern legal terminology) and then apply "strict scrutiny" to any law that disadvantages any one of those groups. In this way, strict scrutiny requires that the Court be satisfied the legislature is pursuing an important governmental purpose *and* that the law is narrowly tailored to meet its objective. If the objective is either unimportant or can be achieved in a way that does not disadvantage a minority, then the law or regulation denies equal protection and is struck down.

Beginning in the 1950s, the Warren Court applied suspect classification/strict scrutiny against a range of laws disadvantaging various groups. Its most famous case, of course, was *Brown v. Board of Education,* which declared legally segregated public schools to be a denial of equal protection.[58] Subsequent cases extended *Brown* by striking down laws mandating segregated public facilities, and in 1967 the Court overturned a Virginia statute outlawing interracial marriage.[59] The Court also broadened its conception of suspect classification to bring other groups under the protection of "heightened," though not "strict," scrutiny, specifically women,[60] the mentally retarded,[61] non-marital children,[62] and aliens.[63]

Democratic proceduralism proposes to understand suspect classification/strict scrutiny analysis of equal protection as an extension of its commitment to perfecting the political process.[64] Laws are rejected because the motives of those who passed them are tainted by prejudice, and suspect classification/strict scrutiny is the method used to detect when the process has been tainted by bad motives. First, laws harming a suspect classification trigger strict scrutiny; then, once this is triggered, the Court asks itself if the law's purpose is sufficiently important and if that purpose could have been achieved in a way that did not harm the protected group. This familiar procedure, according to the proceduralist, is best understood as a mechanism justices use to locate and then eliminate prejudice. But how, then, are judges to distinguish those groups deserving special protection against "unfriendly legislation" from ones that do not trigger strict scrutiny? Clearly, for example, laws putting muggers in jail do not reflect prejudice; but on what basis are proceduralists to distinguish laws of that sort from ones that *are* based on prejudice? We will first look at Justice Stone's recommendation that the Court focus its attention on "discrete and insular minorities." Seeing the weaknesses in that approach, we then consider the nature of prejudice itself and the ways a proceduralist court might seek to eliminate it, consistent with judicial neutrality.

Consider the example of laws "disadvantaging" negligent doctors by insisting they compensate victims of their malpractice or the earlier example of a law sending muggers to jail. Obviously from the proceduralist's perspective these two are not incompatible with the equal protection clause, just as laws requiring segregated schools *do* indicate prejudice. But what justifies that proceduralist claim?

Muggers and negligent doctors are obviously *minorities,* numerically speaking, so it seems that for Justice Stone the key to determining if the law is based on prejudice lies in the twin concepts of "discrete" and "insular." Understood that way, Footnote 4 instructs judges concerned about eliminating prejudice to apply strict scrutiny whenever a law disadvantages a discrete and insular minority. The paradigm of such a discrete and insular group is a small, isolated racial or ethnic minority. But what, more precisely, is meant by the two terms?

By "discrete" Stone presumably meant to single out people who are easily identified as being in a particular group—African-Americans and Asians, for example.[65] The opposite of discrete, in this sense, is anonymous, and since negligent doctors and muggers are anonymous rather than discrete, Stone seems on the right track. The term "insular," in turn, suggests a group that has little contact with others; it is the opposite of diffuse. And here again, muggers and negligent doctors would fall outside of the groups deserving special judicial protection. Is Footnote 4 correct, then, in equating groups that are likely victims of prejudice with ones whose members are both discrete and insular? Have we identified the right test?

A point in favor of Stone's suggestion is the common assumption that prejudice flourishes where members of group are easily identifiable as outsiders and there is little or no interaction between them and the rest of society. If nothing else, religious and racial ghettos should tell us that. (It is perhaps worth noting here that *Carolene Products* was decided in 1938, a time when Jews, Gypsies, and many homosexuals were being murdered in Germany.) The plausibility of the assumption evaporates, however, on closer scrutiny. First, it is too broad: We can readily imagine many groups that are both discrete and insular yet are *not* subject to significant prejudice. Consider, for example, Roman Catholic nuns. Few in society are more insular, and their distinctive clothing, clearly distinguishing them from others, also makes them discrete. Yet it is implausible to suggest that they now need the special protection strict scrutiny affords.

Besides being too broad, Stone's test is also too narrow. Some groups that clearly *do* need protection *lack* the characteristics of discreteness or insularity. For example, women, though discrete, are anything but insular, yet it seems clear they too need judicial protection against discrimination by male-dominated legislatures. Or to take an even clearer example, consider the case of homosexuals. Far from living in ghettos, they are physically distributed throughout the population and associate on a daily basis with non-homosexuals. But in another sense, of course, they are insular; though not geographically isolated, many homosexuals have little or no contact *qua minority* with the majority. Many who work with homosexuals are unaware of that fact. In that sense, a closeted lesbian would be as insular as if she lived in a ghetto, and therefore Stone's analysis would recommend strict scrutiny if she also meets the other test. Discreteness, however, is another story. Gay men and lesbian women (notwithstanding traditional stereotypes), unlike blacks, women, and nuns, cannot be readily identified as homosexuals. Anonymity, not discreteness, marks them.

So if we assume, as I have, that women and homosexuals, who are often the victims of prejudice and laws disadvantaging them, should be protected by equal protection analysis, then we must look beyond discreteness and insularity for an account of the "suspect classifications" that trigger strict scrutiny. Judges cannot identify groups victimized by prejudice by looking just at those two characteristics. But then how *are* they to identify the groups needing special protection, given proceduralism's commitment to exercising judicial review without invoking judgments about values and rights?

Since discreteness and insularity cannot serve as a marker for groups that are in need of special protection afforded by suspect classification/strict scrutiny, the only alternative seems to be for judges to confront the question of prejudice directly, asking first if they have reason to believe a group might be the object of prejudice. Judges would first be asked, based on their historical and social sense, to decide which groups are likely to be subject to unreasonable hatred or dislike and then to determine if a law disadvantaging that group reflects that historical prejudice. Since not all laws harming such groups are based on prejudice, the Court would then apply strict scrutiny in the normal way in order to decide if a law is compatible with equal protection.

Let's assume, then, that we define prejudice as an attitude of unreasonable hatred or dislike of an individual or group—often, though not always, in virtue of some religious, racial, or ethnic characteristic. Since hatred and dislike of muggers, though prevalent, is not unreasonable, they would not be a suspect classification; laws sending them to jail do not trigger strict scrutiny in the first place. And furthermore, even if strict scrutiny were triggered, such laws would presumably survive because they serve important government purposes (such as deterrence) that cannot otherwise be achieved. Nor would laws requiring negligent doctors to compensate victims of their malpractice be subject to strict scrutiny (doctors are not historical victims in this society of prejudice), but even if such laws were subjected to strict scrutiny, again judges know that there are important purposes served by them. However, African-Americans and other racial or ethnic minorities clearly *have* often been subjects of unreasonable hatred and dislike, and therefore laws disadvantaging them would trigger strict scrutiny. So if a law harming them does not fulfill a substantial government purpose or is not narrowly tailored to meet its objective, a judge would infer the law is a reflection of prejudice and strike it down.

Yet although it is better than Stone's emphasis on discreteness and insularity, this approach too cannot serve the proceduralist's purpose. Consider again a judge who is asked to decide whether anti-sodomy laws, placing a particular burden on homosexuals, are compatible with the equal protection clause. To answer that, according to proceduralism, the judge must first decide if members of the group in question traditionally have been victims of prejudice.[66] But how is a judge then to make such a judgment *neutrally*, that is, independently of her larger views on the morality of homosexuality and the rights of homosexuals? If the judge's moral conviction is that there is nothing morally objectionable about homosexual acts or that in any event consenting adult homosexuals have the right to perform the acts, then historical opposition to homosexuals will naturally be seen as an expression of prejudice, and strict scrutiny will be triggered. But if the judge is convinced homosexuality is *not* a legitimate form of sexual expression and that homosexuals have no moral right to practice it, then these historical attitudes will not be viewed as prejudice, and strict scrutiny will not be triggered.

Similar problems arise at the second stage, once strict scrutiny is applied and the judge is asked to decide if the law serves an important government purpose and is narrowly tailored to meet its goal. A judge who thinks homosexuality is wrong may for that reason conclude the law serves an important purpose—deterring immoral behavior. But if the judge thinks there is nothing morally objectionable about homosexual acts, or that homosexuals have a right to engage in them whether they are right or wrong, then the claim that the law is a legitimate instance of legislative enforcement of morality would be rejected on grounds that the law is an expression of prejudice.[67]

I began with the thought that the questions of the entitlement of homosexuals to special judicial protection and the eventual survival of anti-sodomy laws under strict scrutiny both depend on whether the condemnation of homosexuality is based on prejudice, understood to mean unreasonable hatred and dislike. But, I argued, those questions cannot be answered independently of a judge's position on substantive moral questions. No amount of talk about perfecting the democratic process can hide the fact that judges who undertake to root out prejudice from the political process must confront substantive moral questions.

Though an important example, homosexuality is only one of many substantive moral judgments that must be made by judges who rely on this second approach to strict scrutiny. Consider an anti-abortion law. Suppose we agree that women are a suspect classification and have decided to subject the law to strict scrutiny. We then ask if the state has a legitimate purpose in imposing the burden of that law on women. Again the answer must at least in part depend on the judge's moral and political views on the rights of a fetus and on the right of a woman to control reproduction. If fetuses are thought to have a right to life—the same right as young children, say—then laws protecting fetuses will not be likely to be viewed as a reflection of prejudice against women. But if a fetus is seen as having no more rights than a tonsil or other piece of human tissue, then the law serves no legitimate purpose and should probably be struck down as an irrational expression of male legislators' attitudes toward women and their role in the family. And once again we see that judges who follow democratic proceduralism must inevitably take positions, acknowledged or not, about morality and rights.

Perhaps, however, the proceduralist could respond as follows. Suppose a judge is considering the constitutionality of a law banning homosexuality or abortion but does not herself believe there is anything wrong with these practices. Nonetheless, the proceduralist judge might conclude, she should ignore her own moral views and therefore allow the law to stand because it is a result of the majority simply exercising its (different) moral judgment. The response, in other words, is that although it may *seem* members of the legislature were motivated by prejudice against homosexuals and women in these cases, in fact they are not; rather, they are acting on the basis of a moral position the judge rejects. But since it is not the proceduralist judge's responsibility to enforce her moral views, she should not reject the law.[68]

This response by the proceduralist also cannot succeed, however. Recall, for example, that segregation laws were defended in the same terms as we are now imagining the legislature defending its ban on homosexuality. That legislation, it was argued, also does not reflect prejudice but rather the sincere but admittedly controversial moral judgment that racial mixing is wrong. What this shows (since virtually all laws struck down on equal protection grounds could be defended on some moral ground or other) is that equal protection analysis would be useless if judges let laws stand whenever they reflect the moral views of the community, regardless of the merits of those views. Unlike laws disadvantaging muggers and negligent doctors, segregation laws expressed *both* the prevailing morality and the prejudices of the voters who enacted them. Versions of democratic proceduralism that prevent judges from overturning a law on the ground that it reflects a moral view different from the judge's own would leave judges without the resources necessary to achieve the proceduralist's original understanding of the equal protection clause: elimination of prejudice from the political process.

Neither approach we have considered is adequate to the task set for proceduralism of finding a value-neutral method whereby judges can eliminate prejudice. Discreteness and insularity cannot serve to identify groups needing special protection, and prejudice cannot be identified in a morally neutral way. Whether the law reflects prejudice depends on the appropriateness of the negative attitude it represents, so that a judge cannot hope to know if laws reflect prejudice without assessing the reasonableness of the dislike that motivated legislators to adopt the law.

The version of democratic proceduralism we have been testing does not provide an attractive, workable account of judicial review and constitutional interpretation. For democratic processes to be self-legitimizing, on the model of pure procedural justice, they must fulfill Footnote 4's promise to protect minorities. But this cannot be done, I argued, if proceduralism is to remain true to its commitment to judicial neutrality. Proceduralism founders, in other words, because it cannot provide adequate protection of minoritiesOA without violating its central tenet—that interpreters of the Constitution must eschew value judgments in favor of perfecting the democratic process.

Strong Proceduralism

Perhaps, however, we have not given proceduralism its due. In this section I will develop an alternative version of proceduralism that, while admitting judges cannot remain neutral if they seek to eliminate prejudice, argues that this concern with prejudice is unnecessary to protect minorities. If we focus more attention on the requirement that the political process be fair and open, according to the argument, the problems that the standard version of proceduralism encounters in rooting out prejudice do not arise.

Proceduralism, as I have characterized it, depends on the understanding of democratic forms as examples of pure procedural justice; that is, as if it were a game in which there is no independent criterion of justice. Assuming the system is genuinely democratic, in the sense that regular elections are both open and fair, the legitimacy of the outcome is assured. Openness, I said, requires that each citizen be given the opportunity to participate in the process by voting and running for office, and fairness requires that the influence voters are able to exercise is distributed correctly, specifically that each voter be allowed to speak out and cast one equally weighted vote. As we saw, the Court has often seemed to act in just the way proceduralism recommends, by extending the franchise to new groups, requiring reapportionment, and protecting citizens who criticize public officials or policies from infringement of their freedom of speech.

But it might be argued that this familiar conception of democratic procedures does not take seriously enough the ideal of political fairness, that is, the requirement that political power be distributed correctly. For the "standard" procedural position we have been testing, democratic fairness means providing individuals, in the ways I have specified, with an equal opportunity to participate in the democratic process. Suppose, however, that fairness demanded not just an equal opportunity to participate but an equal opportunity to *influence* the outcome. That would provide a different, strengthened conception of democratic proceduralism.

Behind strong proceduralism, then, is the thought that for democratic processes to be truly fair and thereby express genuine political equality, the political process must strive to assure that each citizen can have as much influence on the outcome as any other citizen. The vote, although important, is only a part of the political decision-making process, which also includes discussion and debate leading up to elections as well as the lawmaking process itself.

Continuing the game analogy, we can see that strong proceduralism differs from the standard version in the same way that a lottery differs from bridge or poker. In games like poker it is assumed that fairness is not violated when people lose the game as a result of individual characteristics and talents such as a good memory or an unexpressive "poker" face. As in other examples of pure procedural justice, here there is no test of the right outcome independent of the process, and justice is achieved as long as people do not cheat. The fact that one player is naturally gifted at remembering cards or even has enough money to cover a large bet while another is forced to withdraw if the stakes get too high is not regarded as a defect in the procedure. Other games however, such as lotteries, exemplify a stronger notion of fairness: Here each person has exactly the same chance to win regardless of particular talents or other characteristics. Nobody is disadvantaged in a lottery by an honest face, poor memory, or inability to cover a bet, so that each person's chance of winning is the same as everybody else's. For the strong proceduralist, then, the ideal of pure procedural justice is the lottery, not a poker game. In addition to an equal opportunity to participate (understood as the right to speak, run for office, and cast an equally weighted vote), strong proceduralism demands that everybody be given an equal opportunity to *influence* the outcome of the process. By focusing only on participation while ignoring the opportunity to exert influence, standard proceduralism assumes natural differences do not affect the fairness of the political process; strong proceduralism, however, seeks to compensate for the differences among people that create unequal opportunities to influence political decisions.

Modern democratic politics falls short of this second, stronger conception of political fairness in two respects. First, people's ability to influence the political outcome is influenced by their social and economic situation. Wealthy citizens can purchase access to the media in order to press their political agenda as well as offer large contributions to candidates willing to listen sympathetically to their positions or vote in ways that they wish. Similarly, some people are able to use their economic and social standing to political advantage. They may have friends in positions of power or their socioeconomic or cultural background may enhance their ability to exert political influence. On the other extreme, those who are at the bottom of the socioeconomic ladder experience political disadvantages in a democracy, including, in extreme cases, an inability to read or to take the time away from jobs and family that could increase their ability to exert political influence. In addition to these socially constructed advantages and disadvantages, people differ in a second group of ways that are not (entirely) socially created such as race, gender, ethnic group, intelligence, and articulateness, as well as in more extreme natural disadvantages like mental and physical handicaps.

Clearly, then, the strong proceduralist's ideal could never be fully realized in practice. Characteristics such a good speaking voice, superior intelligence, articulateness, and an attractive appearance will affect people's capacity to exert influence in any democratic society and cannot be completely eliminated. Whether other characteristics like race, gender, and ethnic background are advantages or disadvantages depends on the social realities in which persons find themselves. The strong proceduralist's point, however, is that to the extent society does not achieve a reasonable approximation of the ideal that each should have an equal opportunity to influence the outcome, democratic procedures do not exemplify pure procedural justice and therefore are not self-justifying.

Now standard proceduralism's major problem, recall, was its inability to address the disadvantages faced by minorities and others whose important interests are insufficiently protected in a democratic electoral system. Strong proceduralism, however, is in a better position than standard proceduralism to protect vulnerable minorities just because of its deeper conception of democratic fairness. Publicly financed elections and strict limits on campaign contributions are obvious examples of reforms demanded by strong proceduralism, since inequalities in wealth can play a large role in shaping the amount of influence a person can exert. Ross Perot exercises far more than an equal share of political influence, while many of the poor exercise far less—neither of which is compatible with strong proceduralism's vision of a fair electoral process. But beyond that, strong proceduralism also requires serious efforts at providing equal educational opportunity for all citizens, including minorities. Knowledge may not *be* power, but like wealth, illiteracy, and ignorance, it has important political consequences. Furthermore, poverty itself is also a political disadvantage from the perspective of strong proceduralism: People who must work at extra jobs just to feed and provide clothing and shelter for themselves and their families are hardly in a position to expend time and energy working for political candidates or running for office. A serious commitment to securing an equal opportunity for everyone to exert influence in the political process would therefore require that at least a reasonable economic minimum be provided.

Racial minorities could also win special protection under this revised version of proceduralism. Laws preventing members of minorities from earning a decent living by excluding them from well-paying jobs can be attacked on the ground that they affect the educational and other opportunities of people and thereby tilt the political system in favor of other groups. Extending the argument further, into psychology, it could also be argued that segregation and other discriminatory practices are destructive of people's self-esteem, and for that reason they too undermine political fairness. By teaching some citizens that their viewpoints are not worthy of serious consideration and reducing their self-confidence and sense of worth, segregation and other race laws destroy character traits that can be an important part of an active, successful public life.

Minorities could be protected in other ways as well. One possibility, termed "cumulative voting," means that instead of giving each citizen one vote in an election where, for instance, there are five seats open, each person should have five votes that can be distributed any way the voter wishes. Minority candidates might then win elections they would otherwise lose if enough voters cast their multiple votes for them, just as white politicians might be motivated not to ignore minority voters in hopes of securing some of their votes. Similar procedures might also be put in place in the legislature itself, so that minority (and other) representatives could cast multiple votes for laws that are of special concern to their constituents. There are other, more extreme possibilities as well, such as giving minority representatives multiple votes or even the power to veto bills that are of particular importance to their constituents.[69]

In these ways, strong proceduralism tries to offer a different, more attractive version of proceduralism—one that provides a neutral method for addressing minority rights. Instead of asking judges to assess the motives of legislators in order to root out prejudice as a means of assuring democratic fairness—an approach that runs afoul of proceduralism's commitment to political neutrality—strong democratic proceduralism protects minorities in other ways. For strong proceduralism, the equal protection clause rests not on ideals of racial equality and the commitment to eliminate prejudice itself from the political process but instead on a commitment to assuring equality of opportunity to *influence* (and not just to participate in) political outcomes.[70] From that perspective, segregation and other laws that destroy a sense of self-esteem for some citizens and under-mine equality of educational opportunity undermine the system's fairness by less-ening the capacity of those citizens to exert equal political influence. Strong proceduralism thus takes seriously the arguments that unequal educational op-portunity, or even economic inequality itself, is an unconstitutional denial of equal protection.[71] Strong proceduralists would thus have reason to support the conclusion in *Brown v. Board of Education* (1954).[72] Other forms of segregation and discrimination might also be attacked on grounds that they adversely affect people's self-esteem and thus their ability to influence political decisions and, fi-nally, it is also possible to adjust the political process using devices like cumulative voting to assure more equal influence. Strong proceduralism therefore has more resources at hand with which to protect minorities and others whose interests may not be protected in standard proceduralism; both segregation and large in-equalities in wealth may be challenged on the basis of their impact on the political process. Strong proceduralism's central claim is that if, and only if, the process is genuinely fair, in the same way that a lottery is fair, will it exemplify pure proce-dural justice. Once it is clear, however, that the process itself secures an equal op-portunity for all citizens to influence the process, the outcome's legitimacy is as-sured.

Though in many ways it is a more plausible conception of the democratic ideal than standard versions of proceduralism, strong proceduralism still does not suc-ceed, by itself, in offering an attractive, workable vision of judicial review and constitutional democracy.[73] There are various reasons for this that I wish to point out, some practical and some theoretical. First, it is not at all clear how some of strong proceduralism's proposals would actually work. Among the proposals strong proceduralism offers to achieve equal opportunity to influence political outcomes is the idea of designing electoral districts to assure minority participa-tion as well, perhaps, as providing minority legislators extra votes or a veto over legislation affecting their constituents. But how, then, is it to be decided which groups are to be given such special protection? If Asian-Americans and Latinos are included along with African-Americans, then should Korean-Americans, Chinese-Americans, Cuban-Americans, Mexican-Americans, and so on, also be assured proportional representation? And what about women, homosexuals, and the poor? Women constitute more than 50 percent of the population, so should they be assured at least fifty senators? Asian-Americans now make up about 3 per-cent of the U.S. population, so should they be assured three senators and fourteen representatives?

A deeper problem, lying behind these questions, is how we are to decide which people need such special procedures in order to secure equal influence. If we as-sume membership in certain groups is sufficient to warrant such protections, then how is the group to be identified? It is far from clear whether that can be done without again raising the same value-laden issues involving prejudice that confronted standard proceduralism.

In addition to these problems of identifying those who deserve special concern in a way that is compatible with judicial neutrality, we might also wonder about the political assumptions and consequences of the strong proceduralist. Proceduralists tend to see the electoral process through the lens of the market, as a competition among groups with conflicting interests, and also to assume that these interests follow mainly racial and ethnic lines. Yet neither of these assumptions is entirely true. Although voters obviously do sometimes vote on the basis of private *interests,* their votes also express their *judgments* about major issues of public concern. Issues of equality, rights, and justice are central to public debate and the electoral process, yet proceduralism focuses only on political influence and power. Nor is it correct that people's interests follow racial or ethnic lines; Asian-Americans, Latinos, and African-Americans can be found occupying the entire political spectrum. Yet none of this fits neatly with strong proceduralism's suggestion that electoral politics can be made fair simply by assuring that groups have a proportional share of influence.

In a more theoretical vein, it is not clear that even the strong proceduralist really can get all she wants out of the commitment to democratic fairness and thereby avoid the standard proceduralist's problems in dealing with prejudice. According to strong proceduralism, laws violating religious or other rights, including ones based on prejudice, are of no concern, constitutionally, unless they also adversely affect the fairness and openness of the political processes. There is a serious question, however, whether such laws could, in fact, be rejected solely on the grounds of political fairness. Such laws, in fact, may not have the *political* impact envisioned, and thus (assuming they *should* be rejected) the strong proceduralist would have no grounds to do so.

Furthermore, even if strong proceduralism's approach to problems of individual rights and discrimination *could* reach the right conclusion, there is an important sense in which the theory misses the real point behind those ideals. In limiting itself to *political* problems of such laws, strong proceduralism must strain to find constitutional grounds on which to protect rights and attack discrimination—grounds that have little to do with the actual issues raised by such laws. By limiting itself to procedural objections against segregated educational facilities or laws violating religious freedom, proceduralism seems to overlook the heart of what is wrong with those laws in favor of its more narrow (but admittedly important) concerns about political influence. Put another way, it seems that even if laws violating minority rights did not have an adverse impact on people's ability to influence the political process, such laws would still be objectionable on non-proceduralist grounds—assuming, of course, we had on hand an adequate account of rights.[74]

These objections to democratic proceduralism suggest, then, that we must look beyond the model of pure procedural justice. No democratic procedure, however fair, can guarantee that the outcome will be acceptable, and we must therefore ex-

pand the search for a theory of judicial review and interpretation to include visions of politics that appeal not to the social contract agreed to among the framers
and enforced by judicial review or even just to the virtues of fairness and equality
and consent inherent in the democratic process. We need to look, therefore, at the
capacity of the political process to produce the right sort of laws (ones that respect
individual rights like freedom of religion, privacy, and racial equality) and also at
the role judicial review might play in such a conception of democratic government. Before exploring these alternatives, however, we must take a step back to
consider a view that, along with originalism and democratic proceduralism, challenges the possibility of building a constitutional theory on individual rights.
Skeptical about the existence of moral rights and about the power of political and
legal argument to constrain those who interpret the Constitution, Critical Legal
Studies goes beyond the theories we have discussed so far and denies both the
possibility and the importance of the search for a coherent, attractive conception
of judicial review and constitutional interpretation. These problems will lead to
discussions of the nature of rights and the prospects of a rational, objective defense of rights, as well as the possibility and importance of legal coherence, and
the ideal of the rule of law.

3

Critical Legal Studies
and the Denial of Law

Democratic proceduralism seemed a promising solution to the problems of the role of judicial review and the methods of constitutional interpretation. By limiting themselves to the task of assuring that the political process is genuinely democratic, open, and fair, the proceduralist argued, judges exercising judicial review could provide an important political function while at the same time not overstepping the bounds of their legitimate authority. So like original intent, democratic proceduralism also sought to develop a conception of constitutional interpretation and judicial review in which judges would eschew their own moral views; but instead of deference to the historical intentions of the framers, proceduralism proposed that judges leave controversial moral judgments to the democratic process.

But both originalism and democratic proceduralism failed, I have argued, to provide a workable, attractive conception of judicial review. Given those failures, we are left with two options. One possibility (to be discussed in the last two chapters) is to construct an interpretive theory that avoids the criticisms of judicial activism that motivate originalism and proceduralism. The second option, discussed here in the context of Critical Legal Studies, is in a sense more radical because it rejects as unworkable all attempts to provide a theory of constitutional interpretation that will guide judges to make sound decisions.

Critical Legal Studies, or CLS as it is often termed, is an important, controversial theory that has emerged in recent years. It poses a challenge to constitutional theory at a number of points, arguing that law is contradictory and incoherent and that the "rule of law" is a myth. Judges are not, claims CLS, constrained either by precedents or by concepts but instead may roam freely across the judicial landscape, reaching whatever decision on whatever theoretical base they choose. In that sense, CLS can be understood not simply as another interpretive theory, competing on the same plane with the two I have discussed, but as an attack on the possibility of such theories at all. That is not to say, however, that CLS has nothing to say about constitutional interpretation—only that it denies the claim that judges' decisions are guided by law and legal theory. Political ideology, not law, is the true basis of legal deliberations according to CLS.

After describing the historical roots of CLS, particularly its connections with legal realism, I next consider the basis of the key CLS claim of legal incoherence, especially as it relates to the rule of law, along with how that incoherence leads CLS to its skeptical conclusions. The motivation behind the charge that law is incoherent, I argue, is a pervasive skepticism about the existence of pre-political human rights and, indeed, about the power of moral argument in general.[1] Rejecting the claim that human rights can be rationally defended, CLS (in common with original intent and democratic proceduralism) contends that assertions of rights are just disguised expressions of political power and personal preference. In response to these CLS claims, I first distinguish three different types of rights— legal, conventional, and human—and then consider what it means to claim that any sort of right "exists" along with the merits of the charge that there are no such things as human or moral rights existing independent of law and convention. This discussion of the twin claims of legal incoherence and rights skepticism leads finally to issues of moral subjectivism and objectivity as well as consideration of the importance of the ideal of the rule of law and the consequences of CLS's rejection of it.

Given its understanding of law and constitutional interpretation, I argue, CLS is left with only one conclusion: that judges should accept the reality of the power and discretion they exercise and think pragmatically about the impact of their decisions on the future. Instead of attempting to rule in ways that are consistent with the best theoretical understanding of the Constitution, argues CLS, judges should focus their gaze directly on the moral and political consequences of their decisions. Pragmatic consideration of the future should be their watchword rather than legal theory and rights.[2]

Legal Discretion and Judicial Pragmatism

Historically, Critical Legal Studies shares much in common with an earlier, distinctively American conception of law and legal argument known as legal realism.[3] Legal realists emerged in the 1920s, exerting an important influence on the intellectual legal community and beyond.[4] The realists' enemy was what they termed "legal formalism"—a view they characterized as holding that law is a mechanical, deductive procedure in which general rules are applied, without reference to values, to specific cases.[5] Formalists were also thought by realists to believe that legal concepts map in some way an unchanging, objective moral reality, so that in describing the rules of negligence, criminal responsibility, contract, and so on, judges do not "invent" their legal conclusions but rather "discover" them.

Rejecting these (alleged) formalist claims, realists stressed the wide discretion judges exercise both in deciding what the law requires and in determining the "facts" of a case.[6] Jerome Frank, for example, suggested that rules found in past decisions are "merely words" and therefore cannot control how a judge decides to rule.[7] The law, he therefore concluded, is best understood not as a system of rules but instead as nothing more than all the individual decisions made in the past and a prediction of how a given judge might decide in the future.[8] In addition to believing in wide and sometimes unbounded judicial discretion, realists also stressed the impossibility of separating political and philosophical ideas from legal interpretation. Since law is not a deductive system and judges are free to reach decisions as they wish, it is inevitable that each judge's personal moral and political ideas, biases, economic and political attitudes, and interests will shape judicial decisions.

But besides these critical claims, the realists also had wider aspirations for law, seeking to shape it in ways that accorded with the latest social scientific findings. They saw themselves as progressives; law, they believed, should not be used to protect the powerful against the weak, as they charged formalists had done. Skeptical about legal reasoning and the capacity for guiding judges of abstract concepts often found in the common law, statutes, and the Constitution, realists sought to replace these abstractions with more specific and therefore less flexible guidelines. Thus, realists worked to reform the law across a wide range of issues, including consumer protection, wills, marriage and family, and insurance, all in accord with their progressive sympathies. They sought, in Bruce Ackerman's words, to "craft legal rules to fit very particularized fact patterns."[9] Such particularity was required by their view of judicial discretion, since without very specific guidelines judges are left free to use those more general, indeterminate legal materials in ways that do not accord with the realist's progressive social agenda.

Critical Legal Studies is in many ways the contemporary heir to this legal realist tradition. CLS shares with realists the rejection of formalism, agreeing with them that law is generally indeterminate: Neither the general language of statutes and constitutional rules nor concern with earlier precedents restrains a judge's wide discretion. Judges are free to rule as they wish without the constraining force of legal materials and argument. David Kairys, for example, writes about the inability of *precedents* to control or even limit judicial discretion. Past decisions, he claims, are "largely reduced to rationalizations, not factors meaningfully contributing to the result; they support rather than determine the principles and outcomes adopted by judges."[10] Writing about contract law, Clare Dalton describes the inability of *concepts* to provide legal answers. Legal categories, she claims, are "empty vessels" into which can be poured whatever moral or political views the interpreter may wish.[11] One of CLS's most ardent defenders, Mark Tushnet, summarizes this position in suggesting that in fact all of the materials of legal doctrine "are almost measureless, and the acceptable techniques of legal reasoning. ... are so flexible that they allow us to assemble diverse precedents into whatever pattern we choose."[12]

Nor do legal or interpretive *principles,* or *theory,* provide judges with the road map to correct legal answers that is envisioned by formalists. Stanley Fish, for example, writes of those who invoke general legal principles in defense of their decision: "At the moment of their invocation, 'principles' would be doing rhetorical, not theoretical, work, contributing to an argument rather than presiding over it. Such principles (and there are loads of them) form part of the arsenal available to a lawyer or judge ... and the skill of deploying them is the skill of knowing ... just when to pull them off the shelf and insert them in your discourse. Once inserted, they are just like other items in the storehouse, pieces of verbal artillery whose effectiveness will be a function of the discursive moment."[13] And of legal theory, Fish writes that although it "may sometimes be a component of legal opinion writing and discussion it will not usually be the driving force of the performance; rather it will appear in response to demands of a moment seen strategically, a moment when the practitioner asks himself or herself, 'What might I insert here that would give my arguments more weight?'"[14] All these writers are suggesting, in concert with the legal realists who wrote early in this century, that what is normally thought to be various elements of law—precedents, concepts, principles, and interpretive theory itself—are in reality just rationalizations used to justify what is essentially a political decision by a judge. Legal arguments, in Fish's terminology, are nothing more than the "arsenal" a judge has available to be deployed in whatever way and toward whatever political end the judge chooses.

Though sharing that skepticism about the power of legal argument to constrain, realism and CLS differ in one important respect. The early realists saw law mainly from the point of view of individual judges, so that judicial discretion depended on the judge's personality and other individual traits. They often spoke of the importance of a judge's "intuition" in deciding cases. Judge Joseph Hutcheson, for example, claimed that the key to the judicial process occurs when the judge has an "intuitive sense of what is right or wrong for that cause."[15] Jerome Frank also echoed this emphasis on the role of *individual* judges and their peculiar attitudes in understanding law: Their power, he wrote, is the power to "individualize and to legislate judicially."[16]

Although agreeing that judges exercise wide discretion, CLS tends to think of law and its operation in larger, more ideological terms than did the realists, focusing on the warring political perspectives living within law rather than on the individual judge's personality or values. For CLS, then, a judge's specific "intuitions" (as Hutcheson termed them) are less important to understanding the law than are the political ideologies that compete just under the surface of legal opinions and argument. In that way, CLS tends to view law from a distance, at a greater level of abstraction: To understand law requires looking beyond the individual judge's attitudes, as realists emphasized, to the underlying ideological, class, and other conflicts that are fought out in law and that find expression in the law's ongoing development. None of that is to say, however, that CLS denies the indeterminacy of law; the point, rather, is that the indeterminacy exists at a higher level of abstraction; judges are still free to rule in any way they wish, unconstrained by law, in accord with whatever ideological scheme the judge adopts.

Assuming, for the moment, that CLS scholars are correct in claiming that judges exercise wide discretion by choosing among the different, competing ideological viewpoints embedded in law, how then do they think judges should exercise that discretion? What follows, if anything, regarding judicial review and constitutional interpretation? The answer has already been suggested: Like their realist ancestors, CLS scholars tend to see courts and legal interpretation as vehicles for social change; wise judges acknowledge the discretion they enjoy and exercise it "pragmatically" and in ways that provide for the best future.[17] What constitutes that "best" future is controversial, of course, and will depend on a judge's particular ideological commitments. Indeed, those who share this broadly pragmatic approach to legal decisionmaking will often differ among themselves about specific cases as well as on larger, ideological questions.[18]

The fact that law is indeterminate does not mean, however, that CLS must approve whatever interpretation a judge chooses—only that the dispute be understood as political in nature rather than merely "legal." Thus some judicial decisions will be compatible with CLS political goals, others will not; defenders of CLS can and do support affirmative action, the extension of women's rights, the constitutional right to privacy, and a more equitable distribution of wealth. Some in CLS go further, offering more theoretical proposals concerning the direction law should take. Mark Tushnet, for example, argues for more "decentralization" of political and economic power along the lines of recent participatory democrats and communitarians.[19] None of that is incompatible with their continuing denial of the possibility that any "grand theory" (as Tushnet terms it) can succeed. Judges remain free to decide as they wish, without the constraints of previous cases, abstract legal concepts, or constitutional theory.

Viewed in that light, CLS can be thought of not as offering another account of legal interpretation, competing on the same plane with originalism and proceduralism, but as rejecting the possibility of legal interpretation itself in favor of legal pragmatism. Those who seek a coherent, philosophically attractive account of the Constitution that presents it as a reasonable effort to achieve worthy objectives seek what cannot be had. And so, faced with the indeterminacy and incoherence of law, judges do well simply to act in whatever way best advances their political ideals.[20] The first claim of CLS—legal incoherence —thus leads naturally to its anti-theoretical, pragmatic account of legal decisionmaking. Unconstrained by an inevitably contradictory body of legal materials, judges are left to rule in whatever ways they wish. Pragmatism replaces legal formalism, and judges are free to help construct the best future, however they understand it.

To begin our discussion of these different CLS themes, I will first consider various arguments offered in defense of legal indeterminacy, along with the consequences of CLS rejection of the rule of law. Then in later sections I will consider the connections between legal indeterminacy and the CLS critique of rights and the related topic of moral objectivity, returning finally to reconsider the nature and possibility of the rule of law in light of the CLS critique.

Legal Indeterminacy and the Rule of Law

The rule of law is often thought to mark a distinction between a law-governed regime, on one hand, and one that exercises arbitrary power, on the other. If law is indeterminate, however, and judges have the wide or even complete discretion envisioned by CLS, then it seems to follow that law is nothing more than the arbitrary exercise of power. Claims that judges are bound by the Constitution would seem little more than a facade, since judges can rule in any fashion they want. One defender of CLS, Joseph Singer, puts the point bluntly: "While traditional legal theorists acknowledge the inevitability and desirability of some indeterminacy, traditional legal theory [also] requires a relatively large amount of determinacy as a fundamental premise of the rule of law. Our legal system, however, has never satisfied this goal."[21] This rejection of the rule of law is founded, ultimately, on the premise that legal interpretation cannot be distinguished from politics—a view that I have been defending as well. One reason many in CLS use to defend legal indeterminacy is skepticism about rights and the objectivity of political argument, a topic to which we will turn shortly. But another argument, also familiar in the literature of CLS, rests legal indeterminacy not on subjectivity but rather on the inherent political conflicts found within and between those who make and interpret it. Duncan Kennedy, for example, argues that the law's incoherence flows from the fact that those in power themselves have conflicting political feelings and attitudes; contradictions in law mirror our own internal ambivalence. Kennedy argues that embedded in the private law of contract, tort, and property, for example, are different visions of human relationships, reflecting the conflicting feelings people have between the value of "altruism" on one hand and "individualism" on the other.[22] Neither social and political ideal, he argues, can be ignored if one is to give an adequate account of legal doctrine and precedent.

Roberto Unger takes this analysis a step further, arguing that legal incoherence follows from the conflicting moral and political visions not only *within* but *between* those who construct and interpret the law. "The many conflicts of interests and vision that lawmaking involves," he writes, "are fought out by countless minds and wills working at cross purposes." Because the law emerges from political conflict, he claims, legal coherence is impossible. In order for law to be coherent, he suggests, there "would have to be the vehicle of an immanent moral rationality whose message would be articulated by a single cohesive theory. This daring and implausible sanctification of the actual is in fact undertaken by the dominant legal theories."[23] Since such an "immanent moral rationality" does not exist, the goal of locating a single, coherent theory of the Constitution or any other area of law is doomed from the start, and law is indeterminate. The reason, Unger claims, rests with the diversity of viewpoints among those who are responsible for writing and then interpreting the law. Rather than a single, coherent system, the law more nearly resembles a "patchwork" of incompatible statutes, doctrines, and precedents. Indeed, nothing else but incoherence, he thinks, could result from a process in which many people holding conflicting ideological views make and interpret the law.[24]

The reasons why Unger might think this are not hard to imagine. Laws are constructed at different times by legislators whose political ideologies vary widely and who are sometimes forced to compromise with other legislators whose views they do not share. Beyond that, law is then interpreted by judges whose political beliefs may also diverge from both those who wrote the law and earlier judges whose interpretations they are now free to accept, distinguish from current cases, modify, or reject altogether. Given those origins, it seems inevitable that law should be as CLS predicts.

Nor, of course, do these two sources of indeterminacy contradict each other; indeed, a defender of CLS might point out, the conflicting (internal) political attitudes and the fact that law is a patchwork created by different individuals and groups complement each other. As a result, concludes CLS, law speaks in many voices rather than one voice, and judges are left free to rule in almost any way they wish. Precedents and other legal materials will be sufficiently incoherent and self-contradictory that interpreters will find in them virtually any position that the judge is inclined to take. If some few extreme positions *are* ruled out (an Islamic republic or a dictatorship of the proletariat, for instance), it is also likely that no judge would be tempted by them in any event. Judges, after all, are products of the same legal and political culture that created the precedents, statutes, Constitution, and other materials they are now charged with interpreting.

To this argument that law is contradictory and therefore judges are unconstrained, CLS scholars often add the further claim that even if the rule of law could be achieved, it would not be a worthy ideal. That is because, says CLS, appeals to the rule of law support and enforce existing, unequal relations of political and economic power. David Kairys, for example, writes in his introduction to an influential collection of CLS essays that the "legitimacy" of the law is a natural expression of the "distorted notion of government by law, not people."[25] Appeals to the rule of law, he is suggesting, hide the fact that judges exercise arbitrary, political power and in that way legitimize existing political and economic relations. So, for CLS the ideal of the rule of law is not just unrealistic; it shores up the existing, illegitimate political order, hiding the reality behind the throne—that in the place of reason and neutrality is raw political power.

I want to argue, however, that this CLS critique is mistaken in at least two ways. I will first consider the claim that the ideal of legal determinacy and coherence is unrealistic because of law's inherently political content combined with the fact that law inevitably presents a patchwork of conflicting ideological ideals rather than a single, coherent vision of constitutional democracy and judicial review. This argument leads next to a discussion of the ideal of the rule of law and why it might be thought, contrary to CLS, to be a worthy ideal that should be protected for its own sake.

One initial response to the CLS claim that law is incoherent because of its origins in compromise and conflicting ideologies is simply to point out that those who would seek the best theory of constitutional interpretation need not deny that there is at least some conflict in the law. Assuming, as we surely must, that Kennedy and Unger are correct in thinking that there are inevitable inconsistencies and tensions within the law, it simply does not follow that there is no single, best theory of constitutional interpretation. What it does suggest, however, is that no single theory can realistically hope to bring *every* decision within its scope. But why does this fact, if it is a fact, mean that no theory is better than any other or that any attempt to defend one theory against the others is doomed? Any interpretive theory will almost inevitably view some past decisions as mistakes, though different theories would undoubtedly disagree about which decisions are mistaken and which are not. *If* interpretive theories had to accept the assumption that every past decision was correctly decided, then Kennedy and Unger might be correct in thinking that none could succeed. But that is not what is required of such theories; indeed, defenders of different interpretive theories have often been more than willing to criticize past decisions, as the discussions of originalism and democratic proceduralism clearly illustrate.

The question, then, is not really whether there will be incoherence in law—everybody agrees there will be some—but whether the amount and depth of the conflict is sufficient to establish legal indeterminacy. Political disagreement among law's interpreters and authors does not, by itself, prove that it is impossible to find an acceptable theory of constitutional interpretation and it does not show that judges are "unconstrained" by legal materials. Still, however, it might seem that Kennedy and Unger have at least created a *presumption* in favor of legal incoherence and indeterminacy, given the fact that law both reflects individual ambivalence and is created over time by legislators and judges representing divergent political ideologies.

But this CLS argument again moves too quickly, for in addition to the forces it describes that tend toward incoherence there also exist other factors that will tend to force law in the opposite direction, toward consistency. What I have in mind is the familiar thought that besides seeking to express their political ideals in law, judges also seek—again as a matter of political morality—to *avoid* legal incoherence. This would be the case if legislators and judges had a sense that contradictions in law are to be avoided for their own sake, in order to protect consistency and the rule of law. But do they have such a sense?

Ronald Dworkin suggests they do, using as an illustration what he terms a "checkerboard statute."[26] Consider, he suggests, a law that strikes a compromise between pro-choice and pro-life forces by allowing women born in odd years to get abortions while those born in even years are denied them. Legislators, we may well suppose, would tend to reject such a statute. Forced to choose between it and a law that gives no protection to a fetus (or women's choice), a legislator might reluctantly accept such a compromise as the lesser of the two evils—but the point is that it would, in fact, be regarded as an evil by almost everybody. Or consider other examples: Suppose the law provided for women prisoners to vote and not male prisoners or required negligent heart doctors to pay full compensation while eye surgeons enjoyed caps on their liability. These and other laws are objectionable not just because they treat two groups differently—laws do that all the time—but because they make arbitrary, indefensible distinctions between them.

The point, then, is that if, as seems likely, both judges and legislators would be inclined to reject legal incoherence, then perhaps we have an argument that can block the inference that CLS has advanced from the fact that laws grow out of conflicting ideologies to the conclusion that law must inevitably be deeply and pervasively incoherent. The fact that coherence is regarded as an *independent* virtue by lawmakers and judges constitutes a counterweight to the tendency, emphasized by Kennedy and Unger, toward incoherence.[27]

So the fact that an interpretive theory can always count some earlier decisions as mistakes along with the desire of lawmakers and judges to seek coherence suggest that CLS's claim of legal incoherence cannot be simply assumed. Indeterminacy must be defended on the ground, by entering into the actual details of the law and answering those who claim to establish its coherence. Defenders of incoherence must consider the arguments on behalf of legal coherence one by one, on their own merits. Nor, of course, would it follow from the fact that no theory as yet has been advanced that shows the law to be coherent mean that coherence is beyond reach; perhaps legal theorists have not yet found the right account. The Kennedy/Unger argument does not establish, by itself, the indeterminacy of law.

That leads to the second CLS idea I have described—that the rule of law would not be a worthy objective even if it were attainable. To answer that, we will need to consider carefully the nature of the rule of law as well as the merits of the CLS criticisms of it along with the reasons why others have felt this in fact *is* an independent political ideal. If, as I will argue, the rule of law is an important ideal that does not, as CLS claims, encourage the mistaken attitude that any legal system, however oppressive, is legitimate, then we have further evidence against legal indeterminacy. For in that case not only will it be the case that legislators and judges have a commitment to avoid indeterminacy (as the checkerboard statute suggests), but that commitment to the rule of law would then be a reasonable one.

First, it must be admitted that there is a distinction, sometimes overlooked by the rule of law's more ardent defenders, between the ideal of the rule of law and freedom from unwarranted governmental power. A favorite target of CLS, John Locke, invites that charge when he writes that "freedom of men under government is to have a standing rule to live by, common to every one of that society and made by the legislative power erected in it, a liberty to follow my own will in all things where the rule prescribes not, and not to be subject to the inconstant, uncertain, unknown, arbitrary will of another man."[28] This remark is typical of some defenders of the ideal of the rule of law, especially political conservatives. Friedrich Hayek, for example, expresses a similar view in his well-known attack on socialism. Nothing, he writes, "distinguishes more clearly conditions in a free country from those in a country under arbitrary government than the observance in the former of the great principles known as the Rule of Law."[29] It is important to note, however, that Locke and Hayek are really making two points: Besides defining the rule of law (under which, as Locke puts it, people are not subject to inconstant, uncertain, unknown, or arbitrary rules), they also contend that the rule of law is sufficient for "freedom" to flourish. But is that correct? What, precisely, is the relationship between freedom and the rule of law?

Locke says, rightly in my view, that the rule of law includes the requirements that laws be (relatively) constant or unchanging, precisely defined, known to all, and applied consistently. Yet it is far from clear how those requirements, by themselves, can assure political freedom. Even the most totalitarian and oppressive society might follow the rule of law in the sense of being sure its oppressive and unjust rules are consistently applied, precisely defined, and so on. The most that can be said, therefore, is that the rule of law is a *necessary* condition for the existence of freedom; not that it is sufficient, as Locke and Hayek also suggest.

Having distinguished these two, however, the CLS claim emerges even more starkly. "Surely," we can envision the defender of CLS saying, "the rule of law should not be regarded as an independent political ideal, distinct from all others such as freedom and democracy." To respond to that, we first need to say something about the nature of law itself, for I want to argue not only that the rule of law is a virtue but also that, rightly understood, it is a necessary condition even for the existence of law.

What then is law? Following John Rawls, suppose we think of law as, roughly, a system of rules and other standards, backed by the coercive power of the state, that is addressed to persons in order to enable and encourage them to regulate their conduct.[30] Laws inform people how fast they may go on the highways, how much to pay in taxes, how to make a will or contract, and the extent and limits of their free speech rights, to give only a few examples.[31] They also specify the consequences of failure to follow those rules (for example, fines, prison, compensation to injured parties, or simply the failure to create a binding, legally valid contract or will).

The connection between these thoughts about law in general and the rule of law, then, is that for a legal rule to succeed in addressing persons for purposes of providing guidance, it *must* exhibit to a sufficient extent the characteristics of constancy, clarity of definition, and publicity. Otherwise, at least in the extreme, there can be no legal system at all.[32] Secret rules, for example, could not serve as a guide for citizens; nor could a system of constantly changing rules or rules that are inconsistent or vaguely written establish a genuine system of law.[33]

This does not mean, of course, that there cannot be *some* changes in laws, some vagueness, and some ignorance on the part of citizens regarding what the law requires. No system can perfectly achieve the rule of law. But if all laws are constantly changing, for example, then in that sense law itself is in jeopardy, just as it would be if the rules were unknown to the public. The rule of law is thus a condition of the existence of law itself. In an entirely indeterminate system in which judges acted completely independently of previous judicial decisions and enactments of legislatures or other political bodies, then the law, in the sense of a system of rules addressed to people allowing them to regulate their conduct, would not exist. The CLS claim of indeterminacy therefore cuts more deeply than may at first appear: It follows from at least the more radical versions of the indeterminacy thesis that law is, in fact, a myth.

This fact that, in the extreme, indeterminacy destroys law itself leads us back to the second question I posed and the claim that the rule of law is an independent political ideal. Rightly understood, I want to suggest, the rule of law actually expresses *two* important moral ideals. The first is "formal" justice, or what might be termed equality of citizenship. Here the idea, deeply rooted in the law, is that all citizens are entitled to fair and impartial treatment at the hands of government. For example, if one person is not prosecuted for an act, then the principle of fair equality requires that others also not be prosecuted *unless* there is a relevant difference in the cases. Similarly, if one person receives compensation for damages caused by a negligent doctor, then fair equality requires that another citizen on whom similar malpractice was performed also be compensated. If government fails to live up to this ideal, arbitrarily punishing some or compensating others without regard to how those similarly situated are treated, then the government's claim to political legitimacy is undermined.

This is not to deny, however, that it will often be difficult to know what constitutes "similar treatment" for "similarly situated" people; there is much room for argument about what similarities are relevant and what ones do not warrant differential treatment. The checkerboard statute allowing abortions only for women born in odd years is an easy case; but what about denying victims of a professor's negligence the right to sue, but allowing patients and clients to sue doctors and lawyers? Or if women are given paid leave from work to care for children, shouldn't fathers be granted leave as well? But whatever the difficulties inherent in these judgments, the fact remains that if the law treats persons differently and there is no reasonable basis on which to justify that differential treatment, it has failed to live up to an important, independent political ideal; that is, to treat all citizens equally. It is primarily for that reason, I think, that the "checkerboard" statutes described earlier seem offensive to legislators and judges.

The second moral ideal that is expressed by the rule of law is often termed "fair notice," and it applies primarily in the criminal context. It is the notion that people should be held liable for actions only where they could have been expected to behave as the law expects. This means, however, that the legal system must state clearly what it requires and forbids so that people can act accordingly. In that sense, the due process provisions in the Fifth and Fourteenth Amendments requiring that all levels of government not deprive citizens of "life, liberty or property" without "due process of law" can be seen as the constitutionalization of this second aspect of the ideal of the rule of law. Those provisions demand, in other words, that before a person can be deprived of life, liberty, or property by government, she must have been given sufficient opportunity to conform to the law. This means, among other things, giving adequate notice of the law's existence and reasonable clarity as to what the law demands—exactly the same ideals Locke identified as part of the rule of law. If the law is deeply and pervasively incoherent and judges exercise unbounded authority to rule in whatever fashion their own political ideologies recommend, as CLS thinks, then fair notice can never be achieved.

Legal indeterminacy is not, therefore, to be welcomed, and judges or legislators who reject checkerboard statutes and work to achieve legal coherence are on solid ground. In the extreme, indeterminacy jeopardizes the very existence of law and the legal system. And even in less extreme forms, it undermines two values inherent in the ideal of the rule of law: equal citizenship and due process. So I conclude that although the rule of law cannot guarantee political legitimacy, as Locke and Hayek seemed to suggest, neither can full political legitimacy be achieved *without* the rule of law. If this is correct, then it also provides further reason to be skeptical of the CLS claim that indeterminacy is an inevitable consequence of law's origins among people with conflicting ideological commitments. Not only is the rule of law widely *believed* important, blocking the Kennedy/Unger argument that legal indeterminacy follows directly from law's political character, but judges and legislators have *good reason* to insist that the rule of law is a virtue and choose to protect it even when it conflicts with freedoms or rights they also think important.

Skepticism and Rights

We come, then, to the final basis on which it might be argued that legal indeterminacy is inevitable and the rule of law impossible: rights skepticism. Both CLS and realism emphasize the role that moral and political ideals play in constitutional interpretation. In one sense, of course, these claims are not at odds with the view of interpretation I have defended. Indeed, I argued, value judgments enter constitutional interpretation at two levels: in the judges' identification of the purposes and justifications of individual rights and, further, in their thinking about the purpose of judicial review itself. That is because, as Madison and Wilson stressed, interpretation seeks to present the Constitution as a reasonable effort to achieve genuinely worthy ends—a claim that is itself deeply political and, of course, controversial.

The language of liberties and rights pervades legal discourse. Besides the Constitution's claim to protect freedom of speech and religion, the right to due process of law, rights against self-incrimination and cruel and unusual punishment, and so on, the civil law also includes concepts such as rights of contract, the right to property, and the right to be compensated when injured. Such concepts are not, of course, self-defining; when judges are called on to interpret broad, general terms in the Constitution that protect rights, they inevitably rely on value judgments.

One of CLS's most important constitutional scholars, Mark Tushnet, draws the following conclusion from this.[34] Nobody, he points out, thinks that rights can be exercised regardless of the consequences on others, which means that judges must often weigh rights against competing interests as well as against other rights. But in recommending that judges "balance" the different interests at stake, says Tushnet, legal theorists set judges free to limit or expand a right in whatever way they see fit, showing again that the law is indeterminate.

Take, for example, the question of abortion and freedom of choice. By finding a legitimate governmental interest in protecting prenatal life, judges can then hold that it outweighs the woman's right to choose, turning courts free to decide abortion cases in accord with their own political values, unbounded by law. So, for example, while the Supreme Court has not explicitly rejected *Roe v. Wade*,[35] protecting a woman's right to get an abortion, it has restricted freedom of choice by allowing states to require that a woman listen to pro-life material, wait for twenty-four hours before getting the abortion, and get the consent of a parent if she is a minor.[36] CLS would point out that nothing prevents the Supreme Court from doing that or from not doing it, which shows once more the law's indeterminacy.

Besides appealing to other values against which a right may be balanced, courts can also limit one right by holding that it conflicts with another, more important right. Examples of this abound; indeed it is hard to think of a right that would not, under some circumstances, come into conflict with another. Freedom of speech can conflict with the right to property (Can the state prevent people from posting campaign signs on telephone poles or in parks?), with the right to privacy (Can a candidate sue a newspaper for printing false information about her personal life or for going through her garbage?), and with public safety (as Holmes famously pointed out, nobody can falsely cry "fire" in a crowded theater). Like realists before him, Tushnet finds rampant indeterminacy in these disputes about the definition and limits of constitutional rights.

Besides balancing explicitly protected constitutional rights against other values as well as other rights, human rights also enter the picture in various ways. A judge might think that it is wise, insofar as possible, to understand explicit, constitutionally enumerated rights as attempts to secure citizens' human rights against government. If a judge takes that position, however, then clearly her interpretation of the constitutional right will be influenced by what she takes to be the meaning and limits of the underlying *human* right it aims to secure. Human rights can also enter the interpreter's thinking in another context as well, as judges consider whether the Constitution protects unenumerated rights. Both the Ninth and Fourteenth Amendments can easily be taken to mean that besides explicit rights the Constitution also protects others that are not specifically identified, suggesting another way in which a judge's political values may influence legal thinking. Human rights can be used to give substance and shape to both enumerated rights and to those provisions that seem to protect unenumerated ones as well.

The implications of all this for CLS are summarized by Mark Kelman: "What 'rights consciousness' allows is for us to believe that we ... will fuse with people as long as they respect our rights; we will insist on that separateness guaranteed us by our rights. That rights are in some deep sense so indeterminate as to be illusory—that [problems] ... inevitably recur in *defining* rights, which may demand in an oscillating contradictory fashion more or less concern for others, more or less capacity to call on others to be concerned for us—never fully negates their [supposed] role."[37] These thoughts are not new, of course. As we have seen, Robert Bork and William Rehnquist relied on similar arguments to defend original intent, claiming that judges who rely on arguments about preexisting human or moral rights violate the important requirement that judges remain neutral. Although these conservative originalists speak of such rights as mere expressions of "preferences" and CLS speaks of the "indeterminacy of rights discourse" while pointing out that defenders of rights often have a conservative political agenda, both sides agree that appeals to pre-political human rights do not rationally constrain judges.

All of this may be seen as even more grist for the indeterminist's mill. Not only have we admitted that political morality plays a role in choosing one interpretive theory over another, but now we have added the idea that judges can put human rights into the mix when considering the meaning of enumerated rights as well as in seeking to protect unenumerated constitutional rights.

The importance of rights to legal discourse is therefore at the heart of CLS's claim of legal indeterminacy once one adds the further claim that there is no such thing as moral truth and that genuine objectivity about such questions is impossible. Since there is no right or best answer to moral and political questions and reason cannot resolve such disputes, the decision to weigh one purpose more heavily than another, or to include human rights among those purposes, or to choose to be guided by a particular interpretive theory is nothing more than an act of unconstrained judicial will.

The response to that important, difficult challenge will occupy the rest of this chapter and, in a sense, the remaining ones as well. The strategy is to focus first on challenges to human rights in general, for here, it is often thought, the skeptic's challenge is most difficult to meet. How, it is asked, is it possible in the late twentieth century to take seriously claims that pre-political, human rights exist? Indeed, as we have already seen, some hold that appeals to such rights *must* constitute nothing more than expressions of personal attitudes, class bias or self-interest. This discussion will lead us on to broader issues of moral skepticism and, eventually, to a reassessment of the CLS claim that law is indeterminate. First, however, it is important to see clearly what is involved in the claim that human and other types of rights "exist," since it is here, I want to suggest, that the CLS critics often go wrong.

The Nature and Varieties of Rights

The claim that a person "has" a right is not like saying she has either a Buick or a headache. Whatever they are, rights are neither physical objects nor mental states. But what then *is* a right? And what can it mean to "have" one? To begin to answer these questions, it is helpful first to consider such claims in the context of law and *legal* rights; then I will turn to other forms, including pre-political human rights.

The first thing to note is that legal rights can take many forms: Sally may be said to have a legal right to the hat she just bought, to vote, to be paid by her employer, or to speak her mind on political matters. It would be helpful, then, if these legal rights could be categorized. A standard analysis divides rights into roughly these major groups: (1) *liberty rights,* for example the right to move to California or put up a sign on the lawn supporting a political candidate; (2) *claim rights* that somebody do something specific, for example that the doctor compensate the patient or that the signatory to an agreement abide by its terms; (3) *power rights* making it possible for people to contract to work for McDonald's, to get married, or to leave their property to others after they die; and (4) *immunity rights* that allow members of Congress to say whatever they wish on the floor of the House or Senate without fear of civil or criminal penalty.[38] The first category, liberty rights, indicates the absence of a restriction on a person's conduct. Claim rights involve specific benefits to be received, while the third class of rights, power rights, provides the capacity to change legal relationships, for example by signing a contract, giving away or selling property, or getting married. Immunity rights protect people against various forms of legal sanction.

Returning then to the question of the nature of rights, I want to suggest that in each of these four circumstances if one person enjoys a legal right, that person thereby enjoys a legal *advantage* of some kind. The nature of that advantage varies, though in each case it is either a liberty, a claim, a power, or an immunity. These are "advantages" in the sense that if a conflict arises between people, the person who possesses a right is for that reason better off than the one who does not have it. The right holder may have other, even more important disadvantages, of course; my point is only that the right, viewed in itself, is an advantage.

To see more clearly the kind of advantages legal rights provide depends on seeing the link between rights and duties. Consider, for example, Sally's (liberty) right to move to California. To say she has such a legal *right* implies that others have a variety of legal *duties* not to interfere with her. They cannot prevent her from moving by locking her up, for example, or by putting up a blockade. Besides those duties, Sally's legal right to move also implies that third parties have other legal duties toward her. If, for instance, somebody does try to lock her up or puts up a blockade, then Sally's legal (liberty) right gives her the further advantage that legal authorities (police and courts) have the duty to stop them. Claiming a legal right, then, means one person has certain advantages over others—advantages that take the form of duties owed to the right holder.[39]

The same may be said for the other types of rights: they too are *advantages*—they constitute *duties of others* toward the right holder. To say Sally has the (claim) right to be compensated by her negligent doctor, for instance, implies the doctor has a legal duty to pay her and that the authorities also have the duty to help Sally collect should the doctor refuse to pay. If Sally has the (power) right to sign a contract, then that also suggests others have duties of various sorts: not to interfere with her in making the contract, for instance, and to help her if somebody should try to interfere.

It is also important to note that statements of legal rights can be false as well as true. Sally can *say* she has a power right to buy a slave, a liberty right to burn her neighbor's house, or a claim right that strangers give her money if she asks for it. In our legal system, however, each of those statements would be false: Nobody has the legal duty to give her money just because she asks, let her burn down a house, or allow her to buy a slave; nor are officials obligated to help her if others refuse to give her money or try to prevent her from burning a house or buying a slave.

Legal rights can of course vary from one system to another. In the old Confederacy, whites *could* buy slaves, just as we can imagine a system that allowed a person (an emperor, perhaps) to burn down houses. Whether one has a particular legal right depends on the duties that the law imposes on others, and, as these examples also illustrate, there is no assurance that the advantages bestowed by legal rights will be distributed evenly or fairly.

Legal rights are therefore best understood as shorthand claims about others' legal duties. If legal duties of the right type exist, then the corresponding legal right "exists." But what, then, about human rights? In what sense might they, too, be said to "exist?" To answer that, we must first distinguish political rights from what might be termed "conventional" rights. To ask if a *conventional* right exists is similar to asking whether a legal right exists, except the former focuses on the society's *moral system* as opposed to its legal system. (I use the term "conventional" here to stress that conventional rights are ones that just happen, conventionally, to be acknowledged by society.) Conventional rights exist, in other words, when the generally accepted moral code of society teaches that its members have the requisite sorts of duties. Thus, for example, people in our society can be said to have the conventional right not to be lied to, except in unusual circumstances: This is because the moral code accepted by society teaches that others have the duty not to lie except in unusual circumstances.[40]

Sometimes, of course, there may be questions about just what conventional rights people do have. Members of society may subscribe to slightly different moral codes, for example, or an agreed-upon moral code may change through time and with it people's conventional rights. When this change takes place, it may be unclear for a period just what rights conventional morality gives to people, or there may not be enough agreement to say whether people have a certain conventional right. Homosexuality and premarital sex are obvious examples, since it is unclear whether according to today's conventional morality people have a duty not to do these things. Some would presumably think that people should not perform such acts; others would claim they have a right *to* do so. Given that there is sufficiently wide disagreement about such questions, the best thing to say might be that there is insufficient moral consensus and conventional morality takes no position. In that sense, it may not be clear whether people have a particular conventional right in a given society at a particular time.

We now turn to a third form of rights, often termed human or moral. We may begin to see what these involve, and how they differ from legal and conventional rights, by considering the following case. Today, whites living in the South have neither the conventional right nor the legal right that African-Americans step aside if they meet on the sidewalk, though years ago whites did have such rights. But now suppose that Sally, living in the old South, refused to step aside, raising the question of whether either conventional morality or law in fact *should* give whites such a right. Her implicit claim, in other words, would be that whatever rights law and conventional morality may give them, whites cannot legitimately or correctly claim that she in fact has such a duty; such a claim would be unjustified or unwarranted.[41] Put differently, the point is that even if Sally violated another's conventional or legal right, one could still ask a meaningful and often important question: Did she *in fact* have the duty that law and convention claimed she had in the sense that the demands made by moral convention and law were justified?[42]

Initially, then, we may say that human rights represent the standpoint from which to critically assess conventional and legal rights. Those who deny human rights are, in effect, denying that any such standard is true or best, so that law and conventional morality cannot be rationally criticized. Defenders of human rights are thus committed to the possibility that reasonable, objective grounds are available on which to defend and criticize legal and conventional rights. Violations of human rights can therefore be seen as instances in which legal power is exercised to establish an unjustified or unwarranted duty or obligation. So given what was said earlier about the "existence" of legal and conventional rights and their connections with legal and conventional moral duties, human rights may now be understood as the claim that conventional and legal systems *should*, morally, impose the relevant sorts of duties on people. Human rights, in other words, are moral requirements imposed on law and convention. Precisely *how* such requirements may be justified, if they can be, is an open question to which we will return in due course. For the present, however, we may simply note that for a *human* right such as free speech to exist, for instance, implies that there are good reasons for thinking that law and conventional morality *should* impose duties on those who would restrict others' speech and, perhaps, also that officials should be required to inject themselves on the side of the speaker when people attempt to interfere.[43]

Human rights also limit the *range* of justifications that can be offered for conventional and legal rights; not all claims that law (or conventional morality) ought to respect rights rest on the existence of human rights against such interference. Recall, for instance, that both original intent and democratic proceduralism also think that claims legal rights exist are (sometimes) justified: for originalism the justification depends on history, and for proceduralism it is process. Neither view, however, defends legal rights on the ground that they are also *human* rights government should protect. Freedom of religion was defended by originalism as a self-incapacitating limitation on power that the people accept, while for proceduralism its justification must somehow be tied to the preservation or furtherance of free and open democratic processes. Neither of these ways of thinking sees the right to free exercise as a substantive *human* right: It is either a limit that the people have tacitly accepted or else a procedural necessity. Both originalism and proceduralism deny, in other words, that freedom of religion deserves protection on substantive moral grounds, independent of history and process, and therefore do not think human rights exist.[44]

Given the various types of rights, we are now able to see the sense in which the three types of rights we have distinguished—legal, conventional, and human— bestow advantages on their possessors. The way in which it is to Sally's advantage to have a *legal* right has already been suggested: When she has such a legal right (i.e., when it "exists") and she finds herself in a certain sort of conflict with others, she can call on political officials to use the force of the state to make them fulfill their legal duties toward her. Because the power of the state stands behind legal rights, they can be very great advantages indeed. Being able to call on the police and the courts to prevent people from harming us or taking our property or re-quiring them to compensate when they injure us or to abide by their agreements makes a huge difference in one's life.

Conventional rights provide advantages that are in some ways analogous to le-gal rights. When others do not respect conventional rights they are subject to blame, ostracism, criticism, and various other informal social sanctions normally imposed on those who do not meet what the social moral code understands as their duties. And, again as for legal rights, possessors of conventional rights may have the further advantage that third parties are obligated to help them. A society like ours that includes in its social moral code a child's (conventional) right not to be abused imposes duties not just on parents but also on the rest of us to inter-vene, at least to the extent of making legal authorities aware of the situation and sometimes also to interfere directly on the child's behalf. Somebody who know-ingly allowed abuse to continue would be the subject of blame and criticism, and so, in that way, conventional rights are also an important advantage for their pos-sessor.

But what, then, can be said about the advantages provided by *human* rights? Much of the time, of course, legal and conventional rights will track human rights, and when they do human rights will also carry with them the advantages of legal and conventional rights. However, there is no assurance either law or con-vention will, in fact, respect people's human rights. In what sense, then, are hu-man rights, standing alone, advantages?

To see the answer to that question, return to the case of Sally, who, we assume, refuses to step aside when meeting a white person on the sidewalk, as required by both the accepted moral conventions and the law. Let's also assume that whites do not, in fact, have the moral right that Sally step aside, and, furthermore, that Sally has a moral right not to step aside. That means, then, that the legal and conven-tional rights given to whites are not justified and, furthermore, that Sally would be justified in refusing to do as law and convention require. In what sense, then, is Sally advantaged simply in virtue of her possessing human right? The answer must be that although she lacks the *practical* advantages legal and conventional rights confer, Sally nonetheless has a *moral* advantage and is better off just for that reason. But what sense can be made of such a "moral" advantage if, as we are imagining, it is respected by neither law nor conventional morality?

The answer is that having it be the case that law and convention are unjustified in imposing this burden on her is a moral advantage in two different senses. One reason having the moral right is an advantage is that she may be able to turn it into a legal or conventional right. The fact that neither convention nor law is justified, finally, in demanding that she step aside gives her a potentially important weapon with which to attack both conventions and laws. Whether she can succeed in turning the human right into a practical advantage is, of course, an open question. It depends on her, those around her, and her historical circumstances. So although the moral right is not yet a practical advantage, the fact that one has morality "on one's side," so to speak, is generally good in the sense that it is a weapon that can be used against those who would maintain existing legal and conventional rights when such rights should not exist.

Besides the possibility of turning a human right to practical advantage in the future, a moral right is also an advantage in another sense. Just by virtue of the fact that she, rather than convention or law, is justified, we might say, Sally has another advantage. Some might claim that the fact of being justified, morally, is even *more* important than convention and law, so that Sally is better off even if she is never able to turn it into a practical advantage since being morally right is its "own reward," so to speak.[45] Others might think she is only slightly advantaged in virtue of having the moral right on her side, believing that here at least practical advantages outweigh moral ones. But whatever one thinks about that dispute, it does seem wrong to say she has *no* advantage at all just in virtue of having the political right on her side in the conflict, even leaving aside the possibility she may succeed in turning the political right into a practical advantage.

But now let's vary the case once again and suppose Sally does not know she has the right to refuse to step aside. Maybe she has lived under racist oppression for so long that she has become servile, believing it a duty of blacks to defer to whites. In those circumstances, it may seem, Sally's human right is not an advantage to her.

In one sense, I agree with this conclusion. Rights, as I said earlier, are advantages *when people come in conflict with each other,* and Sally is not now in conflict with those asking her to step aside. Having a right is thus not an advantage at all times and in all circumstances, but only against a background of disagreement or conflict. Indeed, there are many much more ordinary cases where rights are not advantages because there is no conflict: Think of all the legal rights we have but do not want to exercise (to move to Alaska and live in a tent, for example). The advantages rights provide become important when people both want something and face opposition from others. Still, however, there remains an important sense that even the legal right to live in a tent in Alaska is an advantage, though only *hypothetically* so. *If* the person who had the right were to want to exercise it, then the law would support her in the face of opposition. Unknown or unwanted rights are thus like having a weapon that one does not know exists but might someday learn about. Under the circumstances, having the legal right is not a present advantage, but still it is better to have it than not because it could become an advantage should conflicts later emerge.

The same can be said for Sally and human rights. Though today she may servilely accept her inferior legal and conventional status and also may not believe she has the human right on her side, she nonetheless still does have an advantage. There is no *moral duty* for her to be servile and, therefore, if she wanted to stop she would be justified in doing so. Human rights are thus hypothetical advantages in much the same way legal rights are.

None of this has shown, however, that human rights actually exist or has met the CLS charge that legal indeterminacy is the inevitable consequence of the fact that legal decisions often rest on moral and political claims about rights. But having now a securer sense of what is involved in claiming human and other rights exist, we are in a better position to assess those related claims. In fact, of course, people have offered different, sometimes incompatible arguments against those who claim that human rights exist as well as against those who wish to defend, as I do, the ideal of the rule of law while at the same time acknowledging that judges often rely on them in making legal decisions. Some reject rights for political reasons; others reject them because they think no rights of any sort exist. After looking briefly at both of those claims, we then turn to human rights specifically and to the charge that they cannot exist because they rely on untenable assumptions about moral truth and objectivity. That skeptical position is unwarranted, I will argue, so that the rule of law is not an impossible ideal.

The Critical Legal Studies Critique of Rights

Sometimes skepticism about human and other rights is politically motivated, based on the way rights have been used in the past. For CLS, this familiar argument takes the form that rights "discourse," as it is termed, serves the interests of those groups that enjoy political power against the legitimate demands of the powerless. Rights to contract, for example, were invoked by judges against New Deal and Progressive efforts to secure minimum wages and improve the conditions of workers. In a similar vein, property rights were used to defend slave owners in their efforts to keep their human property.[46] These examples (and there are many others) serve that purpose well since few would argue these days that Congress is powerless to regulate markets and nobody defends the right to own people. But why should defenders of rights think that instances where the Court has in the past been misguided in its conception of human rights mean courts are always or even generally misguided, let alone that there is something inherent in the discourse that biases discussion against the powerless? Defenders of human rights can, and often do, agree that the Court's opposition to minimum wages and other workplace regulations was a mistake. But the fact that judges have sometimes been wrong in thinking something is a human right is no argument against rights in general; and it does not, by itself, indicate that the Courts ought not rely on them. There are plenty of other examples, such as the equal protection decisions holding students have a right against being forced to attend segregated schools and securing the right to vote as well as the privacy decisions upholding the right to use contraceptives and the right to freedom of choice; and one can just as well claim rights to equality of opportunity, health care, and a job as rights to be free of economic regulations or to keep one's property. So here, at least, are important cases in which rights discourse was of real value to Progressives.[47] No defender of human rights must think judges should protect rights that do not exist.

Another, deeper CLS criticism of rights discourse can be seen, dialectically, as a response to that last point. While admitting that occasionally human rights can be of service to Progressives, nevertheless, it might be argued by CLS, there is a strong tendency, based on the nature of rights discourse itself, for it to have the opposite effect. That is because, according to the argument, rights are grounded in an unacceptably individualistic conception of society and politics that denies the importance of community in favor of a picture of separate individuals pursuing their own interests and bound to each other only by the requirements that they not interfere in one another's lives.[48] Yet such a conception, it is argued, is an inaccurate description of how people experience themselves that encourages the feelings of alienation and distance characteristic of Western, capitalist societies. Peter Gabel defends that sort of view when he writes: "Seen as a whole, therefore the 'world' of this rights-based schema is one in which originally passive and disconnected individuals enter into relations with each other because they are allowed to. ... This picture of the world is but an abstract representation of our own alienated effort to distance ourselves from each other by representing our false selves as our real selves."[49] I will have more to say on this as we look more carefully at different conceptions of rights in the next two chapters, but offhand it is at least unclear why, in general, rights should be thought to serve better the political cause of conservatives than that of reformers or radicals. The bare notion of rights, as the previous section showed, is silent about the philosophical *grounding* of the obligations that constitute a given right just as it leaves open exactly what rights exist. There is no reason that rights must be defended in the individualist and contractualist fashion Gabel envisions nor, I will argue, must a contractualist assume "disconnected individuals" trying to "distance" themselves from each other. Gabel's picture of the political world as seen through the eyes of those who defend rights is not uncommon, of course; but neither is that Hobbesian view inevitable. How those accounts might look, however, must await the next two chapters.

It remains open to CLS at this point, however, to move from political to philosophical grounds, arguing that rights do not, in fact, exist. And it is this argument, we will see, that reintroduces the issues with which I began the chapter: legal incoherence and the rule of law.

Objectivity, Justification,
and Moral Skepticism

One skeptical strategy, of course, would be to await the arguments offered on behalf of human rights and to show they do not succeed—a possibility I shall take seriously in the chapters that follow. Others, however, have claimed to know, before hearing any argument that human rights exist, that such an argument *must* be mistaken. This may be either because there are no rights at all—human, legal, *or* conventional—or else because those who claim human rights exist assume, incorrectly, that there are moral "facts" or "objective" moral truths. If either of those claims is correct, then the CLS charge of legal indeterminacy would be vindicated—at least insofar as judges rely on human rights and moral argument, as many do, to interpret the Constitution. Nor, moreover, would a judge who defends her more general interpretive theory on the ground that it shows the Constitution to be a reasonable effort to achieve (genuinely) valuable ends be justified in *that* claim if moral skepticism is correct. For if there are no genuinely worthy ends but only different, equally (un)justified opinions on the subject, then law would again seem to be indeterminate. In place of true or sound answers to legal questions, there would only be different ones—just as CLS has suggested. We will move toward these deeper, more general skeptical claims indirectly, by first looking at the idea that human rights do not exist because rights in general do not exist. Then we will discuss more theoretical arguments flowing out of different versions of moral skepticism.

Consider then the idea that human rights do not exist because no rights of any kind are real, whether legal, conventional, or human. Such an argument depends, I believe, on a misunderstanding of what is involved in claiming a right "exists." To make such an assertion is not to affirm the existence of some strange, magical things that are invoked like charms to ward off evil governments. It involves rather the notion that there are legal, conventional, or moral duties of the relevant sort. Thus, people may be said to have a legal right not to be killed (or, put differently, such a right would truly be said to exist) if individuals have *legal* duties not to kill and officials have legal duties to intervene when they try. It is no more credible to deny that *conventional* rights exist, for here again the claim is best understood not as asserting magical entities but instead ordinary, garden variety obligations, this time of the conventional moral sort. Conventional rights exist because conventional moral duties are enforced; people are, in fact, sometimes subjected to criticism, blame, ostracism, and so forth.

Notice, also, that even if neither the legal system nor conventional morality provided for legal and conventional rights it still would not follow that there are no *human* rights. If one thinks that law and convention *should* impose duties on people, then human rights (in the sense I have understood the concept) would exist; it's just that law and conventional morality ignore them.

So the general point against this first form of rights skepticism is that once it is seen that "rights" are no more mysterious than obligations, the skeptic cannot successfully attack human rights based simply on the general skeptical claim that *no* rights exist of any sort—cannot, that is, unless she wishes also to deny that legal, conventional, and moral *obligations* exist.

Another argument on which a skeptic might rely tries to tie beliefs in human rights to a particular theory of their origin. We should reject human rights, according to this view, because they reflect an outdated and implausible conception of the relationship between morality and religion and also commit their defender to an obviously mistaken view of how we can know them. Asserting human or moral rights, according to this argument, requires adopting the sort of metaphysical picture expressed in the Declaration of Independence where (following John Locke[50]) such rights are said to reflect a "self-evident" truth that people are *"endowed by their creator"* with certain "inalienable rights." But, says the skeptic, even assuming God exists one surely cannot claim in the late twentieth century to have direct access to God's intentions, let alone to know these things as "self-evident" truths. None of that, however, is likely to bother the defender of human rights. Perhaps there is another, better account of human rights that does not rely on a two-century-old theory whose metaphysical and religious assumptions are now widely rejected or at least questioned. It is as if a person who has become skeptical of the *creationist* account of the origin of natural species mistakenly concludes that therefore species do not exist at all. The correct conclusion, of course, would be that *either* species do not exist or there is some other, more reasonable way to explain them.

Still, however, it may be thought that all of this has missed the point since although it must be agreed legal and conventional rights exist, human ones do not. That is because, according to this familiar argument, there is no such thing as genuine, or "objective," moral obligations of the sort that would establish human rights. We noted earlier, for example, that both Robert Bork and William Rehnquist claimed the choice of one right over another is no different from a subjective expression of taste or personal preference, which can be compared to the love of "granite rocks and barberry bushes," as Rehnquist put it.[51]

Filling in the argument, we can imagine the subjectivist pointing out that statements about rights, values, duties, and so on are "subjectivist" in the sense that they do not say anything objectively true about the natural, physical world but instead reflect personal attitudes dressed up in apparently "objective" claims about the world. A complete and full description of the natural world, according to this view, would exclude all evaluative or moral properties; they are mere expressions of personal taste or preferences. Moral utterances, whether they involve how best to live one's private life or the human rights that governments morally ought to respect, are not assertions of "fact" but instead express the feelings and attitudes of the speaker. To say that Hitler was "evil" is not to claim anything that is objectively true about him; words like "evil," "good," and "wrong" do not refer to objective properties in the real world. In what follows I will offer only a few brief comments on these issues and then consider their implications for the question of legal indeterminacy.

Suppose, to begin, that the subjectivist we have been describing insists on a distinction between matters of "fact" that, she claims, are susceptible of scientific confirmation and questions involving values and morality that cannot be scientifically tested. The idea, then, would be that statements about values are subjective because they cannot be proven or tested scientifically, although other statements that are not subjective *can* be so tested.

In thinking about this claim, however, it is important first to note that people make many types of claims, besides moral ones, that do not seem confirmable by science in any ordinary sense. Physics, chemistry, and biology cannot tell us that slavery was among the important causes of the U.S. Civil War, for example. History is argumentative and seems to involve "facts" without being scientific. The response to somebody who claims slavery was not an important cause of the Civil War is to ask for evidence, listen to it, and offer counterarguments that are appropriate to historical discourse. Did Lincoln lead the country to war because he had a deep, personal commitment to abolitionism, or was his support of the abolitionist position simply part of a strategy to win the war? If slavery was not a major cause, can anything else explain it? Or is the most sensible position that there were many causes, including slavery? Each position requires reasoned defense against the alternatives. To the extent personal interests and preferences are offered in place of reasons, the person is electing not to participate in the discourse—not, that is, to "do" history.

In addition to historical issues, scientists also cannot use their instruments to answer *philosophical* questions about the nature of their own scientific theories and explanations, let alone the nature of knowledge and truth themselves. Asked to explain what a scientific theory is or whether scientific entities like electrons or numbers are real, a scientist is driven out of the laboratory to philosophy and history books. But having now turned what seem to be a variety of non-scientific issues of history and philosophy into the realm of "fact" rather that "value," it has now become far less clear exactly what the distinction amounts to. Nor, therefore, is it as clear as it seemed why value claims are not at least "in principle" susceptible to confirmation (since we are no longer requiring that matters of fact be *scientifically* confirmable).

Beyond questioning whether scientific testing marks the distinction between matters of fact and non-fact, we might also wonder why it is the case, as the subjectivist may claim, that only certain types of assertions (including historical and philosophical as well as scientific ones) can be correct or incorrect, true or false although value and moral claims cannot. Viewed *from the inside* it certainly does not look or feel that way; considering whether to accept or reject a moral, legal, or political argument does not seem to those who make such a decision to be simply a question of deciding how we happen to feel at the moment. Disagreement about affirmative action, for instance, raises an array of important and difficult questions including the importance of compensation for past injustice to groups, the merits of ignoring race when assigning jobs and in admissions, whether groups can have rights, and the proper response to situations in which an innocent person is asked to pay for others' wrongdoing. It simply does not square with our understanding of the moral domain and our role in it to describe such problems as merely inquiring into our "attitudes" about the subject, as if we were trying to decide if we like some new food. To enter into the world of political and moral discussion is not to leave the world of reason behind in favor of purely personal taste.

The claim that democratic procedures are self-legitimizing, for instance, or that people tacitly consent to an original social contract commits one to defending the judgment in the common currency of moral and political argument. Indeed, it would be quite odd for somebody who just claimed democratic governments have special claims to legitimacy to respond when asked why she thinks that with the remark, "Oh, well, all I meant was to express my personal feelings toward democracy; I meant nothing more." Such a person, we might conclude, did not really mean what she said: Although acting and speaking as if she were participating in the common moral arena, in fact she meant only to express feelings without making any further claim on what others should do or believe. In other words, from the perspective of moral participants, morality and politics rest on the practical assumption, not shared by matters of merely personal taste, that there *is* a correct answer, and that reason-giving and argument are the means by which such answers are to be pursued.[52] Indeed, many of us have had the experience of coming to see that our earlier moral or political ideas were confused or mistaken—an experience that seems at odds with this subjectivist picture.

My alternative suggestion, then, is that instead of trying to mark a sharp boundary between facts, which are objective and testable by science, and values, which are merely subjective, we should instead think of morality, literature, law, philosophy, art, and politics as requiring assessment in terms suitable for each type of discourse—assessment that is not correctly viewed as "subjective." Viewed from *within* the discourse of literary or music interpretation, for instance, critics discuss and debate the degree to which works live up to their (shared) standards of excellence, just as we argue and debate matters of justice, fairness, and rights. People also sometimes disagree about the criteria themselves that are used; they may differ, for instance, about artistic excellence itself. Some, for example, may believe political content is an important component to successful literary works; others may argue it is a distraction. Yet these disagreements about the correct standards by which to judge art are themselves the subject of reasonable debate and discussion, though at a different level from interpretive disagreements about particular works. The discovery of such deep disagreement over correct standards does not lead to subjectivism, however; it just means critics then move to that level, prepared to defend their standards themselves as well as their judgments about an individual work.

The same may be said about historical argument and, of course, about legal interpretation. It is commonplace, after uncovering a disagreement about how best to interpret a single constitutional provision, to find that the real issue involves deeper divisions in constitutional theory. But having learned that, people do not stop thinking and either fight or go drinking together. The issue simply shifts to the merits of their competing theories. Or, to take an example from another area of law, a judge may be asked to weigh arguments from both defense and prosecutors about whether a killer was or was not legally insane. Those arguments may or may not reflect lawyers' disagreement about the proper tests for such excuses. If they do, then that question, too, is subject to reasoned discussion and debate. In that way anybody entering the realms of artistic and legal interpretation gives up the option, if they wish to be taken seriously by others who participate in the discourse, of asserting their personal preferences in place of giving reasons. The terms of the discourse itself demands that people seek justifications from the impartial arena of reason-giving rather than merely asserting their preferences.

Often, of course, people's views may be influenced by personal interests or desires, but it does not follow from that fact that personal bias is *all* there is.[53] Indeed, the fact that concepts like "bias" and "rationalization" play an important role in our shared argumentative practices indicates the extent to which participants *assume* not only that judgments need not all be based on self-interest but also that the appropriate argumentative standards *demand* that people seek to reach for a more impartial standpoint from which to argue. (None of this is to deny, however, that questions in art, politics, morality, philosophy, history, and other areas are occasions of wide and sometimes deep disagreement, for plainly they are.)

Another argument, besides the claim that values are non-scientific and therefore mere expressions of personal attitudes, focuses on the fact of moral and political disagreement.[54] Morality and politics, we know, are deeply controversial and the subject of wide dispute, and therefore, according to this argument, we have reason to doubt whether such assertions can be objective or true. Though it must be admitted that there is also wide disagreement within both science and common sense, still, it is claimed, the disagreement about morality and politics is more fundamental or pervasive.

It is important, however, that in weighing this familiar claim we not exaggerate the lack of agreement in moral and political matters. Few now defend racial segregation, let alone slavery. True, there remain many intractable moral and political problems, but there is also wide disagreement among scientists, mathematicians, and historians as well as philosophers of science. Further, we may wonder why the mere fact of controversy and disagreement, even if it is far greater in politics and morality than other areas, should constitute evidence that moral statements are subjective. Maybe reaching agreement about how people should live together is an especially difficult problem for human beings—harder, even, than learning how nature works. Self-interest, after all, is often at stake when confronting political and moral issues, and that fact by itself could make impartial consideration of such questions especially difficult as compared with understanding how gravity or the cell works.

We are also all aware, of course, that if we had been raised differently we might now hold very different moral views. But why should we think that this fact constitutes good reason to doubt the soundness of our current views or the fact that they rest on good reasons? We would also, presumably, have different scientific, historical, and other beliefs were we raised in a different culture at a different time; does that mean we would be wise to doubt the soundness or objectivity of our beliefs that the earth revolves around the sun, that black holes exist, or that germs cause disease?

Instead of pursuing these questions further, however, I want to conclude this section by looking more closely at the subjectivist's position and asking whether, even it were accepted that morality is fundamentally about "attitudes" rather than "facts," we are led to the sort of subjectivism and indeterminacy envisioned by CLS. Many people, often termed "non-cognitivists," argue that, in fact, they can accommodate the arguments against subjectivism I have been describing while at the same time holding to the underlying position that there are no moral facts and that morality is, finally, about sentiments and attitudes. But what, then, for the non-cognitivist, *is* the link between morality and the attitudes people have that allows them to walk the line between the claim that moral properties are "real" and the subjectivism that I have been criticizing?

The answer depends on making a distinction between genuinely moral attitudes and ones that are personal or biased. To understand morality, according to the non-cognitivist view I will now weigh, we must think of attitudes not of the person making the moral claim but instead of a person whose attitudes or sentiments reflect a more universal standpoint. If we do that, according to the argument, we will then avoid the errors of subjectivism and at the same time be able to agree that there are no "objective" moral properties existing independently of human feelings. But how are we to identify this "genuine" moral attitude if not simply by describing the attitude of the person uttering the moral statement? David Hume answers this way: "When a man denominates another his *enemy*, his *rival*, his *antagonist*, his *adversary*, he is understood to speak the language of self-love, and to express sentiments, peculiar to himself, and arising from his particular circumstances and situation. But when he bestows on any man the epithets of *vicious* or *odious* or *depraved*, he then speaks another language, and expresses sentiments, in which, he expects, all his audience are to concur with him. He must choose a point of view, common to him and others: He must move some universal principle of the human frame, and touch a string, to which all mankind have an accord and symphony."[55] Hume is suggesting, then, that although morality does involve "sentiments," they are attitudes of a special kind, differing from the self-interested ones any particular person may have toward some action or government. To take the *moral* standpoint, as when we condemn people as vicious or depraved, expresses attitudes that are in some sense universal and shared rather than individual and selfish. But how, then, is the non-cognitivist to distinguish between the speaker's potentially self-interested attitudes, on one hand, and moral attitudes that express a "point of view ... common to him and others," as Hume puts it, on the other? What, more specifically, would the non-cognitivist look for in people's attitudes if she wished to distinguish moral attitudes from whatever ones an individual or group happen to have? The answer, according to many non-cognitivists, falls in three parts.[56]

First, a non-cognitivist would want to follow Hume's suggestion and assure that genuine moral attitudes are not *biased,* in the sense that they are unduly influenced by personal interest or "self-love." If so, then the attitude is not impartial and does not express sentiments that are "common" to all, as Hume put it.[57] Impartiality is central, in that sense, to morality. Second, it seems clear the moral attitudes should not be *uninformed* in the sense that they are based on mistaken or insufficient information. Attitudes that express the moral viewpoint should, ideally, be based on complete, relevant information rather than on mistaken beliefs or incomplete knowledge. Nor, third, would a non-cognitivist identify moral attitudes with ones that are based on *faulty reasoning.* Attitudes that reflect erroneous statistical methods, for example, would not do the work for the non-cognitivist, nor would ones that reflect other logical errors. So instead of the non-cognitivist looking to individual or even social attitudes, the suggestion here is that she shift the focus to attitudes that are not defective in any of these three respects.

Armed with these three limitations, the non-cognitivist's claim is that we can understand morality in terms of attitudes rather than facts while at the same time avoiding the charge that non-cognitivism can make no sense of moral improvement, moral reasoning, and moral mistakes. The non-cognitivist accomplishes this by arguing that morality involves the "qualified" attitudes of a well-informed, impartial, and rational observer—what Roderick Firth and others term an "ideal observer."[58]

Following this general approach, the non-cognitivist would then be able to say that "Slavery is wrong" should be understood not just as an expression of personal or group disapproval but rather as expressing the thought that an ideally impartial, informed, and rational observer *would* disapprove of slavery. So if some person's (or group's) approval of slavery, for instance, depended on misinformation about what life is like under such a system or (what is perhaps more likely) did not reflect genuine impartiality, then that attitude is not the "correct" moral attitude. In that way, the non-cognitivist could claim *both* that there are no moral facts and that slavery is objectively unjust, regardless of whether a particular individual society or individual approves of it. Moral claims may be, in a sense, either mistaken or correct yet at the same time not be true in the same way that the statement "Clouds are water molecules" is true; the latter, but not the former, is a claim about properties of things existing in the natural world independent of human attitudes. So even granting that moral facts do not exist, it would not follow that every moral attitude is as reasonable as every other, that there is no right answer to a moral problem, or that there is no moral progress. Instead, according to the ideal observer non-cognitivist, moral objectivity, progress, and argument can each be understood in terms of attitudes that an impartial, fully informed, and rational observer would have. The fact that history has almost universally rejected slavery is true moral progress, and the statement "Slavery is wrong" is objectively correct, because an ideal observer would have a negative attitude toward slavery. Sense can even be made by non-cognitivism of moral "truth" as long as it is understood in terms of attitudes of an ideal observer rather than as claims about natural facts existing independently of human attitudes and sentiments.[59]

This way of understanding morality is thus analogous to one familiar way of understanding other, non-moral properties such as bitterness, sweetness, or redness. Consider, for instance, an apple. An apple's being tart or red depends, crucially, on how it appears to a typical or "ideal" human observer—that is, to somebody who is not sick with a head cold, colorblind, looking at it under abnormal light, and so on. Its having properties like being red and its appearing a certain way to people in certain ideal conditions are in that sense the same thing. Being red or tart depends, crucially, on how the apple appears or tastes to normally functioning human beings.

These arguments are not to deny, of course, that it is the apple's underlying molecular structure combined with how light waves behave when entering the eye that determines that normal humans see it as red; the point, rather, is that the property of redness cannot be understood independently of our notion of a well-functioning, normal human perceiver functioning under certain, ideal conditions. According to the ideal observer theory, then, having a certain color property and having a moral property are in a sense similar: Both are objective (we can be mistaken about them), yet both also depend on how things *seem* or look to certain (ideally situated) persons.[60]

The lesson, therefore, is that if the non-cognitivist follows this approach, then she will be led away from the conclusion that morality is "subjective" and toward the idea that there is, indeed, a right or best answer to moral questions. The non-cognitivist's claim that morality is tied to attitudes rather than "objective" properties in the natural world that are independent of human beings therefore does not lead inevitably to the subjectivist's conclusion that evidence and argument have no role to play in politics and morality or that morality is (simply) an expression of individual or cultural attitudes. To the contrary, once it is acknowledged that sound moral judgments reflect the attitudes of an ideally impartial, rational, and well-informed observer then rationality, information, and impartiality are in fact at center stage. Whether people actually have human rights of a certain sort will then depend, as I have argued, on whether legal systems that do not protect such rights are justified. But that, in turn, would depend on the attitudes that an ideal observer would have toward institutions that deny or affirm such rights in law.

It is worth noting, finally, that there is nothing in the ideal observer theory to *guarantee* that every moral question will have only one right answer. It is possible, and perhaps even likely, that on some questions a fully informed, rational, and impartial observer may not have strong feelings one way or another. If there are such moral dilemmas that cannot be resolved by more information, more careful thought, or more complete elimination of bias, then the best thing to say is that moral argument runs out, lacking sufficient resources to guide even the ideal agent.

Moral Objectivity
and the Rule of Law

One of CLS's arguments for legal indeterminacy, we have seen, rests on the premise that legal interpretation inevitably requires value judgments of various sorts, often including appeals to human rights, and that such judgments are in some sense subjective. Viewed clearly, CLS claims, statements about rights, like other value judgments on which constitutional interpreters rely, are merely expressions of personal attitudes that also tend to reinforce existing political and economic relations. Legal argument, CLS concludes, leads to legal incoherence. I have argued, however, that we are not driven to such a skeptical position. Skepticism about rights often rests on a mistaken conception of the nature of rights in general or of their political effects or else on unwarranted assumptions about the "subjectivity" of morality in general. Even non-cognitivists who make a sharp distinction between forms of discourse that describe the natural world and other forms that rest on attitudes cannot sustain the claim that morality is isolated from argument and evidence or even that there is no such thing as the best or correct moral answer.

This suggests, though it does not prove, that it is possible for political and moral argument to constrain judges, whether one is a moral realist who believes moral properties are genuine or a defender of the ideal observer theory who denies they are real. On both views, judges are not "free" to choose whatever interpretive method or specific interpretation they wish.[61] Constitutional interpretation, though it does require *judgment*—including an assessment of political and moral arguments—is not simply a matter of individual, subjective preferences or attitudes lying beyond the capacity of reason and argument. Because these charges of subjectivity are unwarranted, in other words, it remains at least possible that there is one correct or best answer to legal questions rather than an indefinite number of personal preferences imposed by judges in an incoherent, arbitrary fashion.

None of this means, however, that the ideal of the rule of law will *always* be achieved or even that it can, *in fact,* ever be fully and completely realized. For one thing, as I have already noted, it is possible that some moral and political problems will not have a single, correct answer. Even a perfectly informed, impartial, and rational observer might conceivably be indifferent, having neither a positive or negative attitude with respect to a particular political or moral issue. And, moreover, even granting that there is one uniquely right answer to a question, it does not follow that judges will identify and act on it. Personal bias, ignorance, and confusion will undoubtedly continue to infect the law, even on the most optimistic moral realist or ideal observer assumptions. Resting final authority in a central appeals court can and will help, of course, but there is no assurance that even a single court will arrive at the right solution.

The claim of legal indeterminacy therefore cannot be either sustained or refuted without careful consideration of the actual state of the law and of alternative accounts that seek to make it coherent. Whether a given set of precedents, rules, institutions, and other legal practices *can* be integrated into such a coherent, attractive vision of constitutional government and then be extended to new cases depends, finally, on the details of the argument. The debate cannot be settled without looking at the legal and philosophical arguments *from the inside,* and success cannot be either assured or ruled out without going through the process of actually weighing both the legal and political arguments advanced on a theory's behalf, just as was done with original intent and democratic proceduralism. Legal coherence is not an inevitable outcome of these reflections, but neither is it impossible.

Both theories yet to be considered, utilitarianism and democratic contractualism, affirm this commitment—rejected by CLS—to locate an attractive, coherent account of judicial review and constitutional interpretation that can guide judges seeking to protect the rule of law. But although hoping, each in their own way, to see the Constitution as a reasonable effort to achieve worthy objectives, they also reject the originalist's and proceduralist's demand that judges set aside their substantive political judgments about a law's merits in favor of either historical intentions or procedural purity. And unlike all three of the theories considered so far, neither utilitarianism nor democratic contractualism is skeptical about the existence of moral rights. The first of these two that I will discuss, utilitarianism, places a commitment to maximizing the general welfare at center stage, arguing that judicial review and constitutional interpretation are best understood as part of a larger theory that assesses law and government in terms of their tendency to increase utility.

4

Promoting the General Welfare: Utilitarianism, Law, and Economics

This chapter represents a kind of watershed. Until now, I have been focusing on the philosophical assumptions and arguments behind three familiar legal theories: original intent, democratic proceduralism, and CLS. The jurisprudence of original intent, I have argued, understands judicial review and constitutional interpretation in terms of the social contract while democratic proceduralism looks to the self-justifying character of democratic processes themselves. In discussing Critical Legal Studies, however, we were led into the different though no less philosophical terrain of rights skepticism and the importance of the rule of law. The remaining chapters view matters from the opposite direction. Instead of beginning with legal theories in order to assess how they understand the purposes of democratic government, I am concerned primarily with exploring the legal and constitutional implications of two familiar political theories, utilitarianism and social contract. As before, however, my most basic claim is that these issues are intimately linked: How we understand judicial review and constitutional interpretation both shapes and is shaped by our philosophical vision of the purposes of government and the justification of democracy.

In addition to establishing justice and securing the blessings of liberty, the Preamble to the U.S. Constitution also speaks of another purpose of government: to promote the general welfare. According to the utilitarian view we are now going to consider, the commitment to welfare is the most fundamental of all the aims of government. Once that is understood and accepted, claims the utilitarian, all the other ideals, including rights, democracy, and the rule of law, can then be derived from that one basic commitment.

One helpful way to think about the differences between utilitarianism and the other positions that were discussed in earlier chapters is in terms of time. Defenders of original intent look backward, to history, claiming political legitimacy flows from the fact that the people consent to the social contract. Judicial review is justified since judges are enforcing the contract that the people imposed on themselves. Proceduralism, however, casts its gaze on the present, claiming that since genuinely democratic forms constitute a fair compromise and treat each citizen as a political equal, the results of that process are assured legitimacy. Judicial review is important according to *this* model insofar as it helps perfect that democratic process by making it truly fair, open, and (according to standard proceduralism) also free of prejudice. Because of its skepticism about the possibility of interpretive theory's project to offer an attractive, coherent account of constitutional law, CLS—I argued—invites judges to look to the future. Given that judges exercise wide, unbounded discretion, claimed CLS, responsible judges ought to seek the best future.

Utilitarianism both agrees and disagrees with different aspects of these three theories. In contrast to both originalism and proceduralism, it argues that judicial review and democratic government in general can win legitimacy only on the grounds that they provide the best future, understood in terms of promoting or increasing the general welfare. The utilitarian, in common with the pragmatist, therefore rejects the originalist and proceduralist claim that judges should remain morally neutral and focus on either history or democratic procedures themselves. The utilitarian parts company with the pragmatist, however, because the utilitarian does not reject the possibility that constitutional theory might succeed in providing a coherent, attractive vision of the law that can guide judges' deliberations. In that sense, utilitarianism shares in the goal of originalism and proceduralism. It differs greatly from them, however, because its conception of judicial review and constitutional interpretation rests on what utilitarianism takes to be the foundation of political morality: a commitment to increase total welfare.[1]

Viewed from the perspective of the need to identify a constitutional structure that can fairly and effectively govern a religiously and culturally diverse people with different moral ideals and religious obligations, utilitarianism suggests that government must promote the welfare of all persons equally. What that welfare will consist in may vary among individuals. For some, that will include practicing a particular religion; for others, their good may involve acquiring wealth or political power. But whatever differences exist among people, the utilitarian first seeks a conception of the general welfare that is applicable regardless of these differences and then hopes, with that as a basis, to describe the institutions, laws, and practices that will promote it. It is in this light, according to the utilitarian, that we should think about the purposes of judicial review and the interpretive method judges should employ.[2]

Utilitarians therefore agree that increasing total welfare is the final test of political institutions and practices, so that law is conceived instrumentally, as a means to achieve an end.[3] But within those parameters, utilitarians differ over many questions, including what welfare consists in and the most effective strategy to maximize it. We begin our discussion of utilitarianism and judicial review by asking why law should be conceived of as a matter of maximizing welfare. On what basis, we will ask, might it be thought reasonable to think that welfare comprises the ultimate test of political and legal institutions and practices? Then we will weigh different theories of utility, focusing first on the debate between the preference, or desire theory, on one hand, and what has traditionally been called the hedonistic account of welfare, on the other. That dispute leads, in turn, to a discussion of law and economics. But disagreement over the grounding of the theory and the best way to understand the general good are only two of the problems faced by the utilitarian, so we will then consider the role of judicial review in utilitarian jurisprudence along with the related question of how the Constitution should be read. The chapter concludes with a brief discussion of some of the limits and objections to utilitarianism as an account of constitutional democracy and in particular of judicial review.

Why Utilitarianism

There are many, well-trod routes to utilitarianism, and it is not part of my project here even to describe them all, let alone resolve the many questions about their relative merits. I do want to indicate, in broad outline, what I take to be at least one of the more typical approaches; what follows is also the view, I think, that comes closest to the motivations of the doctrine's classical defenders.[4] The starting place for this view, which we see in Hobbes, Bentham, and James Mill, is to note that people generally take an abiding interest in their own welfare, seeking at every turn to get what they want from the world and each other. But why, then, should people care about others? Answers to this also vary, but often we find in utilitarianism an appeal to people's natural sympathy and benevolent concern for others—sympathy that, it is argued, is neither unnatural nor irrational.

Explanations for this sympathetic concern vary. Some understand such behavior in terms of evolution, pointing out that a desire to help others can be explained in terms of its long-term advantages for the progress of the species.[5] Others argue that we come to care about others through an inevitable process of psychological conditioning in which we associate others' pain behavior, like screaming, with (our own) unpleasant experiences and that this in turn causes us to develop negative feelings toward pain behavior in others.[6] And there are some who think that concern for another's welfare is beyond rational argument.[7]

Whatever sympathy's origins, these utilitarians stress, there is no reason to conclude people motivated by desires for the welfare of others act irrationally. In fact, assuming that among a person's desires is one to see others happy, it might be irrational for him *not* to consider their welfare in a particular case. Parents who take off on a fairly unimportant vacation trip, for instance, and spend money they could use on their more important objective of providing for a child's college, act irrationally. They would get more of what they desire if they saved the money for the child's education rather than spending it on themselves.

Behind this point, however, is another, deeper one about moral motivation. T.M. Scanlon[8] has suggested that the key to classical utilitarianism is sympathetic concern, or what Hume termed the "sentiments."[9] As noted before, whether for evolutionary or psychological reasons it seems clear that we often do wish not only that our own lives should flourish but that others would also not suffer and, indeed, that their lives would also go well. Scanlon expresses the point this way: For classical utilitarians, he says, the "natural source of moral motivation" is "the tendency to be moved by changes in aggregate well-being" and this, in turn, is "what natural sympathy becomes when it is corrected by rational reflection."[10]

Assuming, then, that sympathy is a rational and perhaps even inevitable human emotion that is central for understanding morality, the utilitarian is now in a position to extend the argument along the lines suggested by Hume's remarks discussed in the last chapter. Hume said it is essential in thinking about morality to distinguish between the "self-interested" viewpoint, which others cannot be expected to share, and the moral standpoint, which he characterizes as "universal." But if that is the case, a utilitarian may now argue, it leads directly to the welfare maximizing standard since, viewed objectively and impartially, no person's welfare or good is *intrinsically* more valuable than another's. The pain of one child in Los Angeles and another in Detroit, if equally severe, are equally important from the impartial moral standpoint, so that an ideal observer sympathetic to the suffering of others would have the same negative attitude toward each.

Though critically important, however, impartiality is only one of three features that an ideal moral observer may reasonably be thought to possess; others are full information and rationality. If the choice of the utilitarian principle depended on mistakes about some important factual matter or errors of reasoning, then the case for the principle would at least intuitively seem to be undermined.[11]

It also seems, finally, that sympathy must be added to the description of the ideal observer since if impartiality is taken to mean disinterestedness, in the sense that the person takes no interest in her own or anybody else's welfare, then it is not clear *any* moral principle would be chosen.[12] Being impartial, the ideal observer cannot care more about her own welfare than anybody else's, and if she also isn't concerned for others, then what *does* she care about? Lacking the benevolent desire to see other people made happy, in other words, the completely impartial, disinterested person may have no reason to care about anything including the choice of a moral principle.

In this way, then, utilitarians reach what seems the reasonable claim that could be agreed to by all members of a religiously and culturally diverse society—that the welfare or good of each citizen, however it may be achieved in different contexts, is of central moral importance. Indeed, says the utilitarian, facts about what welfare is and how it can be maximized are in the end the only important moral facts. All other moral and political problems are reducible, finally, to questions about how to promote the collective well-being of individuals.[13]

Utilitarians sometimes also emphasize the scientific, objective nature of their theory, contrasting it with mythical social contracts and the speculative excesses of theologians. Utilitarians look to history, economics, psychology, and all the other social and natural sciences in deciding how best to promote the common good. In that way, utilitarianism is sensitive to how the world actually operates and to the various historical and cultural circumstances in which people find themselves. Thus, what would be right in one society at a particular time would not necessarily be best for another society or even the same one under different circumstances—everything depends on the actual social consequences of various political and social forms in their specific historical and cultural context. In that way, utilitarianism focuses all available intellectual resources on the future, considering the past only to the extent that doing so is part of a sound strategy to promote the general welfare.

The Nature of Welfare

Utilitarianism holds that politics, like all of morality, rests on the sympathetic concern for the general welfare. If the theory is to succeed it must both explain what welfare consists in and how it is to be "maximized." Viewed from its own perspective, in other words, the first task is to give an account of the states of affairs in the world that is to count as intrinsically worthwhile or valuable; then, second, utilitarians must offer a strategy for increasing the aggregate amount of welfare or value as it has now been defined.

On the first problem, the nature of welfare, utilitarians often seek a single, comprehensive conception of the "good" by focusing on either pleasure or on desires. The former, hedonistic theory holds that pleasant experiences (and the absence of unpleasant ones) are the basis of a valuable, worthwhile life, so that the reason knowledge, love, and so on are (usually) thought to be part of such a life is that they lead either directly or indirectly to pleasure.

One problem with this approach, however, is that it seems wrong to suppose people do many of the things they do and value what they value merely because getting them will bring pleasure to themselves or others. Great artists and writers, for example, notoriously suffer in creating their works, yet it would be wrong, surely, to conclude they therefore do not find the experience of producing art a valuable one. Nor, of course, would it be right to think that they do it because, and only because, they hope the work will give pleasure to others. This suggests, then, that utilitarians may be better advised to look at valuable experiences in general rather than simply at pleasant ones, as the hedonist recommends.

Another argument I want now to consider[14] serves both to strengthen the point that pleasure is not the only valuable experience and to sharpen the distinction I just suggested between the hedonistic and experience theories. Consider then the following possibility, suggested in a recent interview with a scientist working on the mechanisms of the brain and on what is sometimes termed "virtual reality." Suppose, he said, there existed a latex rubber body sheath, attached to a large computer, that could be slipped over the entire body so that it perfectly covered the skin. Imagine further that attached to this rubber membrane is a huge computer that enabled the person in the body sheath to have whatever pleasant experience he or she desired.[15] Now the question is not whether people would refuse to get into such a "virtual reality machine," for I assume many would—at least temporarily. The point I want to focus on, rather, is that in doing so something of value is lost, suggesting that there is more of value than pleasure, as hedonism suggests. People might even choose to stay in the machine because the pleasure they get from it outweighs whatever importance they place on other experiences they also value, but again that is irrelevant to the basic point, which is that activities and experiences in addition to pleasure are valued. Creating great art, curing disease, and having friends are valued for more than the pleasure they bring.

Let's assume, then, that the hedonist's conception of welfare—that it consists only of pleasant experiences—is extended to include other sorts of valuable experiences. Now we can imagine, taking the argument one step further, that the machine can do more than create pleasant experiences; it can create any experience whatsoever. Thus, if the artist wants the (admittedly unpleasant) experience of painting a great work, then that too can be had. Indeed, we will assume, people can have any experience they find valuable: winning prizes, ruling the world, being loved by a family, curing cancer, or whatever.

That seems to many a more attractive machine, reinforcing the earlier point that more experiences are of value than just those that involve pleasure. But still the question should be asked whether this machine can provide everything that the utilitarian would count as good or valuable. Robert Nozick has suggested that, in fact, there would still be something lacking because, he says, people not only want the enjoyable *experience* of *seeming* to live worthy lives or doing valuable things, they want *actually* to do them. The virtual reality machine, though providing an experience that is impossible to distinguish from actually being loved, curing diseases, or ruling the world, cannot make the experience real—and that, according to Nozick, is also valuable in itself. So the fact that the virtual reality machine lacks something even though it provides experiences that are indistinguishable, subjectively, from real ones suggests there is more of value at stake here than whatever value or utility an experience can possess. (Note, however, that the critic is not saying that *only* real experiences are valuable but instead making the weaker claim that being real adds additional value.)

Friends of the experience theory could agree, of course, that it would be better if experiences such as curing cancer were genuine because having a cure would then be able to improve other people's lives by eliminating painful and other bad experiences. It is therefore important to emphasize that the criticism of the experience theory is that the mere having of such unreal experiences as envisioned in the virtual reality machine is less valuable simply because the experience is unreal, not because others' lives are less valuable in virtue of the fact cancer is not really cured and great art is not actually produced, independent of any other facts about the case. The claim, in short, is that non-veridical experiences are less worthwhile, intrinsically, than veridical ones.

Two responses are available to defenders of the experience theory. First, one might simply deny that "real" experiences are better than unreal ones. Consider, for instance, the enjoyment sadists get from experiences that, if they were real, would actually do great harm. It seems clear that for cases such as the sadist there would not be any increase in value if the experience were genuine rather than in the "unreal" situation of the machine. This suggests, contrary to Nozick, that genuinely creating great art and curing diseases are better or more valuable than merely "experiencing" such events only because others will benefit from the art or the cure if they are real. There is nothing intrinsic to the experience itself that makes it more valuable.

Another response the experience theorist might make is to question whether the critic's conception of the "reality" of ordinary experiences can bear the weight that is put on it by the objection to the theory. If one believes, for example, that mental experiences like seeing, hearing, believing, and desiring are nothing more than physical states of the brain, then it will be difficult to distinguish the virtual reality machine and the mental life of humans. In neither case do we experience the world "as it is," either because secondary properties like color are not real properties of things over and above their molecular structure or, more radically, because only subatomic particles truly exist and macro-objects like trees and tables are mere collections of smaller ones. Thus, according to this view, when we seem to see colored objects, in reality we see no such thing, so that our normal mental states are not "real" in any sense that would allow us to distinguish them sharply from states we would have in the virtual reality machine, as the critic of the experience theory supposes.

I will assume, therefore, that the utilitarian would extend the original, hedonist theory to include not only pleasure but other experiences as well, but would not take the further step we have been discussing and claim such experiences are better merely because they are veridical. Instead of thinking of utility as pleasure, so that unpleasant experiences like creating art would have no intrinsic worth, the utilitarian defender of the experience theory claims that any experience that is desired, whether pleasant or not, is valuable, just as having any unwanted experience decreases welfare.

It may seem, having said that experiences are valuable only if also desired, that the utilitarian should then take another short step and reject the experience theory completely in favor of the desire theory. One reason for this might be based on skepticism about the possibility of measuring or weighing utility if it is understood in terms of experiences. How, it may be asked, could a utilitarian compare different experiences in order to structure political institutions and practices so as to "maximize" what is enjoyable or valuable about them? It is implausible, according to the objection, to think of all the various experiences we desire as actually having something in common, called "enjoyment," unless we are thinking simply of the fact they are desired. A pleasing meal, a good book, an intellectually challenging debate, a brilliant concert, a win at racquetball, making love, and an intimate conversation with a friend are all experiences people seek, but it does not seem that they have a common element that can be measured and compared with other experiences. But if that is true, then how can the utilitarian know if a good meal, say, is a more valuable experience than a concert or racquetball game?

In fact, as we have already noted, the situation is even more problematic for the experience theory. Besides comparing or weighing the welfare of each individual person, utilitarians must also make decisions affecting the collective welfare of many persons. Not only must different experiences had by the same individual be compared, but the utilitarian commitment to maximizing *total* welfare requires an account of how to weigh the effects of decisions on different people.

Perhaps, then, the utilitarian should turn from thinking that welfare is tied to experiences to the desire or preference theory and the idea that maximizing welfare consists in fulfilling the strongest desires of the largest number of people. In that way utilitarianism may seem in a better position to perform the required interpersonal comparisons, making the problems of measurement more manageable. Instead of weighing the value of different experiences, we now need only inquire how political institutions and practices will affect people's preferences and desires. The desire utilitarian's basic commitment is thus to maximizing desire-satisfaction, without any requirement that the experience associated with fulfilling desires is valuable or the person enjoys the experience of having desires satisfied.

But how then is the desire utilitarian to do interpersonal comparisons, that is, measure the strength of desires? The answer must presumably come in the form of behavior; people indicate the presence of desires, as well as the strength of those desires, by what they say and do. But what behavior, specifically, should we look to as an indicator of the existence and strength of desires? Some have thought that economic analysis is useful here, since it offers a conception of welfare that is measurable yet also attractive from the desire utilitarian's viewpoint. We will next consider that claim and then return in light of that discussion to reconsider the dispute between desire and experience views of utility.

Economic Analysis

Economic analysis begins with the assumption that the utilitarian should focus on people's *revealed* desires or preferences, seeking to fulfill the largest number possible of the strongest ones.[16] Because we lack an easy method to compare the utility of different experiences, we may therefore use economics to provide a more workable account of individual welfare; this technique may avoid or at least reduce the problems associated with measurement by focusing on people's revealed preferences and seeking to maximize society's total wealth. But how, precisely, might that go?

Begin by considering the idea of a market. Suppose (as once happened to me in a seminar) that members of a group are randomly handed a different sandwich; one is tuna, others are BLT, chicken, and cheese. Given an initial distribution of goods, if people can voluntarily trade with each other, then the resulting distribution will increase utility—a fact we can know without having to compare experiences, as the utilitarian seemed required to do before.[17] This new situation, after trades are made, is "Pareto superior" to the pre-trade distribution since at least one person is made better off while nobody's situation is worsened. And we know this without having to compare the value of the experiences each would have had given different sandwich distributions. We left it to them, they traded, and as a result there is more total welfare than before. Note, also, that when people stop trading, the situation is a "Pareto optimal" or "efficient" one, in the sense that the distribution of sandwiches cannot be improved by making one person's situation better without hurting somebody else.

Unfortunately, however, in the real world trading may stop before efficiency is achieved. In the sandwich case, it was easy to get information about possible traders and to reach and enforce agreements. But often such "transaction costs" (the costs of actually reaching an agreement) can be substantial and may prevent the market from reaching an efficient distribution. Suppose, for example, that there are hundreds of people instead of only four and that the only one who likes tuna has not been given the one tuna sandwich. Because the costs associated with finding that one person and making the trade outstrip the benefits to both of the potential traders, they would not be able to make the bargain and there will be less total utility as a result.

But now note another fact about the sandwich case and transaction costs: If the transfer of sandwiches between the tuna lover and tuna hater were somehow to take place via a miracle, for instance, or if a dictator were to force the transfer, then that too would constitute a Pareto improvement, creating more total utility. This means that utilitarians must think beyond the trades people *actually* make to the ones they *would* make in a world where transaction costs are zero. Such hypothetical trades—ones the parties would have made but for the high costs of making the agreement—are of interest to the economist because of the possibility that the market will not reach efficiency due to high transaction costs.

This allows us, then, to extend the idea of maximizing utility through revealed economic preferences one step further, though it will take us beyond simple Pareto improvements to situations in which some people are actually made worse off. Suppose Jones has the only tuna sandwich, but that Smith (who has no sandwich) would happily pay Jones at least as much for it as Jones would want in a trade. Absent transaction costs, therefore, the sandwich would be sold. But notice also that this means it would increase "wealth," as economists say, for Smith to have the sandwich rather than Jones, *whether Smith buys it or Jones is forced to give it to him.* Although forced redistribution to Smith makes Jones worse off and does not create any more sandwiches (or anything else), it would nevertheless increase total "wealth" because the *value* of the goods has been increased. This is because the tuna sandwich has greater value in Jones's hands than in Smith's—a fact that we can know even though we have gone beyond mere Pareto improvements. Given that Smith *would be* willing to give more to Jones than Jones would demand

in a trade, the new distribution pattern increases social wealth even though no actual trade took place and it is not a Pareto improvement.[18]

The legal implications of these ideas can be brought out by considering the following case. Suppose a person who shipped goods on a barge that sank in a storm
sues the barge owner for compensation.[19] At trial it is determined the barge
owner did not require a pilot to be on the barge while it was being towed in the
storm, even though that could be done at little cost, and furthermore that if one
had been on board, this and other accidents would have been avoided. Who then
should win the lawsuit and pay for the lost cargo—the cargo owner or the barge
owner?

Assume the cost to the barge owner of hiring pilots is $100 per towing, and
there is one chance in ten of saving $5,000 in cargo. But suppose also that without
pilots it would cost shippers $500 to buy insurance or otherwise protect against
the risk of a storm. Now obviously the economically efficient solution is for there
to be pilots: The cargo owners could compensate the ship owners fully for the
$100 and still come out $400 ahead. So in order to get that (efficient) result—having pilots on barges—the judge should hold the barge owner liable for the damages. The ship owner acted inefficiently—she should have hired somebody to
guide the barge through storms rather than risking the cargo—and the new rule
will encourage more efficient actions in the future.

Another important fact brought out by the case is this: *Absent transaction costs*
the two parties, ship owner and cargo owner, would have agreed on their own to
hire a pilot no matter how the judge ruled.[20] If the ship owner is not legally liable,
then cargo owners would be willing to pay the ship owner anywhere up to $500 to
have pilots, and (since pilots cost only $100) the two will reach a bargain some-
where between the two figures, so that economic efficiency will be achieved. The
reason that was not done before, we assume, is transaction costs: It was too costly
for the parties to find each other and then negotiate the agreement.

This conclusion is relevant to a judge who wants the wealth maximizing result,
that is, that there be pilots on the barges. The economically minded utilitarian
judge, concerned to maximize utility, does not care, of course, who pays for pilots,
just as long as efficiency is achieved and they are on board. But if the judge decides the cargo owners must pay for their own losses instead of the ship owner,
then the pilots may not get hired because transaction costs are too high for cargo
owners to negotiate the agreement with shipper. That would mean the cargo
owners would have to try to avoid accidents in some less efficient way and there
would be less total utility. Thus, the best way to get the efficient result is to hold
the ship owner responsible rather than the cargo owners. That saves transaction
costs (no lawyers need to be paid to write contracts between shipper and barge
owners guaranteeing they hire pilots), and assures the pilots are hired.

Put another way, judges should "mimic" the market by imagining an auction
in which the right to avoid paying for the loss is auctioned off to the person who
would pay the most for it, and then assign the right to that person.[21] Because
avoiding the accident would be more costly for the cargo owners, they would have

paid more for the right not to bear the loss and should therefore not be assigned liability.

Though analytically useful, this illustration may seem relatively uncontroversial. It will be helpful therefore to look at another example, not drawn from the law of negligence, in order to focus on the philosophical and legal problems law and economics must confront. Suppose a group of farmers has asked for an injunction against a local factory to prevent it from increasing its pollution levels, as it proposes to do. Again we must make economic assumptions; so let's say that the factory can produce $100 worth of goods an hour if it runs slowly and $900 worth of goods if it runs at full speed. But at that maximum output it also strains its filter system, expelling much greater amounts of pollutants. Suppose therefore that the local farmers will lose $600 in damaged crops if the company goes at high speed but lose only $60 in crops if it runs at the slower, less polluting level.[22] The legal question, whether the farmers should get their injunction that prevents the greater level of pollution, can be put in the form of an economic question: Who can most cheaply bear the cost of the pollution—the company or the farmers? By hypothesis, the company would lose $800 ($900 minus $100) if it runs at the slower pace, while the farmers will lose only $540 if the factory is allowed to go at the faster speed ($600 minus $60). So the wealth maximizing outcome is for the factory to work at maximum capacity and produce $900 in economic wealth: The loss to the farmers will only be $540 compared with $800 to the factory if it slows down.

As with the earlier example, were we to assume there are no transaction costs, then it would not matter in terms of total utility what the judge does (though it *would* matter to the individual factory owners and farmers). If the farmers are given the right to stop the higher level of pollution, the factory owners will simply buy the right to pollute at the higher level from the farmers, since the owners could do that and still make a profit. If the farmers do not get the right to stop the pollution, however, then the factory will proceed at the faster rate itself; it would not be worthwhile for the farmers to pay the factory not to pollute, and again the efficient outcome (that is, the factory running at high speed) will be reached.

But now suppose transactions costs are significant, perhaps because the agreement would be costly and difficult to draft or because there are hundreds of farmers who must be contacted, so that there is less to be gained by the parties in trading the right than they would lose in transaction costs. Under those circumstances it will matter very much, from the perspective of maximizing utility, how the judge assigns the right. If it goes to the farmers, they will exercise it (since transaction costs preclude selling the right to the factory) and thereby lose only $60 due to pollution rather than the $600 it would have cost them if the factory had gone at full speed. That is not, however, the utility maximizing outcome, since (we are assuming) the factory loses $800 because it could be producing $900 but now produces only $100. If, however, the judge says the *farmers* must bear the cost and cannot enjoin the factory, then the factory will proceed and utility will be maximized. The farmers will be unhappy, of course, since they will lose $600. But the economic point is again that factory owners would pay more for the right to pollute than farmers would to prevent them (the factory owners *could* compensate them and still make a profit at the faster rate of production).

These results could be different, however, if the economic facts change. Suppose that besides lost production the extra pollution also raises farmers' medical bills by $500. In that event, the economically efficient outcome is reversed, and the judge should assign the right to get an injunction to the farmers. For now it is the farmers who would pay to keep the factory at the slower rate: They will lose $540 in crops plus $500 in medical bills at the faster rate of production, as against a total loss of only $800 to the factory at the slower pace. In that way, economic analysis is both sensitive to the economic facts and only as good as the information on which it is based.

This case, besides exemplifying the economic approach, nicely illustrates the problematic nature of economic analysis from the perspective of utilitarianism.[23] The question to be asked, of course, is whether the economist's concern to achieve efficiency and maximize utility, understood in terms of *wealth*, is an objective that utilitarians would support. Is that the right goal from the perspective of those committed to maximizing total welfare, understood as desire satisfaction? I began my consideration of the economic theory, recall, by discussing Pareto improvements: If people voluntarily trade then the new distribution makes at least one person better off while nobody's position is worsened. That is because the new situation is preferred by at least one person, while nobody desires the older distribution over the new. In that way, the economic theory would seem able to measure strength of desires while avoiding the problems of interpersonal comparisons inherent in the hedonism and the experience theory. But is that right? Does the economic approach I have outlined capture the attractive features of the desire theory? And should a utilitarian therefore support law and economics?

Clearly the answers to these questions are "no." The reason is connected to the fact that economic theory extends beyond Pareto improvements to embrace hypothetical compensation, making the further claim that legal rights should be assigned to those who will benefit from them sufficiently that they could compensate the losers of the litigation, regardless of whether they actually do.

According to the economic argument, judges are to seek efficiency in order to maximize utility by imagining an auction in which rights are sold to whomever would pay the most. Now we may perhaps assume that if somebody is willing to pay more for a concert ticket than a baseball ticket or more for a tuna sandwich than a concert ticket she has a stronger preference for the former. But law and economics asks judges to make comparisons *between* persons, an extension that pretty obviously breaks the link between willingness to pay and strength of desire. The reason is that whether winners could compensate losers is influenced by the initial distribution, that is, by the amount of wealth each person begins with. Suppose, for instance, that one of the costs of pollution is a general decline in the farmers' ability to enjoy their neighborhoods due to the unpleasant smell and ugly appearance of the landscape. If the farmers are wealthy, the factory owners may not be able to outbid them for this right because wealthy farmers would pay more for the clean air than it is worth to the factory owners to pollute. But if the farmers are poor, they may not be able to pay much to keep the air clean.

Something seems to have gone wrong from the utilitarian perspective. If anything should be obvious, it is that poor farmers do not get less welfare from clean air simply because (unlike an otherwise identical group of wealthy farmers) they cannot outbid the factory for the right to pollute. Poor people who are unable to pay to keep pollution out of their environment cannot be presumed to care less about their health or that of their children merely because they cannot pay more for it. (Indeed it seems likely the poor might care even *more* about clean air since they cannot easily avoid pollution's effects by taking long weekends off or staying in an air-conditioned house.) Auctioning rights to those most willing to pay is a poor strategy for a judge wishing to maximize expected total utility in the sense of satisfying the maximum number of people's strongest desires. Even if the utilitarian agrees, in other words, that Pareto improvements increase utility (by making at least one person better off and nobody worse off), this does not justify the economic approach's reliance on *potential* Pareto improvements and imaginary auctions of rights. The fact that winners *could* compensate losers is no guarantee total utility would be increased: If judges imagine what people *would* pay for the right and assign it accordingly, then the result will not be simple Pareto improvements. There will be losers as well as winners. So even if the "wealth" pie grows, the "utility" pie, understood as satisfaction of desires, may be made smaller as a result of the economically minded judge's decision.

None of this is to say, however, that the utilitarian should ignore the economist's advice since absent a significant disparity of wealth between the parties, it probably is utility maximizing for land to be used for higher-value industrial production rather than farming. Weighing costs and benefits is the lifeblood of utilitarianism, but it is welfare, not wealth, that is their measure. The reason that the economist's advice should often be followed is not because the utilitarian thinks increasing wealth is good in itself or even that increasing it will always bring with it anything else of value. The reason, rather, is that competitive markets encourage efficient use of labor and other productive resources. Competition provides incentives that improve efficiency, increasing the size of the economic pie. But there is no reason for the utilitarian to make the further assumption that utility is maximized whenever rights or other things of value go to the person willing to pay the most.

These problems emerge even more starkly as we turn from economic to constitutional issues. Should a judge award the right to free exercise of religion, for example, only to those groups able to outbid the majority for it? If the religious group is small, poor, and unpopular, it seems that the economic theory implies that a judge should refuse to protect its religious freedom. But that seems outrageous; why should willingness to pay determine whether members of a group have the right to practice their religion? A similar point applies to another great First Amendment right: freedom of speech. For the economic theory, the reason behind limits on speech is that speaking is worth less to those wishing to exercise the right (they would pay less for it) than others would pay to have them keep quiet. This may seem fine for situations like Holmes's famous case of falsely yelling "Fire!" in a crowded theater. Yet the fact that a group of wealthy but dangerous speakers could theoretically outbid the victims of the wealthier people's speech hardly shows that giving them the right would maximize utility, any more than the fact that another group would pay less indicates the right is less important to that group.

Since willingness to pay is an imperfect expression of intensity of desire, it might be thought that the economic theory can respond to this simply by imagining, contrary to fact, that the parties had the same wealth at their disposal. Then, it might be argued, the economic theory would be vindicated since the one desiring the right more strongly would also be the one willing to pay more for it. But the problem with such a suggestion is that it seems to have given up whatever advantage the economic argument had in terms of making interpersonal comparisons of utility. The hypothetical question of who would buy if, contrary to fact, resources were equal, although admittedly more relevant from the utilitarian standpoint, is no easier to answer than the original one about which individual or group desires the right more. Indeed, the same evidence that would be appealed to directly by the desire utilitarian as indicating strength of desire would be used by the (revised) economic theory to demonstrate how much would be paid if, contrary to fact, economic wealth were identical. The economic approach has not given us anything new to help determine the strength of desires and make interpersonal comparisons of utility.

Desires, Experiences, and the Problems of Measurement

The economic theory does not offer a conception of welfare that the utilitarian could adopt, and so the utilitarian must again confront the dispute between the desire and experience theories, including the problems of measurement and interpersonal comparisons of utility. In fact, I will argue, the utilitarian is better advised to return to the experience theory despite its problems of measurement. This is the case for several reasons, the most important of which is that the experience theory more accurately captures the utilitarian's underlying moral motivation: a sympathetic, impartial concern for the general welfare of all. This is so for a variety of important reasons.

No utilitarian, it is clear, would claim all desires, however irrational, should be satisfied; weight must be given to the basis of the beliefs on which the desires rest and to the person's level of intellectual development. A child's desire to play in the street would not generate sympathetic utilitarian responses, nor would a temporarily depressed adult's desire to jump from the window or a normal adult's desire to drink from a well if that person was unaware the water was poisoned. Each of these cases suggests that the *reasonableness* of the beliefs on which the desires are based should be considered by the utilitarian motivated by sympathetic concern for others. Perhaps the desire utilitarian should therefore understand welfare to comprise fulfilling only *rational*, or *informed*, desires. But then the question is how to distinguish rational from irrational ones.

Desires are in part at least a reflection of beliefs, so one natural suggestion is that "rational" desires and preferences are the ones that would survive presentation to the person of the correct and relevant information.[24] Thus, if the desire to drink the water disappeared when the individual learned of the well being poisoned, then the desire is uninformed and the utilitarian would not want to meet it. Yet this proposal raises a variety of further questions: How much information must be presented? If we say reasonable beliefs must be able to survive presentation of *all* available and relevant information, then it is not clear how many desires would actually survive, including many of our beliefs that seem clearly rational. If we say they must survive only *some* relevant and available information, then is there not still a sense in which the desire (because it would not survive *full* information) is irrational? And how much information, exactly, must it then withstand to pass the threshold of rationality?

Besides weighing the potential irrationality of desires, the sympathetic utilitarian must also weigh the possibility that the desire is caused by a chemical addiction, for example, or by some other psychological problem. Should the heroin addict's desire, for instance, weigh as heavily as equally strong desires that are not based on addiction?[25] It seems at least plausible to say that chemical addiction, by itself, undermines the claim that fulfilling desires improves welfare, even if the addict's desire is "rational" in the sense that it would not be revised in light of additional relevant information. The fact that it rests on chemical dependence seems to go at least some way toward undermining the tendency of sympathetic observers to want it met.

Still another feature of desires that should worry proponents of this version of utilitarianism, besides irrationality and addiction, is their adaptability: People's desires can be influenced by their beliefs about whether they can expect to get what they want.[26] If something is thought impossible to achieve, people may convince themselves it isn't worth it anyway and, thereby, come to desire it less.[27] Perhaps people adapt this way in order to reduce the psychological frustration of not having what they want. (It is sometimes argued that slaves and other oppressed people manifest this.) Suppose then that we know a desire is "adaptive" in this way, and the only reason something is not desired is that the person has come to think it is unattainable. Again, it seems that the sympathetic utilitarian would want to consider that fact and ignore or at least discount desires that are known to be adaptive. A woman who has lost the will to be free of her husband's dominance through adaptation does not seem to have thereby lost the claim that she would be better off outside his influence.

Besides the concerns about irrational desires, desires based on addiction, and ones that are adaptive, there is another feature about human desires that further undermines the idea that fulfilling them increases welfare. Suppose, for instance, that a person wanted an eloquent eulogy delivered at his funeral; would fulfilling that desire for the now-dead person increase welfare, as the desire utilitarian seems to suggest? Or suppose, to take a different example, that Smith meets a stranger on a train who tells Smith his life story, and as a result Smith forms the desire that the stranger gets what he wants during the remaining years of his life. The two then part ways, never to meet again. As with the eulogy example, it seems that the desire theory leads to the conclusion that Smith's welfare will be affected by what happens to the stranger, since Smith wants him to flourish, whether or not Smith ever hears of him again.[28]

The various objections to the desire theory I have been discussing suggest that the sympathetic, impartial attitude on which utilitarianism rests is best captured in the experience rather than desire theory. The sympathetic attitude on which utilitarianism rests is not engaged when the normal link between desires and experiences is broken or when the desires are irrational or produced by addiction or adaptability. For these reasons, I conclude, utilitarians would do well to look more closely at the experience theory and defend a version of it that avoids hedonism (which holds that all and only pleasant experiences are valuable) as well as the desire theory (which we have just been criticizing).

Suppose we call that middle position the "desirable experience" theory. It shares with hedonism the view that it is only the having certain sorts of experiences that is inherently valuable, rather than getting one's desires met. In that way it avoids the last group of objections against the desire theory by tying value to experiences rather than to (simply) getting what one wants. But then what of the other objections to the desire theory I described: The fact that desires can be irrational or based on chemical addiction and adaptability? In order to address these, I suggest, the utilitarian can distinguish between *desired* and *desirable* experiences: For an experience to be genuinely valuable, it must not just be desired but must be desirable. To be desirable, however, the experience must not be based on mistaken information and the person must not be under the influence of addictive drugs or driven by adaptive psychological processes. Experiences that pass those tests, then, may be thought of as desirable (rather than simply desired), and it is those sorts of experiences that are inherently valuable.

One advantage of this approach, then, is that it occupies a mid-position between the overly broad desire theory and overly narrow hedonism. The desirable experience view does not hold, as the hedonist does, that only *pleasant* experiences are valuable but rather affirms that all desirable experiences, including for instance creating great art, may be intrinsically worthwhile. The desirable experience theory also rejects, however, the desire theory's claim that fulfillment of any desire is worthwhile regardless of concerns about irrationality, addiction, and adaptability. By walking that line between the desire and hedonistic theories, the desirable experience theory can rest securely on the sympathetic attitudes that motivate utilitarianism.[29]

If what I have said so far is correct, however, then the problem that originally led us to the desire theory—the apparent necessity of comparing the value realized by different persons having different types of experiences—presents itself once more. We will shortly consider how *judges* might address that question, given their institutional responsibilities as constitutional interpreters, but first we should address the problem at a more individual level.[30] As we have seen, utilitarianism presupposes that it is neither conceptually incoherent nor practically impossible for decision makers to pursue the ideal of maximizing welfare, and so it must offer an account of welfare and how it can be maximized that is both theoretically attractive and able to give the needed practical guidance to those who intend to follow its mandates. How, then, might the defender of the (desirable) experience theory think that predictions about welfare consequences should, or could, be made?

First, it is important to note that although the utilitarian is committed *in principle* to weighing *all* future consequences, and not just immediate ones that are easily predictable, this does not mean, given the uncertainty of the future, that the utilitarian must somehow know what all those distant consequences are (which obviously cannot be known by anybody). We are entitled to discount potential long-term consequences as they recede into the future for reasons we have already noted: Utilitarianism claims that acts are justified on the basis of expected utility, so that as the envisioned consequences move into the next decade and even the next century, probabilities of any of them actually occurring become more and more remote. Thus, whether the consequence we are contemplating is good or bad, the likelihood of it occurring decreases as time passes, with the result that its practical significance for us approaches zero. A newborn baby might theoretically become either a Hitler or an Einstein; but since we have no way of knowing, today, if that will be true each of those possibilities may be ignored in favor of consequences that, we believe, actually would follow from deciding to take its life.

Another more serious problem, besides how to deal with these remote and long-term consequences, is the familiar issue of weighing or comparing the importance of different consequences that we reasonably expect to follow from our actions.[31] Clearly, no utilitarian is going to claim to be able to turn people making decisions about their own welfare, let alone the welfare of others, into calculating machines, grinding out correct answers. Yet, the utilitarian could point out, we in fact do make comparisons of expected welfare all the time, and usually with reasonable confidence that our decisions are based on good reasons. Think, for instance, of parents deciding whether to move to a new city. One question they will obviously ask—perhaps even the only one—is whether members of the family will be collectively better off in the sense that they will enjoy their new life more than the alternative. From the perspective of desirable experience theory, that amounts to asking whether the experiences of various family members would be more desirable than the experiences they would likely have if the family remained in its current location.

Many factors will weigh in the decision, of course, and responsible people can spend hours thinking about the impact on themselves and their children of leaving friends, the economic benefits and risks, changes in lifestyle, and so on. Yet despite the controversial, often intuitive foundation on which such judgments rest, *from the inside*, that is, from the perspective of a person actually making them, the decisions hardly seem beyond our powers of reason. Though it is not like adding up a grocery bill or using a scale, in fact we do such comparisons all the time as we consider the effects of alternative courses of action on the welfare of ourselves and others. That we may be mistaken does not show that we had no basis on which to make the decision in the first place.

The method used is a complex mixture of factual inquiry and assessment that can be thought to take place in two stages. We first ask what, exactly, the consequences of the options under consideration will be—a process that involves (in the example of moving to a new location) trying to get as much information as possible about jobs, schools, housing, environment, social life, and so on. Each of these consequences, and more, will need to be considered in making the decision. Then, second, we typically try to get vividly before us exactly how we will feel about the various consequences that we have identified, asking how each person's life will be affected. Will the new job(s) be more enjoyable? Will the extra money be worth the extra hours and stress, if those are part of the expected consequences? Will one or more of the children be made miserable by the change in school or friends? Might the child be better off over the long run even if there is considerable unhappiness during the initial period of adjustment? None of these questions is easy, as anybody who has made such a decision knows. But that is not to say, as the anti-utilitarian argues, that such welfare "calculations" are impossible or beyond the power of reason. In fact, we make them constantly, and more or less in the way I have described—by identifying the probable consequences of different options and then imagining, as vividly as possible, how we think those consequences will affect our future lives, understood in the fashion recommended by the experience theory.[32]

Indeed, it seems irresponsible and also probably impossible *not* to weigh the consequences of our decisions. Whether speaking of the consequences on our own welfare, the welfare of friends and our families, or on society as a whole, the alternative—ignoring the available evidence and making decisions without regard for the effects on those whom we care about—seems deeply irrational. However difficult and whatever the uncertainties (and there will often be plenty of each), we have no option except to gather all the relevant information, consider it carefully by imagining as clearly as possible what those consequences will mean for those whose welfare we seek to promote, and then make a decision based on that process. To ignore those factors seems irresponsible, despite the imprecise and intuitive nature of the process.

It is an overstatement, then, to suggest that the difficulties associated with interpersonal comparisons of utility are so overwhelming that the utilitarian theory must be rejected. Although it is often difficult to predict with much certainty the precise consequences of different decisions, as well as to determine the precise impact of those expected consequences on people's life experiences, it does not follow that decisions about consequences are arbitrary or that interpersonal comparisons of welfare are impossible. I conclude, then, that in light of the various problems confronting both the hedonistic and desire theories (including the economic theory), the utilitarian is best interpreted as committed to the claim that increasing total welfare consists in maximizing the relative numbers and level of desirable experiences as compared with the number and degree of experiences that are not desirable.[33]

Assuming, then, that we have reached tentative understanding of the nature of welfare, we now return to issues of constitutional structure and interpretation.[34] The first topic I want to consider is the role of rights in utilitarian legal theory; then we turn to judicial review and particularly to the question of deference to democratically made decisions. In the final sections we look more specifically at questions of constitutional interpretation, focusing here on the actual decision-making process and the role of precedent as well as history.

Rights and Judicial Review

I argued in Chapter 3 that all rights, whether legal, conventional, or human (moral), are best understood as obligations owed the right holder by others. Having a right is therefore an advantage over others, useful in cases of conflict. I wish to show in what follows that utilitarianism, unlike originalism, democratic proceduralism, and CLS, does not assume a skeptical position regarding rights but believes instead that statements about moral rights are either justified or unjustified, correct or incorrect. Indeed, according to the utilitarian, whether or not one "has" a right depends, finally, on a complex assessment of the historical, economic, political, and other relevant facts about how certain states of the natural world (involving well-being) may be brought about or avoided.

It is helpful, however, to begin the discussion by looking at an approach that, though explicitly utilitarian, does not ask judges to think in terms of legal rules and rights. After outlining the weaknesses in that view, both theoretical and practical, I then describe the sense in which moral rights "exist" from the utilitarian perspective as well as the role judicial review might play for the utilitarian concerned to protect such rights against governmental intrusion.

Learned Hand was among the most explicitly utilitarian judges to serve on the bench. Though he never reached the Supreme Court, Judge Hand did sit as an appeals court judge, and while there he heard a major McCarthy-era free speech case, *Dennis v. United States*.[35] The issue in *Dennis* was whether members of the Communist Party of the United States had a constitutionally protected right to express their political views, which included the inevitability of the overthrow of the U.S. government. Hand's approach to the case is often thought a model of utilitarian thinking: Judges, he said, must decide based on their answer to the question "whether the gravity of the 'evil,' discounted by its probability, justifies such invasion of free speech as is necessary to avoid it."[36] In other words, whether speech is constitutionally protected depends entirely on whether the costs of suppressing it outweigh the benefits. Hand's formula also stresses another key point in utilitarian thinking: that these costs and benefits must be discounted by the probability that they will actually occur. So if it is only remotely possible that some harm will result from speech, then the benefit of suppressing it is reduced accordingly. Similarly, the benefits of suppressing a minor harm that will almost certainly follow from the speech, like offending a rather prudish town with sexually explicit literature, could be thought relatively significant since there is no doubt the harm will result if the speech is allowed.

We can thus think of Hand's proposal as a step-by-step process for uncovering the benefits and the costs of deciding for one side or the other in each case. The consequences of each option must first be identified, then discounted by the probability they will actually result from the decision, and then these expected consequences compared with the consequences of ruling the other way after those have also been identified and discounted.

So, to return to the problem Hand faced in *Dennis,* the utilitarian judge following Hand's strategy would first *identify* the various advantages that would be gained if the speech is allowed. Would the Communists' speech facilitate the search for truth through a free exchange of ideas? Would the speech be enjoyed by those who make it or hear it? Might allowing it provide a "safety valve," enabling radical or disaffected groups to vent their anger in non-destructive ways? Then the judge must identify the advantages of suppressing the speech. What are the potential dangers that could be prevented by suppression? Will there be violence if the speakers are not stopped? Might the speech lead to other consequences, including possibly endangering the government itself? The judge must also weigh the costs of suppression to the legal system: Resources will be spent by police, courts, and lawyers that could be used to advantage elsewhere.

Then, having identified the consequences of deciding each way, the judge moves to the second stage where these must be *discounted* based on the probability they will actually occur: The less likely it is that an evil will actually result from speech, the weaker the case for suppression, just as the potential advantages of allowing the speech must also be discounted if they may not actually occur.[37] Then, finally, having identified and discounted all the benefits and costs, the ideal utilitarian judge would *compare* the likely consequences of each possible decision she may make. Which course of action, the judge must ask, would likely produce the most total welfare? At this point, of course, the judge can do little more than hold vividly in her mind just what those expected consequences are and then decide which set of them would be better for her to bring about. This process of identifying, discounting, and comparing the consequences of legal decisions is obviously a complex one, often requiring considerable information; but the key point here is that whatever the difficulties utilitarians confront in making such a decision, Hand's is not the only approach open to a utilitarian judge. Instead of thinking of the utilitarian principle as warranting individual decisions, utilitarian judges could focus instead on the more abstract issue of moral rights and the justification of laws themselves.

It is helpful in developing these ideas to consider a different sort of case than the one Hand confronted. Suppose, for example, that a wealthy man has now died, leaving the bulk of his money for care of his pet dogs. His only surviving family member, a daughter, is poor and asks the court to refuse to honor the will. There is more than enough money in the will, she argues, both to keep the pets comfortable and provide for her. There is also no doubt, however, that the will was drawn in accord with standard procedures: He was of sound mind, there were the proper number of witnesses, and there is no question of its authenticity. What should a utilitarian judge do?

Imagine the judge decides that there would be more total utility produced if the judge simply ignored the will, as one reading of Hand's cost/benefit formula recommends. The daughter needs the money *now*, and the dogs will be cared for in any case. But although that may seem to make good utilitarian sense, it is hardly the standard legal answer. According to normal practice judges enforce legal rules—rules that confer rights on litigants—and they are not free to ignore the rules in a given case even if doing so would maximize expected utility. If rules governing wills require the money to go to the pets, then so be it. That's how the man wanted his inheritance to be handled, and he has a legal right that his will be enforced. So on this reading, Hand's utilitarian formula, which invites judges to decide based on the comparative advantages of each possible outcome, diverges radically from normal legal practice's emphasis on rules rather than the consequences of particular decisions.

A similar point would apply in criminal cases, where judges are again expected to ignore the direct effects of a verdict on the family and friends of the defendant as well as the larger community and focus instead on whether the defendant actually violated the law.[38] Again, any judge who determined guilt or innocence based on the greater expected utility rather than what the law requires would be seen to violate basic principles of legal practice.

In response to these sorts of concerns, utilitarians often insist that one must distinguish two different levels at which the utilitarian principle requiring expected utility to be maximized could enter into the decision, a point that illustrates the traditional distinction between act and rule utilitarianism.[39] Hand's formula suggests the right decision is the one that would maximize expected utility, a view that parallels act utilitarianism. But a second utilitarian position, distinct from this, is that the utilitarian principle enters at the level of *rules*, not individual decisions, so that the right decision would be the one that is required under a rule that, if generally applied, would be justified in the sense that it would maximize expected utility. One of the best known defenders of this rule utilitarian view, Richard Brandt, describes the difference this way: "A rule-utilitarian thinks that right actions are the kind permitted by the moral code optimal for the society of which the agent is a member. An optimal code is one designed to maximize welfare or what is good (thus, utility). This leaves open the possibility that a particular right action may not maximize benefit."[40] Offhand, it seems that rule rather than act utilitarianism is the correct approach for a utilitarian—certainly it seems to describe legal practice more accurately. There are many reasons why this act utilitarian approach should be rejected by the utilitarian—some are specific to particular types of cases, such as wills, but others apply more generally. In this particular instance, it seems clear that current rules governing wills should be enforced rather than act utilitarian rule in part because following normal rules governing wills allows people to control more effectively what will happen to their property, giving them incentives to work and save for the future. Under the act utilitarian approach, however, each decision would depend on who would benefit more from getting the inheritance. The general effect, however, would be to undermine the will-making power—something a utilitarian would presumably believe is not in the long-term interests of society.

Contract law provides another example of the importance of the distinction between act and rule utilitarianism. Suppose the question is whether a person now down on his luck should be required to fulfill the terms of a contract made years ago in which he promised to pay back a loan. The act utilitarian might be tempted to say that the contract should be ignored, thinking that such a decision would maximize expected welfare of the litigants. But again that ignores the distinction between the effects of a system of rules and the effects of a particular decision. A legal rule specifying that agreements will be legally enforced only if *in those circumstances* doing so has greatest expected utility could weaken significantly people's power to make contracts. No longer could the law be counted on to require people to pay back loans—a fact that would have various adverse effects, including reducing or eliminating the amount of money available for borrowing.

So it seems that the act utilitarian position holding that legal justification operates at the level of actual decisions, as suggested by Learned Hand's *Dennis* opinion, is not the one a utilitarian should adopt. Notice, therefore, that it is a mistake to think utilitarians ignore political and moral rights and focus only on the consequences of individual decisions. Utilitarians do take rights seriously. More precisely, to claim somebody has a legal right to something, whether it be a property right, free speech right, or right not to be executed, is justified for the utilitarian if a legal system that effectively maximizes expected welfare would, in fact, enforce that right.[41] Thus, if people have a (utilitarian) right to free speech, then it would maximize expected utility to impose a duty on government or on individual citizens not to interfere with people in the exercise of their speech. If people have a right to property, then society is better off, in terms of total welfare, if acts such as theft and arson are punished. And if the right also exists against the government, then the claim is that society is better off (the general or total welfare would be promoted) if people are allowed freedom of action by government itself, so that officials who try to restrict such behavior should be punished. So utilitarians can speak of rights of one citizen against another as well as rights of citizens against the government. In either case, the issue is the same: Would expected welfare be maximized if the law sought to protect or prevent the behavior by enforcing the relevant rule?

The difference between (rule) utilitarianism and other theories such as natural law is therefore not, as is sometimes said, that the utilitarian lacks an important place for rights; moral rights like freedom of speech, religion, privacy, due process, and so on could play a central role in utilitarian thinking. The difference arises at a deeper level, in answer to the question how the moral right is to be justified and how its boundaries are to be shaped. For the rule utilitarian, unlike other approaches[42] to rights, the answer is instrumental: Rights have no weight, no force, independent of the consequences on the general welfare of imposing such duties on people. Moral rights truly exist when a society that generally enforces them will be a better society, in the sense that more good will likely be realized than if they are not enforced. Both the justification and definition of legal rights, says the rule utilitarian, must reflect this underlying purpose that rights serve.

Supposing then that the utilitarian accepts the rule utilitarian view and believes moral rights, in that sense, do exist; the justification of legal decisions would depend, finally, on whether the decision is compatible with rules that are part of what Brandt terms an "optimal" system. The next question that naturally arises is how all this is relevant to constitutional interpretation. We can begin to fill in the utilitarian theory along these lines by focusing on the implications of what has been said about rights for the practice of judicial review and particularly the utilitarian's attitude toward democratic procedures. Then in the next section we will use another distinction—between direct and indirect utilitarianism—to look more closely at the question of constitutional interpretation including deference to history or precedent, judicial competence, and the maintenence of institutional integrity.

The utilitarian's conception of judicial review must rest, like all law and political institutions, on the role it would play in a larger governmental structure able effectively to promote the general welfare. Whether structures such as federalism, separation of powers, and judicial review, some of which are obviously anti-democratic, could find support among utilitarians depends, in other words, on the expected consequences of those institutions and practices. It is important to keep in mind, then, that democratic procedures themselves as well as whatever limits may be placed on them through such practices as judicial review are warranted, if they are, only instrumentally—as a means to the utilitarian's end. How then might the utilitarian defend the claim that judicial review of legislation, based on a written constitution, promotes the general welfare? Utilitarians have available a range of possible answers.

First, as we have noted, the utilitarian is not a skeptic with respect to moral rights. Some moral claims that law should respect citizens' rights are correct, according to the utilitarian, while others are not. So that at least leaves open the possibility that the utilitarian might find an important role for judicial review if, as seems possible, she were convinced that such an institutional framework would increase the prospects that laws will in fact respect those moral rights and thereby promote the general welfare. But how, exactly, might that argument go for the utilitarian?

To begin, the utilitarian might take a leaf from the democratic proceduralist's book, defending judicial review as a method to perfect democratic procedures including rights to vote, publish, and speak. But instead of envisioning democratic government as a self-legitimizing process that expresses a fair compromise among political equals, as the proceduralist did, the utilitarian's commitment to free speech and voting rights rests on the premise that democratic government is likely to produce laws that maximize welfare. That argument might be filled in along the following lines.[43]

Democratic government often seems attractive to utilitarians due to the dangers and inefficiencies of dictatorships. That authoritarian governments have historically tended to promote the welfare of the few in power at the expense of the common good has seemed obvious to many thinkers over the centuries, often including utilitarians. James Mill, for example, made the problem of forcing those in power to act in accord with the dictates of utilitarian principles the centerpiece of his political reflections.[44] Only by insuring that the interests of those who govern are tied closely to the interests of the governed, Mill argued, can law be expected to serve the *general* welfare rather than the narrow interests of those in power. Among the most important theorists of the U.S. system was Alexis de Tocqueville, who wrote (echoing James Mill) that "democratic laws generally tend to promote the welfare of the greatest possible number; for they emanate from the majority of the citizens, who are subject to error, but who cannot have an interest opposed to their own advantage."[45] In that way, utilitarians can extend general historical observations about the character of dictatorships by arguing that there is a more explicit, theoretical connection between democratic institutions, specifically voting, and maximizing utility.

Taking these thoughts a step further, we can imagine the utilitarian defender of democratic processes pressing the idea that in a democratic system, unlike ones where decisions are made by a minority, each person's well-being is given the same weight, measured in votes, as every other person's. That means, in turn, that the government would be less likely to sacrifice the well-being of the majority for the lesser good of a minority. So absent a benevolent, omniscient dictator who can assure that laws will promote the general welfare, it has seemed to many that democratic practices offer the best hope for enacting laws that will maximize total welfare. In that sense, democratic institutions serve as a mechanism for making social policy in an environment where plausible alternatives are either politically unavailable, risky, or too costly.

Imagine, for example, a town that must decide whether to turn a vacant area into a wildlife habitat or use it for a new park. By putting the decision to a vote, it could then be determined how many people prefer each outcome, which would indicate (the argument continues) the result that will maximize utility. If *elected officials* make the decision, however, then of course the connection between their vote and the welfare of the majority will be more tenuous. There is no assurance the majority of legislators will act in accord with either the public will or the general welfare. Nevertheless, perhaps we can assume that if people are unhappy with the way the town council votes, the council will not be around after the next election and that knowing this, the representatives can generally be counted on to enact laws that would promote the majority's welfare. Assuming all this is true, and democratic procedures tend to yield welfare maximizing laws, then judicial review could play a role in this utilitarian defense of democracy that is substantially similar to the one envisioned by democratic proceduralism, assuring that the political process is open and fair.[46] Laws that emerge from a democratic process will be more likely to reflect the will of the majority and, accordingly, to maximize welfare.

But as I argued in discussing democratic proceduralism, there are no assurances that this would be the case. A direct vote of the majority cannot be counted on to give the correct utilitarian result since each vote is given equal weight. One voter can't pull the voting lever more forcefully and thereby register a stronger desire or greater interest in the outcome than somebody else who really doesn't care much at all about the question. It is sometimes suggested in response that representative democracy, because it provides for logrolling, addresses this problem by allowing groups who care more deeply about a particular question to have their stronger preferences felt in the process. Thus, to use the same example, the stronger wishes of a minority that wants the park would be registered when their representatives trade votes with other groups. Perhaps, for instance, though the park lovers don't support a salary increase for teachers, they might agree to vote for that increase if representatives close to the teachers vote with them for the park. Constituents' desires therefore drive representatives to make compromises with other groups, and the park is secured even though on a straight vote that ignored the *strength* of desires, the park would be lost to developers. Therefore (the argument concludes) as long as logrolling is permitted among representatives, we can assume strong preferences count for more than weak ones, and so the utilitarian defense of democratic procedures stands.

Logrolling in fact, however, provides no assurances about welfare for many reasons. Prominent among them is that although everybody has only one vote and all representatives are free to bargain, there is obviously no guarantee that each person is represented by a lobbying group that is as effective as every other. This can occur for different reasons, one of the most important of which—as discussed in the second chapter—is prejudice; some groups may be unpopular or hated by the majority and therefore not be in an equal bargaining position because coalitions with them may cost votes to the representatives who join with them. Furthermore, candidates need money to win elections, and it is clear that groups able to contribute large amounts to campaigns will have the advantage over poorer groups, as will ones whose members vote in larger than usual numbers or pay close attention to elected officials. Yet no utilitarian should assume that because a rich person contributes ten times more to a lobby, he cares ten times more about the group's projects than a poor person who contributes much less to the opposing group.

No utilitarian can therefore count on democratic government always to gener-ate laws that are compatible even with the desires of the people, let alone their welfare, creating the possibility that judges exercising judicial review are in gen-eral justified not only in protecting democratic rights like voting and speech, as originally thought, but also in overturning laws that fail to meet the substantive utilitarian test. Whether a particular law is justified in the light of rule utilitarian-ism is not, in other words, an issue that can be resolved procedurally, without careful consideration of relevant historical, political, economic, and other evi-dence. It may seem, then, that the utilitarian is driven by the preceding consider-ations about the inherent weaknesses of democratic government toward judicial activism. I want to argue, however, that the real utilitarian picture of constitu-tional interpretation is in fact much more complicated.

Precedent, History, and the Problems of Constitutional Deliberation

Weighing against the theoretical basis for activism I have just outlined are a num-ber of factors that would seem to recommend judicial restraint to a utilitarian. In this section we explore these questions—leading us to weigh issues of relative ca-pacities of different branches to make decisions, the role of precedent and history in constitutional interpretation, and the importance of maintaining institutional integrity.

The process of identifying, discounting, and then comparing the consequences for the public welfare of legal rules is obviously difficult, requiring considerable sociological, political, and historical information. Judges are also vulnerable po-litically; they do not enjoy the legitimizing mantle of having been popularly elected and for that reason are constantly susceptible to the charge that they have usurped or at least abused power. Judges' opinions about the consequences of dif-ferent rules are often likely, for example, to be less informed than a legislature's; and even if judges *are* right in a given instance there may be political and institu-tional costs that outweigh whatever benefits can be expected from overturning a statute on constitutional grounds. The utilitarian, it seems, has good grounds for insisting that judges exercise judicial review cautiously rather than in the activis-tic fashion suggested at the end of the last section.

If these concerns bear out, then we have arrived at the same conclusions about judicial activism and perhaps even original intent that were described in earlier chapters, although this time via a very different route. Instead of urging judicial restraint and neutrality on grounds that judges should enforce the terms of the social contract, as originalists did, here the claim is that, as a matter of fact, judges would be wise to defer to the intentions of the framers on utilitarian grounds.

Aware of their own limitations in assessing the consequences of laws as compared with legislatures and of their limited political capital, judges should ignore their own judgment and overturn laws only if they are clearly incompatible with the framers' original intention. Otherwise, they are open to the charge that they have abused their authority, with the result that the courts and indeed the political system as a whole may suffer over the long term.

These are important considerations that must be sorted out, for there are really a number of different questions that are involved. In order to appreciate the merits of such claims and then to determine how they might fit into the utilitarian framework, it will be useful to analyze the issues in terms of another distinction, also important for utilitarian moral philosophers, that cuts across the earlier distinction between act and rule utilitarianism. Then, with that distinction in mind, we can usefully assess both the nature of the interpretive dispute between activism and restraint and the merits of each position.

Consider, then, the difference between "direct" and "indirect" utilitarianism.[47] Put simply, the idea is that in addition to the question discussed earlier of whether the utilitarian principle of *justification* applies to rules or to individual acts, we also must consider how the process of *deliberation* ought to proceed from the utilitarian perspective. There is, in other words, an important difference between the *justification* of a law or system of laws, on one hand (which the rule utilitarian answers in terms of rules the general enforcement of which would maximize expected utility), and the basis on which judges should subjectively make their actual *decisions,* on the other (which may or may not require them to weigh directly the consequences of rules, precedents, historical intentions, and so on). On one extreme, then, is the "direct" rule utilitarian claim that judges should always, in each case, consider the justification of the rule before making a decision. On the other extreme would be the pure indirect rule utilitarian position that society is better off, all things considered, if judges *never* consider directly the consequences of rules but instead simply apply them without utilitarian reflection on questions of justification. This former, direct rule utilitarian view holds, in other words, that judges should always deliberate and resolve cases by asking directly which rules would, if generally followed, maximize expected utility. The other, indirect view holds that the utilitarian standard is not to be used in deliberation at all but instead functions only at the level of justification, so that judges should set utilitarian concerns about the consequences of rules aside and simply apply the rules they are given. That indirect view remains utilitarian, however, since although the *decision-making process* is *not* based on utilitarian reasoning, the *justification* of the law nevertheless does depend, finally, on the fact that following it generally will maximize welfare. It is also utilitarian in another sense because of the underlying assumption that society is better off if judges do *not* deliberate about the justification of the rules they apply.

Indirect utilitarianism has in common with rule utilitarianism the idea that decisions should be made based on factors other than the consequences of particular acts. Direct rule utilitarians, however, think decisions should be both justified and deliberated about based on the consequences of different rules; indirect rule utilitarians think the judge should ignore questions about justification in the deliberation process (as well as the consequences of individual decisions) and simply apply rules, leaving it to others to determine if the rules are justified. As will become clear shortly, I think that the most reasonable rule utilitarian view is in fact a compromise between the pure direct and indirect versions. The utilitarian must allow some opportunity for a judge to modify or even reject rules that are not welfare maximizing, I will argue, although the extent to which a deliberating judge should look past the rules to consider whether they actually serve the utilitarian ideal, as direct utilitarianism recommends, depends on a range of factors.

My suggestion, then, is that from the utilitarian perspective, issues about judicial competence, original intent, and precedent can profitably be understood as arising in the context of this debate between direct and indirect utilitarianism. Consider, for instance, the example of the will, for here it seems at least at first glance that a rule utilitarian judge would not be satisfied with the indirect view's claim that consequences of rules allowing people to leave wills are beyond the bounds of the judge's deliberation and criticism. Indeed, the rule utilitarian might point out, it would simply be a form of rule worship for the judge to ignore the consequences of blindly applying received rules without considering whether they should be modified in some way. Surely, we can imagine a utilitarian judge thinking, there are times when a rule should include some exception, not previously noted, and that adding the exception is justified because it would maximize utility.

I have already suggested, however, some important objections to this direct utilitarian account, flowing from the limitations on judges' capacity to make the complex utilitarian calculations essential to identifying and comparing the welfare effects of alternative interpretations of rules and (when exercising judicial review) of overturning a law on constitutional grounds. Earlier I argued that it is not impossible in principle to compare "amounts" of utility and even to make interpersonal comparisons, though such judgments, it was admitted, are far from mechanical or precise. Yet that point may seem insufficient to warrant direct utilitarianism since, even granting it is theoretically possible, judges lack the resources, time, and expertise to function in the way the direct utilitarian advocates. Unlike legislators, judges cannot conduct expensive hearings involving the large amounts of resources and time necessary to make reasonable determinations of the consequences of different rules.

This important claim raises a number of different issues that are directly relevant to constitutional interpretation. To focus the discussion, consider again the problem of capital punishment. The Eighth Amendment's ban on "cruel and unusual punishment" gives no indication whether executions fall within that category.[48] Suppose a utilitarian judge is asked to decide whether a law calling for execution of people convicted of murder is constitutional. To answer that, the *direct* rule utilitarian would decide based on a complex set of questions requiring weighing the advantages of the rule and then comparing those with its disadvantages (both discounted based on probabilities) to see which rule would maximize expected utility.[49] If executions either serve no purpose or if the expected harm they cause outweighs the expected benefits, then the utilitarian would conclude such pointless suffering is "cruel and unusual" punishment and prohibited by the Eighth Amendment.[50]

A vast array of factors would have to be weighed by the direct utilitarian judge in making such a calculation, including the savings of tax money needed to keep people in jail (around $40,000 per person per year in New York), the enjoyment of some people at the thought of an executed killer, and, more importantly, the potential lives saved because others are deterred from committing a similar crime. If (as has sometimes been argued) each execution saves something on the order of eight innocent lives through deterrence of other murderers, then the utilitarian will have a strong reason to hold that executions are not "gratuitous" inflictions of pain and are therefore constitutional because a mistake would only mean a convicted murderer was unnecessarily executed rather than some number of innocent citizens' lives lost because a potential murderer was not deterred.[51] It would also be necessary to consider the argument that even in the absence of conclusive evidence that executions deter, it is nevertheless rational to assume they do and allow executions.[52] On the other side are various arguments that rules allowing executions actually decrease utility, including the possibility that innocent people will be executed (a question that can only partly be answered by a review of the historical record) and the risk that executions will encourage social violence. It is also possible that convicted capital offenders might win parole and become productive members of society (as well, of course, as repeating their crime after release from prison).

Obviously these calculations of the costs and benefits of legal rules cannot be done as if weighing two bags of grain on a scale to see which is heavier any more than the comparisons a family makes between the likely consequences of moving to a new city. Yet, as was noted earlier, people do make such decisions about rules as well as individual decisions all the time. Children are told that it is a rule they must be home at a certain time, do their homework before playing, and eat their vegetables—all with the reasonable conviction that the rule will promote their welfare. So this objection against the direct utilitarian is best understood not as the claim that such calculations are in principle impossible but rather that judges are not well-equipped to make them. Indeed, it may seem, a judge in a law library is especially poorly suited to address policy questions regarding the expected consequences of different rules. For that reason, it may be concluded, the utilitarian is well-advised to adopt indirect utilitarianism's demand that judges refuse to undertake such complex calculations and think instead only in terms of the plain language of the Constitution, received precedents, and the historical meaning of "cruel and unusual."

But though there is surely some merit to this objection, the direct utilitarian has a variety of responses. Although agreeing that increasingly complex problems demand sophisticated new methods of analysis, nothing says the judicial system cannot be reformed so that judges are better able to perform their utilitarian role. First, it might be argued, judges can be made more familiar with social-scientific facts and theories as part of their training and background. Indeed, earlier in this century legal realists undertook to reform law school curricula along just those lines, arguing that responsible lawyers and judges need to know far more about social sciences and economic theory than is traditionally taught in law schools.

Legal realists also championed a second reform, which became known as the "Brandeis Brief."[53] This was basically an effort by the legal realists to ask lawyers to help give judges a better understanding of the social and economic consequences of their decisions. So instead of focusing their efforts on formal, legal arguments, lawyers who submitted these briefs typically offered detailed sociological and economic studies in support of their client's legal position. Thus, besides reforming legal education, defenders of direct utilitarianism might also work to overcome some of the intellectual limitations inherent in current legal practice by asking lawyers to focus their arguments on the implications for society's welfare that could be expected if the judge decided that the relevant legal rules should be understood as they are arguing.

So although admittedly posing a difficult task, especially for judges, it does not seem that the direct utilitarian confronts overwhelming practical problems of the sort envisioned by the extreme form of indirect utilitarianism. There is no simple answer to the utilitarian's question about which rules would best maximize expected welfare, of course, or how generally sound rules should be modified in different contexts. But it seems, so far at least, that to avoid the charge of rule worship, the rule utilitarian judge exercising judicial review should at least sometimes consider directly the consequences of rules, asking whether they do, in fact, meet the utilitarian test.

The utilitarian judge would have even less reason for rejecting direct utilitarianism on the grounds that the framers' intentions are a sound indication of the correct answer to this or other constitutional issues. We do know, of course, that the Constitution requires that both national and state governments not deprive citizens of "*life*, liberty or property" without due process of law, clearly implying that the framers envisioned the possibility of capital punishment. But even assuming we have at least in this case overcome the many practical objections to originalism described in Chapter 1, it is still unlikely that a utilitarian judge would be convinced that this piece of history can be of help with the current problem; we have little reason to think the framers' answers were better justified than the ones a current court might reach. Not only do contemporary judges have access to the two centuries of historical experience since the framing, but there exists a vast economic and sociological literature that is relevant to the complex debate over capital punishment's costs and benefits. So even if the framers were asking themselves the right utilitarian questions, contemporary judges are in a better position to give a sound answer. Modern utilitarian judges would therefore have even less reason to trust the framers' utilitarian calculations than those of contemporary legislators.[54]

None of this is to say, however, that the utilitarian should then rush to embrace the direct rule utilitarian's claim that judges should focus their deliberations entirely on the merits of the rules they have been given, allowing no weight in their deliberations for precedent, history, or the position of other branches. There are many reasons for this. Part of the ground for moving back toward indirect utilitarianism is found in the role of precedent; another reason involves a reasonable regard for historical success of the rule; finally, and perhaps most important, are issues of institutional integrity that would incline a utilitarian away from direct utilitarianism in the direction of deference toward both elected branches and, perhaps, to the framers (although not for the reasons just discussed).

First, stare decisis (understood as the faithful application of past rules and precedents) is an important part of any legal system that can be expected to maximize expected utility. As was noted when criticizing act utilitarianism, people must be able to predict what courts will do before they can make financial and other decisions on which the general welfare depends. Not only would practices like will making and contracts be undermined if rules were constantly changed, but other areas of economic and political life such as property and tort would also be radically altered. People developing resources on their land could not predict the results of possible disputes about ownership, and doctors, motorists, and other actors would not be able to predict what would or would not count as negligence on their part if judges were too willing to revise rules in accord with their own understanding of which ones most effectively maximize expected utility.

Uncertainty in the criminal law is perhaps even more damaging since it creates anxiety (to put it mildly) and leads to the sense that people have not been given a chance to conform to law because adequate notice of its requirements was not given. Furthermore, even legal changes that have no impact on commercial or criminal life have costs associated with the reeducation of lawyers and judges, publication of the changes, and general social upheaval that results from often even minor alterations in rules that are the basis of people's legal decisions. For these reasons, a rule utilitarian judge would give some (though not absolute) weight to received rules merely because they are now embedded in legal practice, and therefore be disposed to behave as recommended by the indirect utilitarian.

Furthermore, it might also be argued that despite the many reservations I have expressed about democratic procedures' capacity to yield laws that can pass the utilitarian test, still the fact that the law emerged from a fair and open democratic process constitutes at least a weak presumption in its favor. Judges who take that position, though not feeling bound by legislative enactments, would nonetheless have prima facie reason to uphold the law in the fashion of indirect utilitarianism. Similarly, it might be thought that the mere fact a rule is the product of generations or even centuries of legal and political experience gives some warrant to the presumption that it is the one that will most likely maximize expected utility. The common law, it is sometimes said, operates in something of the fashion of an "invisible hand," so that the laws that survive the test of time are likely to also be ones that have proven over the years to serve well the utilitarian goal.[55]

Another important general reason for utilitarian judges to reject pure direct utilitarianism in favor of the indirect approach to making decisions is the importance of maintaining the authority of political institutions, including both the legislature and the judiciary. This concern takes many forms. If judges are perceived to usurp the legitimate authority of the elected legislature, for example, or are thought too willing to overturn settled law based on their own visions of an ideal society, then society's welfare may eventually suffer. Thus, even if the judge is convinced a particular law should be rejected or modified, it may nonetheless be better to follow precedent rather than risking even greater damage to the political process.[56] This, then, is another reason that a rule utilitarian judge should feel compelled to give weight to received rules, in the fashion of indirect utilitarianism, and to ignore the utilitarian question, Would the general enforcement of the rules maximize expected utility? Both stare decisis and concern to protect institutional integrity exert a powerful moderating influence on direct utilitarian judges who might be tempted to modify or overturn rules in accord with their own sense of the rules' consequences.

Similarly, if people were unwilling to accept a ruling they took to be contrary to the original meaning of the framers, then that too would bear on the important concern of maintaining institutional integrity.[57] Judges who ignore such an important fact and blindly proceed to overturn laws without regard to the fact that the people demand they pay at least some heed to how the framers would have wanted the case to go run the risk of damaging their long-term capacity to exercise power and therefore to contribute positively to the general welfare. So although the framers' intentions are of no use in deciding the merits of an issue like capital punishment, there still may be times when deference to their intentions is the soundest political strategy.

For all these reasons, I conclude that a utilitarian judge would reject the (extreme) direct utilitarian position in favor of indirect utilitarianism, albeit of a modified sort. Concerns about limits on their own ability to evaluate a received rule in regard to welfare maximizing and recognition of the importance of following precedent as well as maintaining institutional integrity all suggest that responsible rule utilitarian judges would tend simply to accept the laws and meanings without (necessarily) asking whether they in fact maximize expected utility. However, I also argued earlier that under certain circumstances judges may sometimes conclude that despite these various concerns, all of which have only prima facie weight, judicial review should be exercised or a precedent should be overturned. The presumption that laws are compatible with the utilitarian ideal is only, after all, a presumption, reflected in the sense judges have that rules should not be modified or rejected except when it is reasonably clear that another rule would function more efficiently. Aware that protecting freedoms of speech, religion, privacy, due process, and so on are central to the overall welfare of society and assuming politically acceptable constitutional and legal arguments are available, a utilitarian Supreme Court might decide that the case is strong enough to outweigh the (indirect utilitarian) presumption against such a decision and overturn a law that obviously harms the public welfare in the name of the Constitution.

From the rule utilitarian perspective, then, it makes good sense for judges to take (and encourage) an attitude of moderate deference to received interpretations of old laws as well as to other branches when considering the constitutionality of new laws. This is especially true, of course, when all the factors I have described are present and judges face well-established, long-standing precedents that have wide support in the other branches as well as deep historical roots. But where the legal issue is less momentous, requiring for instance only that judges consider how an older law or precedent should be applied to a fresh set of circumstances, the direct approach would be more attractive.

Finally, there is no reason (other than ones that have already been mentioned, including especially institutional integrity) for the Court to limit itself to *explicit* constitutional language in exercising judicial review. Whether the Constitution's general concepts like "liberty" should also be relied on to strike down laws would therefore depend, like all other such questions, on balancing the presumption that law is not to be struck down, especially (as discussed here) in ways that run the risk of damaging the Court's authority, against the gain to be made in rejecting the law on such vague constitutional grounds.

The truth, therefore, lies between the direct and indirect accounts; it requires judges to give what Dworkin terms "gravitational force" to rules, though not to the extent that judges completely set aside their own judgments about a law's consequences.[58] The most accurate picture is of a utilitarian judge presuming that a law is constitutional and precedents are to be followed, in the way indirect utilitarianism recommends, but nevertheless being open to the possibility that the presumption may be overridden if the situation requires it.

To conclude our extended discussion of utilitarianism and constitutional interpretation, we may think of the utilitarian maintaining seven central theses.

1. The underlying motivation behind the utilitarian theory is sympathetic concern for the welfare of others, often expressed in terms of the attitudes of a sympathetic, impartial, well-informed and rational observer.
2. Welfare or utility is therefore best understood in terms of the experiences that are desirable rather than either fulfilled desires or economic efficiency.
3. Utilitarianism has sufficient resources available to develop an account of moral rights.
4. The account of moral rights, along with plausible assumptions about the limits of democratically elected legislatures, can explain the role of judicial review.
5. Utilitarian judges exercising judicial review would understand the utilitarian principle to apply not to individual decisions but instead to rules, in the fashion of the rule utilitarian.

6. The ideal decision-making process, as compared with questions of justification, would *normally* follow the model of indirect rather than direct utilitarianism, so that judges would not decide cases by asking anew each time which rule would maximize expected utility but instead would defer to both past decisions and to elected branches, perhaps including historical intentions.

7. This indirect approach rests in large part on concerns about the importance of maintaining consistency and on institutional integrity.

Final assessment of this utilitarian account of judicial review and constitutional interpretation will depend in part of the attractiveness of the alternative and so must be postponed until the next chapter where the contrast between it and democratic contractualism is outlined in detail. We can begin that process, as well as introduce an important theme that will provide a bridge to the discussion that follows, by looking briefly at a constitutional idea that Justice Brennan often referred to in his opinions as the "dignity" of the individual.

Utilitarianism, Dignity, and Procedural Fairness

As we saw in the first section, utilitarians claim that utility calculations occupy the entire field of political morality; the only moral "facts," say utilitarians, are facts about what welfare is and how it can best be maximized. Politics is therefore instrumental: Once it is agreed what the general welfare consists in, institutions and laws are to be assessed in terms of their tendency to achieve that end. This conclusion, as we saw, has often seemed to utilitarians to be a major source of strength. Motivated by sympathetic concern for the welfare and suffering of themselves and others, utilitarians see themselves as placing morality and politics on a solid, empirical footing, replacing the outdated and metaphysical approaches advocated by classical and Christian thinkers. Only if we focus on the actual world and the observable facts about human welfare can we expect, they think, to make moral progress or reach common agreement.

Utilitarianism offers an attractive and powerful theory—one that dominated the moral, political, and legal thinking of the English speaking world for much of the last two hundred years. We will assess it in stages, beginning with the denial that there are other basic principles besides maximizing utility that constitutional interpreters must consider. In this section, I want to begin the assessment of utilitarianism by pointing out two important respects in which that central claim may be questioned. One angle from which to question the utilitarians' key claim was discussed in detail in the context of democratic proceduralism. Utilitarianism views democratic procedures wholly instrumentally—as means to achieve the best results; it does not, in other words, have any room for the proceduralist's claim that fair and open democratic processes have a special, further claim to legitimacy based on the fact that they respect the right of each person affected by the political process to participate in it as an equal.

It is thus important to recall that in criticizing democratic proceduralism I did not claim such procedures fail as a fair compromise or that political fairness in that sense is unimportant. Rather, the point was that one must *also* take into account the outcome of the process, especially in cases involving discrimination and the rights of minorities. But it does not follow from the fact that democratic procedures are not fully self-legitimizing (as proceduralism mistakenly claims) that such procedures are to be assessed *solely* in terms of their consequences, as the utilitarian argues. Insofar then as one is attracted to the view that democratic processes are *inherently* better than others because they represent a fair compromise among political equals and are not just instrumentally more efficient, then to that extent the utilitarian account of democratic government is inadequate. In the next chapter I provide an account of democratic procedures that walks this line between the utilitarian's exclusive reliance on consequences and the proceduralist's claim that democratic procedures are self-justifying.

The second point, which like the first will be explored more fully in the next chapter, involves another respect in which the utilitarian's claim that consequences occupy the entire field is also mistaken. We saw in the last section how a utilitarian would approach the question of capital punishment, asking if such a law can be defended as an efficient crime control measure that strikes the right balance between the benefits and costs to society. If executions are "inefficient" in the sense that they impose greater costs on the person who is executed, his family, and so on than society can expect to gain from deterrence and other potential advantages of the practice, then capital punishment is a violation of the Eighth Amendment's proscription against "cruel and unusual punishment."

I want to argue, however, that this example of the utilitarian approach to constitutional issues, like others I will discuss shortly, is actually a good illustration of the *limitations* of the utilitarian approach to political legitimacy and constitutional interpretation. The issue is whether this conception of judicial review and, specifically, of the Eighth Amendment is defensible. One of the most prominent opponents of executions, former Justice William Brennan, clearly thought there is more to the Eighth Amendment than the utilitarian position allows. He wrote in a 1976 case, for example, that "the Clause forbidding cruel and unusual punishments under our Constitutional system of government embodies in unique degree moral principles restraining the punishments that our civilized society may impose on those persons who transgress its laws. ... Foremost among the 'moral concepts' recognized in our cases and inherent in the Clause is the primary moral principle that the State, even as it punishes, must treat its citizens in a manner consistent with their intrinsic worth as human beings—a punishment must not be so severe as to be degrading to human dignity."[59] Justice Brennan says little to explain what he means by the "intrinsic worth" of human beings or why such punishment is "degrading to human dignity." One thing does seem clear, however: This is not the language of a utilitarian. Brennan expresses a vision of the individual and individual rights that seems to directly contradict the utilitarian's effort to interpret the Constitution solely on the basis of its impact on social utility. There are limits, he says, on what the state may do to the individual, even in the name of the general welfare, and for Brennan that boundary is defined in terms of the respect government must show for the dignity and worth of each individual.

If we assume there is merit to Brennan's claim and that respect for the dignity of the individual is among the basic "moral concepts" embodied in the Constitution, then the utilitarian approach would seem incomplete. Consider, however, the likely response of a utilitarian to Brennan's position. Utilitarianism's founder, Jeremy Bentham, put the point starkly. Anti-utilitarian "theologians," he wrote, "set up a phantom of their own, which only they call Justice. ... But Justice, in the only sense in which it has meaning, is an imaginary personage, feigned for the convenience of discourse, whose dictates are the dictates of utility, applied to certain particular cases ... The dictates of justice are nothing more than a part of the dictates of benevolence."[60] Bentham's response is familiar: In part it challenges those who espouse notions of dignity and justice to give an accounting of the basis on which their claims rest (a problem we will address in the next chapter), and in part it asserts that utilitarian principles can adequately account for all the reasonable limits found on government.

But it is nonetheless unclear at this point that the utilitarian account of political morality is adequate, especially when viewed from the perspective of the cruel and unusual punishment clause. We noted before that the utilitarian purpose of the clause is to be sure, in advance, that punishment is not excessive. Presumably, then, the meaning of "cruel and unusual" should be flexible: As new information becomes available about the effectiveness of different forms of punishment, the Supreme Court should be willing to revise its definition.[61]

The problem with this approach is with what it leaves out of account. According to the utilitarian, the purpose of the cruel and unusual clause is to foreclose inefficient methods of punishment. The framers had in mind the rack and thumb screws but were wise enough not to mention them specifically, leaving it to later interpreters of the clause to consider new forms of punishment like electrocution, poison gas, and lethal injection. But what if the framers' assumptions about medieval torture were wrong? Suppose social scientists were to discover an even more effective deterrent to serious crimes than executions. Torture followed by executions, they report, is the best way to deal effectively with crime. Even giving full weight to the pain and terror caused by their proposal, society would still experience a net gain in utility. But to be most effective, they add, the torture should be done on television. Some viewers would also suffer, they admit, but again this relatively mild cost is more than outweighed by the added deterrent we will be able to purchase with our prime-time telecast.

Now this example, Brennan might say, is really just an extreme way to make the point he wanted to express: There are limits we place on how we will treat fellow citizens that express the worth of each individual and that cannot be understood in purely utilitarian terms. Justice is not, as Bentham said, completely reducible to benevolence, for a benevolent concern to protect innocent lives could lead to gross violations of individual dignity and rights. *Even if* torture could be made cost effective, other moral principles stand in the way.

It is important, however, to note an important distinction, for Brennan and other critics of utilitarianism can easily be understood to be making a stronger claim than is necessary. One way of understanding the anti-utilitarian argument is that concerns about justice and individual dignity place an absolute limit on utilitarian calculations of social benefits and costs, so that no matter how much suffering could be prevented, some forms of punishment are never justified. But this absolutist position is not the only one available to the utilitarian's critic, since a weaker position would claim simply that welfare maximizing strategies do not constitute the *entirety* of political argument. According to this weaker view, then, principles of individual dignity could in theory be outweighed by welfare considerations, though that is not to accept the utilitarian claim that welfare occupies the entire field of political argument. Moral concepts like dignity are important to constitutional interpretation *along with* the utilitarian principle that government should promote the general welfare. This moderate position remains anti-utilitarian, however, because it claims utility considerations do not exhaust political and legal discourse. Benevolence and concern for the welfare of others may be part of political morality, and governments certainly do have a duty to deter crime. Indeed, it may be the case that under extreme conditions it would be acceptable even to offend human dignity in the name of the general welfare.[62] None of that, however, is enough to show Justice Brennan was wrong in his criticism of the utilitarian approach to punishment. Compromising between competing rights or even limiting rights in the name of the general welfare are one thing, but denying they have independent moral importance, beyond serving as instruments to maximize welfare, is quite another.

I am not suggesting that we as yet have on hand anything like a serious alternative to proceduralism or utilitarianism, let alone that these powerful positions are not reaching for important truths. My hope, in what follows, is to identify and develop a different conception of democratic government and judicial review that accounts for the important insights of each while avoiding the objections that have been raised against them—a theory that, as I have suggested, is rooted in Brennan's thought that government must respect individual dignity and equality as well as the proceduralist's point that democratic government has a special claim to legitimacy extending beyond its tendency to yield welfare maximizing laws.

5

Democratic Contractualism and the Search for Equality

In earlier chapters I argued that the choice among competing theories of constitutional interpretation depends, in large part, on their philosophical foundations, in particular their assumptions about the purposes and justification of judicial review in a constitutional democracy. Each interpretive theory (except, of course, CLS, which rejects the possibility of theory in favor of pragmatism) seeks to show the Constitution as a reasonable effort to achieve worthy ends, so that theories of interpretation have what I termed a normative infrastructure. Constitutional interpretation and political philosophy are in that way bound together; interpretive theories cannot be judged independent of their normative, philosophical commitments.

Originalism and democratic proceduralism each stress the potentially antidemocratic features of judicial review, leading them to seek an account of constitutional interpretation that does not undermine self-government and that isolates judges from substantive political and moral debate. Originalism finds this judicial neutrality in the notion of an original contract, enforced by judges; proceduralism in the claim that the power of judicial review exists only to perfect the democratic process. Utilitarianism, however, rejects the claims that judicial review is limited to historical excavation of the framers' intentions or to perfecting democracy and with them the corresponding ideas that political legitimacy rests on an original social contract or on self-justifying democratic processes. Instead, claims the utilitarian, constitutional democracy seeks one basic goal: maximizing the total welfare of society.

But each of these theories fails. Originalism is not a workable theory, nor do its philosophical premises, as I have reconstructed them, withstand scrutiny; judicial review cannot reasonably be understood as a means to enforce the terms of the original social contract. Proceduralism and utilitarianism have also failed; the U.S. Constitution cannot reasonably be defended on the model of pure procedural justice, nor, I suggested, can utilitarianism give an adequate account of individual dignity or the inherent fairness of democratic government. We are left, therefore, with the task of developing a more attractive conception of constitutional interpretation and judicial review—one that takes account of the importance of the general welfare and democratic procedures and also provides a secure justification of dignity and individual rights. Armed with such a conception of constitutional government, we could then proceed to the related questions of the role of judicial review and the proper method of constitutional interpretation.

As will become clear, the approach I will take, though broadly contractualist, understands the social contract and judicial review very differently from original intent.[1] Because of its contractualist foundation, the theory addresses the necessity of governing a religiously, racially, and culturally diverse people more directly than others have done. Under what terms, it asks, can *all* people, whatever their ethnic background, religion, and moral views, reasonably be expected to give their assent to a system of law? The answer will lead us to consider the importance of democratic forms, the place of efforts to promote the general welfare, and the limits imposed on both those by citizens' pre-political moral rights.

I said very little in the last chapter about the non-utilitarian justification of rights or the connection between rights and individual dignity, let alone how those ideas might be woven into a fuller account of constitutional interpretation and judicial review. In Chapter 3 I argued that rights, understood as claims against others, immunities, liberties, or powers, are shorthand statements that others have duties toward the right holder. In that way, each of the three categories of rights—legal, conventional, and moral—gives those who possess them an advantage over others in the event of conflict.

Although utilitarianism, as we saw, does provide an account of moral rights, it will be helpful if we distinguish that conception of moral rights from other, natural right views not usually associated with utilitarianism. As I will use the term, natural rights are a type of moral rights; they are justified intrinsically rather than in the utilitarian fashion as instruments to promote the general welfare. In developing the contractualist theory I will build on that idea and on Justice Brennan's suggestion that individual dignity and equality play an important role in constitutional interpretation. My general strategy is as always to provide an account of the philosophical infrastructure of the theory and then to ask whether, interpreted in that way, it provides a workable, philosophically attractive account of judicial review and constitutional interpretation. First, then, I will explore some comments by James Madison, Louis Brandeis, and others in order to reconstruct the philosophical assumptions behind Brennan's suggestion that constitutional rights are tied to individual dignity. Applying these ideas to the social contract, I then consider the terms such a social contract would reasonably include along with the role judicial review would play if such a conception were adopted. Then in the last sections I turn to questions of law, asking how someone persuaded by this account of constitutional government and judicial review would interpret the Constitution, followed by a brief discussion of two specific constitutional topics along with some objections that may be raised against the democratic contractualist.

Freedom as an Intrinsic
and Instrumental Good

Traditionally, rights to speak freely and to practice a religion have been linked under the general heading freedom of conscience—a right regarded by Madison, Jefferson, and others as among a citizen's most important. John Locke's best-known work at the time of the Constitution's framing was a spirited, forceful defense of freedom of religion.[2] The First Amendment protects freedom of conscience in explicit, bold terms: "Congress shall make no law respecting an establishment of religion, or prohibiting the free exercise thereof; or abridging the freedom of speech, or of the press." Both the utilitarian and proceduralist can defend freedom of conscience, of course, and it will be helpful in beginning to think about the differences between democratic contractualism and other theories we have considered to look briefly at different aspects of this important right.

Justice Hugo Black, for example, expressed a generally utilitarian view in the first case that prohibited mandatory school prayer. Established religions, he wrote, tend "to destroy government and to degrade religion. The history of the governmentally established religion, both in England and in this country, showed that whenever government had allied itself with one particular form of religion, the inevitable result had been that it had incurred the hatred, disrespect, and even contempt of those who held contrary beliefs. That same history showed that many people had lost their respect for any religion that had relied upon the support of government to spread its faith."[3] The proceduralist also offers an account of the establishment clause, emphasizing that unless divisive, even explosive issues such as religious truth are taken off the political agenda, democratic procedures may be jeopardized. Even if we ignore the grave political dangers religious conflicts pose, legislative time and resources would be wasted debating irresolvable questions such as which prayers to allow, how they should be worded, how much public money should go to religious schools, which ones should receive it, and so forth. The establishment clause thus serves the democratic processes by allowing government to address more important, less intractable social problems, and, in the extreme, preventing more serious conflicts from erupting.

The second religion clause, guaranteeing free exercise of religion, has been used, for example, to overturn requirements that all students attend a public rather than a religious school[4] and to overturn the denial of unemployment compensation to a Seventh-Day Adventist who had been fired for refusing to work on Saturday, her Sabbath.[5] Such decisions could also be defended on utilitarian grounds—because the costs to those who might be legally prevented from exercising their religion are greater than the benefits society could gain by preventing such exercise—although other utilitarians may see things differently. Proceduralists also have what they take to be good reasons to protect free exercise, claiming that democratic government is better off by securing a wall between religion and the government. One common proceduralist argument is that where the sources of power are diffused and include strong, independent religious institutions as well as political structures, governmental power is limited and less likely to be abused, making democratic forms more secure.

Although these utilitarian and proceduralist arguments appeal to different basic principles, they have one important fact in common: Each sees freedom of religion as an *instrument,* designed either to promote the general welfare or to facilitate the smooth functioning of democratic government. Yet although important, such means-end analysis of the establishment clause leaves out of account another, important feature of an officially established and publicly supported church. The root idea was expressed by James Madison in terms that are strikingly similar to Brennan's discussion of executions in the last chapter.

In 1779, a decade before the Constitutional Convention, Madison and Jefferson had taken the lead in a movement to disestablish the Episcopal church as Virginia's official religion. This provoked widespread outrage, with Patrick Henry and others expressing concern about the effect of disestablishment on public morals. The debate simmered for six years, and Madison eventually responded with one of the most eloquent statements of the philosophical basis of religious freedom ever written, "Memorial and Remonstrance Against Religious Assessments." Madison's specific target was a bill to expend public funds to "Teachers of the Christian Religion." In attacking the bill, Madison wrote: "Instead of holding forth an asylum to the persecuted, the Bill is itself a signal of persecution. It *degrades from the equal rank of Citizens* all those whose opinions in Religion do not bend to those of the Legislative authority." [6]

This demand that government not degrade the "equal rank" of citizens differs from the instrumental ones of proceduralists and utilitarians; he said, in effect, that to establish an official church over the objections of minorities would not treat everybody as a political equal. It would degrade—treat as inferior—those citizens whose religious convictions run contrary to the one chosen by the government for special treatment.

Madison's suggestion continues to play a role in more recent establishment cases. Explaining why displaying a Christmas creche in front of a city's courthouse violates the establishment clause, Justice Brennan said in a dissenting opinion: "The creche retains a specifically Christian religious meaning. ... But for those who do not share these beliefs, the symbolic re-enactment of the birth of a divine being who has been miraculously incarnated as a man stands as a dramatic reminder of their differences with the Christian faith. ... [To] be so excluded on religious grounds by one's elected government is an insult and an injury." [7] This insult to the status of equal citizenship was again stressed by Justice Brennan in one of the many cases involving state aid to religious schools. In rejecting the aid program, he wrote that it is important to consider "whether the challenged governmental action is sufficiently likely to be perceived by the adherents of the controlling denominations as an endorsement, and the nonadherents as a disapproval, of their individual religious choices." [8] And, finally, Justice Blackmun recently sounded a similar note when he joined in overturning a school-supported graduation prayer. "When the government put its imprimatur on a particular religion," he wrote, "it conveys a message of exclusion to all those who do not adhere to the favored beliefs."[9]

Each of these Justices is giving expression to Madison's ideal that government should not "degrade" some of its citizens but instead respect their "equal rank," suggesting that beyond the instrumental justifications of the utilitarian and proceduralist, violating freedom of religion is also *intrinsically* wrong or unjust, and that the injustice is best understood as a denial of equality of standing or worth as a citizen.

The idea that constitutional rights have intrinsic as well as instrumental importance has also played an important role in the second component of freedom of conscience, freedom of speech. All agree that the Constitution allows many limits on what people say as well as where they say it. Military secrets can be protected, deceptive business advertisements can be prohibited, and advertisements of "murder for hire" can be outlawed. Those are the easy cases; more difficult ones arise when the Nazi Party wants to hold a parade in a Jewish community and the town refuses,[10] when a store claims First Amendment protection for its display of drug paraphernalia,[11] and when political protesters want to burn a draft card[12] or a flag.[13]

In analyzing these cases, we should recall that the Supreme Court distinguishes different categories of speech and has been especially careful to guard its most valued category, political speech, against governmental censorship based on the content of the ideas expressed. Other categories of speech have no constitutional protection at all, such as obscenity, libel, and incitement to imminent lawlessness; still others, such as commercial speech, occupy a middle level of protection. But besides holding that some categories lack constitutional value and are therefore constitutionally unprotected, the Court also allows various restrictions based on the time, place, or manner the speech is delivered. So although speaking on behalf of political candidates is an example of the most protected activity, that protection does not keep governments from banning the speech if it is shouted in a hospital or public library or spray painted on a public building.

We have already seen that the proceduralist's case for protecting political speech is strong and that the Court has often expressed its philosophical commitment to democratic processes in connection with speech. Without vigorous political debate no political system could be open and fair and so could never lay claim to reaching decisions that are a fair compromise among political equals. Utilitarians are also well positioned to defend free speech, as well as to explain the limits allowed on speech by the Court. Time, place, and manner restrictions fit nicely into the utilitarian theory, since each limit can be seen to reflect the judgment that although speech is important in general, the welfare of society would not be served by protecting its exercise in ways that are too costly. The losses incurred by forcing speakers to find other places, times, and manners of expressing themselves are often relatively minor, for example, when compared to the benefits of doing so. It would be one thing to ban Republican candidates from speaking completely; but the cost of requiring them to refrain from spray painting buildings is quite minor compared with the cost of cleaning. Not that all cases are so easy for the utilitarian, of course. For example, the Court has also held that blanket regulations banning advertising are unconstitutional, rejecting the city's argument that the ban was justified on the basis of aesthetics.[14]

The best known utilitarian argument for *protecting* speech is of course John Stuart Mill's;[15] indeed it is so much a part of legal and political culture that Mill's words often find their way into Court opinions.[16] Mill conceives of speech on the model of a competitive market, though his argument extends far beyond economically motivated speech like advertising. Robust, open competition among various viewpoints, Mill thinks, is society's best chance of learning the truth. Open debate allows people to formulate effective economic and political policies, to improve their conceptions of how human lives should be led, and in general serves to increase the state of human knowledge and to improve the lives of everyone. Official dogma, if allowed to stifle dissent, will also stifle progress, with disastrous consequences for the welfare of society.

It seems, then, that both the proceduralist and utilitarian offer a sound defense of free speech; the question I am again raising, however, is not whether these are important arguments but whether they exhaust the case for freedom of speech. Justice Louis Brandeis's opinion in *Whitney v. California* (1927) is the most famous and eloquent account of the role of speech in U.S. law. In this opinion, he describes why freedom of speech is important, and although many of his points resonate with the instrumentalist concerns I have described, he also points out that speech's purpose is not *just* to serve those ends. "Those who won our independence," he writes,

> believed that the final end of the state was to make men free to develop their faculties, and that in its government the deliberative forces should prevail over the arbitrary. They valued liberty as both as an end and as a means. They believed liberty to be the secret of happiness and courage to be the secret of liberty. They believed that freedom to think as you will and to speak as you think are means indispensable to the discovery and spread of political truths; that without free speech and assembly discussion would be futile; that with them discussion affords ordinarily adequate protection against the dissemination of noxious doctrine; that the greatest menace to freedom is an inert people; that public discussion is a political duty; and that this should be a fundamental principle of the American government.[17]

Justice Brandeis thus gives expression to the utilitarian conception (liberty is the "secret of happiness") as well as the proceduralist (speech is "indispensable to the discovery and spread of political truth"). But neither of these, he suggests, is complete. Liberty is also valued, he says, as an *end* as well as a means; not only is it an instrument used to achieve important social objectives, it is also intrinsically important and should be protected for that reason as well. Why it should be thought of in those terms he does not say; but that free speech rests partly on the intrinsic importance of government showing respect for individual liberties is, he says, clear.

So like Justice Brennan's earlier thought that equal dignity (along with such concerns as protecting the innocent) poses limits on the ways government may punish, freedoms of religion and speech too are sometimes defended on the assumption that they have intrinsic as well as instrumental importance. But beyond these general invocations by Brennan and others of "equal dignity" or "worth," little guidance is provided of how we are to understand these inherent, non-instrumental limitations on government. Nevertheless, by widening our net to include freedom of conscience we have begun to see other themes emerge. Equal dignity is not limited to the thought that torturing and maiming people degrades them or in some other way offends their dignity. Whatever it means, the equal worth of citizens must be fairly abstract, expressing a vision of the relationship between citizens and their government that places the individual at center stage in a way that neither utilitarians nor proceduralists can do. But how might that be done? And what connection is there between these notions of equality, dignity, and rights?

Democratic Contractualism

Notice, first, how respect for individual rights and for individual dignity seem, intuitively, to go hand in hand. To have a right, I have argued, means that in case of conflict with another, the right-holder has either a practical or a moral advantage in the form of duties of others toward the holder of the right. To assert a right, then, seems intimately connected with the ideal of respect for the dignity of each individual: Claiming a *right* to vote, protesting sexual harassment, and demanding to be paid wages for work are the opposite of begging, pleading, requesting, and the like. Joel Feinberg puts the point this way: "Having rights enables us to 'stand up like men,' to look others in the eye, and to feel in some fundamental way the equal of anyone. To think of oneself as the holder of rights is not to be unduly but properly proud, to have the minimal self-respect that is necessary to be worthy of the love and esteem of others."[18] Feinberg's suggestion is thus really twofold: When individuals assert their rights, there is also a tendency for them to both *see themselves* and to be *seen by others* as worthy and as fully equal. Think, for instance, of sexual harassment—behavior that until recently was not regarded as a violation of a woman's right but instead as, at most, an unacceptable form of behavior, perhaps on a par with rudeness. As workplace harassment comes to be regarded as the violation of a woman's *right* not to be discriminated against, there is a concomitant tendency also to generate a deeper sense of the dignity and worth of women.

It is important not to misconstrue this point, however. If what I argued earlier is correct, then rights are best understood in terms of the duties of others toward the right-holder, including governments. Women who assert that sexual harassment violates their legal, conventional, or moral rights, on that view, are best understood to assert that others have duties of various sorts, including not to make certain sorts of threats against them or create a hostile work environment. The right may also include the duty of others to intervene on the woman's behalf if people do threaten her. Despite these ties between rights and duties, however, the statement "You have a duty to do X" does not focus attention on the beneficiary of the moral relationship in the same way as does the claim "I have a right to A." That makes a practical difference. Though the right-holder can make the same point in terms of others' duties, by asserting her right the right-holder makes her claim as an equal, not as an inferior who is complaining or pleading with others to fulfill their obligations.

Asserting rights has another aspect that reinforces Feinberg's claim that rights focus on the one to whom the duty is owed: When asserting a right and thereby claiming an advantage in the conflict, there is no suggestion of a willingness to compromise or negotiate. Rather, the idea is that there is a standard of some sort (legal, conventional, or moral) in virtue of which the right-holder is entitled to something—period. The invited response is either to deny that the right exists, thereby engaging in argument, or else to suggest that for some reason the right should not be exercised under the circumstances. But in neither case does the assertion of a right imply there is room for negotiation nor that another is to be given any choice. Rights are strong medicine.

These points do not yet, however, constitute a justification of natural rights (understood, recall, as moral or human rights that are justified intrinsically rather than instrumentally). My point here is the more modest one that the language of rights quite naturally invites the sort of argument I propose to make, based on dignity and equality. But that is only a suggestion, based on the ways the language functions, and not an argument. So my goal in what follows is to develop an account of important rights such as speech, religion, and protection against cruel and unusual punishment that shows why they are of intrinsic value; then in later sections I elaborate on those themes in order to explore the democratic contractualist's view of rights, judicial review, and constitutional interpretation. The account of constitutional democracy and judicial review that I want to develop is rooted in two fundamental ideas: that the Constitution, including judicial review, is best understood on contractualist terms (albeit very different terms than original intent) and that basic rights do not serve as instruments but instead reflect the dignity and worth of all citizens.

I begin the discussion with the notion of consent, for as I have emphasized throughout it is an idea with deep roots in the U.S. political tradition. Both originalism and democratic proceduralism lay claim to it: Originalists find consent in the social contract and the self-incapacitating limits "the people" agreed to and which the Court enforces, while democratic proceduralists understand consent to require that lawmakers be chosen by the people in a fair and open democratic process. Democratic contractualism, like these other theories, also stresses consent though it is understood in still different terms. But what then is consent from that perspective? The answer leads back to a (revised) version of the social contract and to ideas that can be traced to the legal and philosophical views of James Madison, Immanuel Kant, and others.

The controlling principle of government, Madison writes in "Federalist Number 49," is that "the people are the *only* legitimate fountain of power."[19] Yet as we have also seen, Madison was at the same time deeply skeptical of democratic processes, fearful that factions would emerge that would threaten individual rights and undermine the legitimacy of government. Madison tries to resolve these tensions in a well-known letter he wrote to Thomas Jefferson in the wake of the Constitutional Convention. The letter is in response to Jefferson's suggestion, made in an earlier letter to Madison, that there should be a constitutional convention every generation so that the democratic ideal of self-government is fully respected.[20] With respect to ordinary laws passed by the representatives of one generation but that continue in force as later generations come on the scene, Madison says that the fact the majority have not repealed them indicates clearly enough that they tacitly consent to them. But what, then, of the acts by previous generations that cannot be overturned by a (current) majority? Here Madison mentions two different types of laws: the Constitution itself, which requires significantly more than a majority to amend, and debts that are left to be paid off by later generations.

One reason Madison gives for opposing constant revision of constitutional and other laws is practical: He worries about the political consequences of any system that would regularly call into question existing laws, let alone the constitutional structure itself. Here Madison specifically mentions the loss of support for the Constitution and most importantly the dangers that factions would "agitate the public mind" leading to changes that are not "expedient." So again we see Madison's great concern expressed that when the people are involved in government there is the constant danger that "passions, not the reason ... would sit in judgment."[21]

But Madison also responds to Jefferson's proposal in another, more philosophical fashion. In establishing the Constitution, including the principle of majority rule itself, he writes that "*unanimity* was necessary; and rigid theory accordingly presupposes the assent of every individual to the rule which subjects the minority to the will of the majority."[22] But how then could it be said that the Constitution has the *unanimous* consent of the people?[23] Madison considers this question further in his treatise "Memorial and Remonstrance Against Religious Assessments." In arguing against the bill to provide public funds for clergy, Madison expresses his conviction of the importance of natural rights and describes the philosophical basis on which they rest.

He begins with the assertion of individual rights against government, connecting them to his familiar claim that political power rests on popular consent. Rulers, he says, "who are guilty of such an encroachment [on individual liberties] exceed the commission from which they derive their authority, and are Tyrants. The People who submit to it are governed by laws made neither by themselves, nor by an authority derived from them, and are slaves."[24] Again we see Madison stress-

ing that the only sources of authority are laws people have themselves made and
authority "derived" from the people. The former refers, of course, to laws passed
by an *already existing* legislative body elected by the people. But that leaves open
the questions he raised earlier regarding the basis of the authority of the Constitution itself and how *its* authority can be "derived" from the people. Madison answers that question in the following terms: "If 'all men are by nature equally free
and independent,' (Decl. Rights Art. 1) all men are to be considered as entering
into Society on equal conditions; as relinquishing no more, and therefore retaining no less, one than another, of their natural rights. Above all they are to be considered as retaining an 'equal title to the free exercise of religion according to the
dictates of conscience' (Art. 16)."[25]

Madison makes two important suggestions here regarding the "derivation" of
constitutional authority from the people: First, he says, all men are "by nature ...
free and independent" and, second, they "enter into society on equal conditions,"
retaining no more or less than any others. The establishment of an official religion is attacked, then, on clearly contractualist terms: People "enter into society"
as "equals" and thereby define the rights that they are to have, including the rights
against an official, state-supported religion. But instead of an actual contract, on
the model of originalism, Madison is suggesting the social contract may be understood as one people *would* make under certain conditions—namely "equal
conditions" agreed to among "free and independent persons."

This conception of political authority and the social contract can be extended
further if we turn to comments he made in his notes of the Constitutional Convention. That convention, as all knew, was charged only with amending the Articles of Confederation, not establishing an entirely new government, so that the legitimacy of its authority was open to serious question. It is clear, however, that
Madison did not envision the convention as just another political event on a par
with normal political debates. In his notes Madison writes that what distinguished the Constitutional Convention, making it such an extraordinary political
event, was that people were, in his words, "*deliberating in a temperate moment,
and with the experience of other nations before them, on the plan of government.*"[26] So although Madison was the first to acknowledge that factionalism,
partisan advocacy, personal interest, and passion often dominate politics, that
was not all he witnessed at the convention. When issues of fundamental constitutional importance are on the agenda, and the discussion turns to the terms of the
social contract, then not only should people be envisioned as free and independent equals but they should also behave in a fashion appropriate to the task and
deliberate in a "temperate moment."[27]

The question, therefore, is precisely how we are to envision this admittedly
vague Madisonian vision of the Constitution as a contract made among "free and
independent" equals "deliberating in a temperate moment." An answer is provided by one of the Enlightenment's great philosophers, Immanuel Kant. One
cannot, says Kant, think of the social contract as an actual agreement or "fact," as
he put it, since that would mean people could not regard themselves "as bound by

an already existing civil constitution."[28] Instead, says, Kant, the social contract is a "mere idea of reason" that envisions laws "in such a way that they *could* have sprung from the unified will of the entire people and to regard every subject, insofar as he desires to be a citizen, as if he had joined in voting for such a will. ... If a public law is so formulated that an entire people *could not possibly* agree to it (as, e.g., that a particular class of *subjects* has the hereditary privilege of being a ruling class), it is not just."[29] So Kant's important suggestion was that instead of thinking in terms of "tacit" consent to an actual contract, as originalists sometimes did, we should instead ask ourselves the hypothetical question—or "mere idea of reason" as he puts it—of what contract *could have been* agreed to by all citizens. Tying together Kant's idea of a hypothetical contract with Madison's comments, we can now characterize the central problem for social contract theory as constructing the terms of a social contract that free and independent persons joining society as equals *could,* reasonably, be expected to accept. That, then, is how I propose to understand Madison's emphasis on universal consent and "free and independent equals" who "deliberate in a temperate moment."

One way to expand these ideas has been developed with great ingenuity by John Rawls.[30] Following his lead, we might think of deliberations among free and independent equals as taking place among people who ignore, for constitutional purposes, all the factors making them *not* equal—as reasoning, in short, behind a Rawlsian veil of ignorance. Only by setting aside these differences, including religious beliefs and other facts that set us apart, can a diverse people hope to find a constitution and system of laws that all citizens can reasonably accept. The idea, then, is that the constitution is to be chosen under circumstances of equality— that is, by ignoring all the factors setting people at odds with one another— thereby assuring that the results are ones everybody can reasonably accept.

Religious freedoms, which Madison had in mind, illustrate well the power of this approach. No constitution that depends for its justification on particular religious beliefs could win such universal support among diverse citizens, as Madison argues in his "Memorial and Remonstrance Against Religious Assessments." But then, of course, we may wonder what other factors should also be ignored if persons really are to view themselves as free and independent equals entering society on terms nobody can reasonably reject.[31] The answer is that they would ignore all factors that distinguish people from each other and thus do not express their equal status as parties to the social contract. Race and gender,[32] for example, are clearly not characteristics that we share as free and independent equals, nor are wealth and social status any more than our unique talents and special handicaps. The key thought, then, is that any constitution chosen on the ground that it serves the interests of one of those groups could not be acceptable to *all* citizens, viewed as free and independent equals, any more than would one that is based on a particular religious faith. The idea, following Rawls, is that all of these facts would have to be ignored if the terms of the social contract are to win the assent of every citizen in the terms Madison envisions.

But why, then, should people imagine themselves in that unrealistic situation, as free and independent persons whose circumstances are "equal"? Why, in other words, might people think it reasonable to ignore factors that set them against each other in choosing a constitution and laws? Ordinarily, after all, contracts are binding only if they are actually entered into; imaginary contracts people *could* make do not carry the moral weight of actual promises and previously undertaken agreements.[33] Bank officers *could* have agreed to ignore the fact Bill owes them money, and the patient *could* have agreed never to sue her doctor for malpractice; but those facts in no way affect the rights of the bank and the patient. Why then would it matter what agreements free and independent persons hypothetically would make were they to decide to join society as equals?

Answers to that question take two general forms, one practical, the other moral, and I want to explore each. First, on the practical side, we know not only that people have very different moral and religious ideas about how to live their lives, as Madison stresses, but also that such differences have led to deep, intractable political conflict. "Torrents of blood have been spilt in the old world," Madison points out, "by vain attempts of the secular arm to extinguish Religious discord, by proscribing all difference of religious opinions."[34] So given the diversity of society, and the need to reach peaceably a common understanding about laws to govern over such a people, it is at best impractical and at worst disastrous to attempt to do anything besides assure that the government respect individual differences. Because there is no realistic possibility that people can be convinced to reject their religious or philosophical beliefs, the best alternative is to set off the agenda questions such as which church should be allowed to exist and which should be banned.

But besides its practical advantages there are other, moral considerations on behalf of viewing the Constitution as the result of a social contract adopted under the circumstances of free and equal persons deliberating in a temperate moment. This moral side of the argument for appropriate constraints on constitutional choice can be viewed from two different, but related, perspectives. The first rests on the ideal of impartiality. Suppose, for example, that one of the Episcopalians who stands to benefit from the established church Madison attacked in his "Memorial and Remonstrance Against Religious Assessments" were to claim that he is entitled to a constitution giving him special privileges and establishing his faith. Similarly, were he wealthy he might argue for low taxes, or if poor, then higher taxes on the rich, or he might appeal to the fact he is a male, or white, in a similar effort to tailor the choice of the constitution to his advantage.

According to Madison's constitutional vision, however, none of these appeals are possible, and in that way his vision expresses a commitment to the ideal of impartiality. People who choose a constitution in light of crucial information about themselves would not be "deliberating in a temperate moment" and the constitution's impartiality would thereby be compromised. The resulting constitution would not be a reasonable compromise among different individuals viewed as free and independent equals but instead would reflect the particular needs, characteristics, and social conditions of one group and in that way would sacrifice impartiality.

That commitment to the ideal of impartiality might be justified in either of two ways. Some might defend it on the ground that it provides a reasonable method by which to come to an understanding of moral truth. Just as one might expect jurors to give a more accurate assessment of the defendant's actions if they are not biased than if they were disposed to favor or harm the defendant, so too it might be claimed people choosing the terms of social cooperation are more likely to arrive at the (genuinely) best ones if they are uninfluenced by personal interest. Though impartiality cannot *assure* correct answers, whether in a court of law or outside, it does increase the likelihood that the constitution and laws will be, in fact, the right ones.

But impartiality can also be defended in another way, by those who are skeptical about the existence of moral truth and think morality must be "constructed" rather than discovered.[35] In Chapter 3, when discussing non-cognitivism and the ideal observer, we noted that impartiality is often thought important by those who see morality as expressions of attitudes. Defenders of that non-cognitivist view, I argued, should reject the suggestion that the best or soundest moral judgments be identified with the attitudes of any actual person, or even any particular group, in favor of the idea that sound moral claims reflect the attitudes of an ideally rational, informed, and impartial observer. Viewing impartiality as central to moral attitudes, however, parallels the requirement that the constitution be chosen by free and independent equals who are unaware of who they are and so cannot tailor the terms of the social contract to their own advantage. But instead of envisioning the ideal observer as a sympathetic and neutral advocate of maximizing total welfare, as utilitarians do, the contractualist thinks in terms of equal persons deliberating in a position that structurally prevents bias from arising. Those who believe that moral truths are expressions of the attitudes of an impartial, well-informed, and rational observer, in other words, can see Madison's conception of the social contract chosen in a "temperate moment" as a natural method by which to give content to their theory.[36]

Besides impartiality, deliberation among free and independent equals also expresses a second moral ideal. As Rawls emphasizes, the factors it leaves out of consideration in constitutional design are "morally arbitrary." No one, Rawls points out, "deserves his place in the distribution of native endowments, any more than one deserves one's initial starting place in society. The assertion that a man deserves the superior character that enables him to make the effort to cultivate his abilities is equally problematic; for his character depends in large part upon fortunate family and social circumstances for which he can claim no credit."[37] So besides the *practical* advantages associated with requiring constitutional deliberations to take place without relying on factors that set people against each other, and the fact that impartiality is assured, such limits also guarantee that the social contract does not reflect "morally arbitrary" facts such as race, gender, and class. It represents, in other words, a commitment on the part of society to set aside factors such as natural talents, handicaps, class, and so on because none of these—whether an advantage or a disadvantage—is deserved. Only when deliberation takes place under conditions of equality are people prevented from either cashing in on or being hurt by morally arbitrary factors that should play no role in the design of a constitution.

These various practical and moral advantages of the contractualist model lead to a final point, expressed in Justice Brennan's thought that law must reflect each person's dignity and worth. The commitment to understand the Constitution in these contractualist terms demands it be justified to everybody and in that way also insists that each citizen be treated with equal dignity and respect. Ignoring religion, race, gender, class, and other characteristics that differentiate among citizens expresses the (abstract) notion of treating people as equal, free, and independent citizens. Put another way, were people not able to justify it to all, the Constitution would *in that way* deny their equal dignity and worth, so that the ideal that government respect citizens' equal worth and dignity is also expressed by democratic contractualism's requirement that the Constitution and laws be able to be justified to each person, under reasonable circumstances. In that sense, the constitution can truly be said to flow, as Madison put it, from "authority derived from [the people] themselves."

The import of these various considerations can be brought into focus by considering the Constitution's most spectacular failure: its provision for the continued existence of chattel slavery. Slave states were unwilling to compromise on the issue, leaving framers who opposed slavery facing a dilemma: Either compromise what they took to be a basic constitutional and moral principle or accept that there would be no union. Faced with that choice, together with the realization that slavery would not be abolished if they rejected union, the Constitutional Convention reached its compromise. In the contractualist terms I have been describing, this constitutional failure should be understood in the following way. Unlike the First Amendment's guarantees of freedom of speech and religion, which constituted a *refusal* to appeal to particular religious and moral convictions, the provision for chattel slavery illustrates the Southerners' refusal to deliberate as free and independent persons entering society as equals. Instead, their insistence that the Constitution not abolish slavery (and, indeed, that the practice be given special constitutional protection) was based on information about race and economic interests that should, ideally, have been excluded if the social contract was to be justifiable to everyone.

At its deepest level, then, democratic contractualism is not founded on sympathetic concern for the well-being of others, as with utilitarianism, but rather on the desire of people to know that as they pursue their interests and projects they are doing so in accord with a constitution and laws that all others would acknowledge as reasonable (or at least would not reasonably reject.)[38] That desire—to act in accord with a constitutional system that is acceptable to all—provides the deep motivation behind social contract theory; it is founded on a commitment on the part of all citizens, especially those who benefit most under the legal system, to live by laws that they can justify to all others.

The sense in which democratic contractualism places the problem of governing a religiously and culturally diverse population at center stage should now be clear. Although other theories sought in their own way to address that problem, contractualism's commitment to finding a constitution and laws that are accept-able from everybody's perspective reflects awareness of both the practical and moral problems posed by diversity as well as a desire to confront the problems it poses directly. Were it not for factors such as religious, ethnic, and racial diversity, neither the practical nor the moral arguments for democratic contractualism would be of significance. But because society includes people with different values, religions, economic circumstances, races, and cultures, there is no alterna-tive but to set such factors aside if we are to find a constitutional regime that can successfully be defended to all.

All of this is, of course, excessively abstract. In order to see how the Constitu-tion should be interpreted according to democratic contractualism, as opposed to originalism, utilitarianism, and democratic proceduralism, we must next flesh out the actual terms of the social contract. What terms, specifically, would free and independent equals agree to if reasoning in a Madisonian temperate mo-ment? The discussion so far has indicated only what the social contractors are to *ignore,* and given no indication of what they desire of government or what further demands they would press against each other in establishing the constitutional structure and laws to govern themselves. We need to know, then, much more about the contractors and how they are motivated. Furthermore, in order to ap-ply the contractualist's project to judicial review and constitutional interpreta-tion, we must also say more about the specific limits on government that the con-tractors would adopt and how they might be implemented. What limits, in other words, would they place on governmental power? And assuming they would also opt for judicial review, how would they want those charged with interpreting those constitutional limits to approach their interpretive responsibilities?

The Terms of the Social Contract

Following Madison's suggestion (understood in the ways suggested by Kant and Rawls), we are to imagine people considering the basic terms of the social con-tract *before* there is a specific constitution establishing a government and defining its powers. In limiting the discussion to the demands prospective *citizens* can make against each other, I mean to distinguish this question from all the many other claims people make of each other when they occupy other roles and capaci-ties: Children's demands on parents, and parents' on children, the demands of employers and employees on each other as well as the mutual demands of wives, husbands, and friends are all of a different sort. But what then are the demands prospective *citizens* can legitimately press on each other in the establishment of society's constitution and laws? I want to argue that there are two broad demands free and independent equals deliberating in a Madisonian temperate moment could make, based on two different interests such citizens can reasonably be thought to have. The first demand is an *equal opportunity to realize their ideals of the good life*; the second is an *equal opportunity to participate in the democratic process.*[39]

I will turn first to citizens' demands that they be given an opportunity to realize their ideal of the good. Behind this idea lies the important fact that persons, viewed as free and independent, know that in society they will in fact *desire* to pursue some set of religious or other goals. People's ideas about how they wish to live will vary widely, of course; they may include different combinations of religious beliefs, family values, and the acquisition of power, money, and knowledge—to name only a few. So although people do not know the particulars of their own values, they do assume they will have some system of ideals about the good and they will therefore have an interest in making sure that they can fulfill it under the constitution they choose. What, exactly, their ideas will be they are to ignore; that they will have them, however, they assume.

Based on that interest, then, they would all want for themselves the *means* necessary to a secure and worthy life according to whatever standards they may have. But how can they know what that involves without knowing what their specific ideas of the good will be? The answer, found in the Preamble to the U.S. Constitution, is that the new government was to serve two key objectives: to promote the "general welfare" and to "secure the blessings of liberty for ourselves and our posterity." Those two represent the first part of the democratic contractualist's answer to what free and independent persons entering society as equals would want. They indicate, in other words, what it means for government to provide citizens the equal opportunity to realize their idea of the good life. (As we will see, the second demand, to participate in the political process as an equal, arises from another interest citizens who join society as free and independent equals would have.)

We begin, then, with the blessings of liberty and what will be for many an extremely important element of their ideas of the good—religious practices and beliefs. Since they are entering society as equals, citizens know they could be anybody, including a member of a religious minority. Under such circumstances, people would know that the risks of not protecting religious freedom at the outset are great because they may be a member of a despised minority unable to practice their religion. The advantages gained by *not* protecting minorities and allowing the majority to pass laws preventing free exercise of religion would therefore not be worth the risk, especially when there is an easy way to protect everybody.[40] So since they cannot know their chances of being in a minority and the risks would be great, people would take what is in effect the conservative strategy of securing basic rights to protect their religious beliefs and practices. Potential benefits they might get from repressing a minority, if they are in the majority, would not be worth the risk of suffering religious oppression.

What then of freedom of speech? These are important because besides knowing they will have a vision of the good life, people entering society as equals also know they are "free and independent," which means they have the capacity and potentially the desire to *revise* and even *reject* their religious and other fundamental values. Given that fact, they would want to see that the decisions they might make in matters of such fundamental importance are taken in light of available information about their choices—something they could not hope to achieve without free and open public debate. Free speech would therefore be broadly conceived and include more than merely political issues, as proceduralists suppose. Moral and religious discussion would also be protected, as would imaginative literature, in order to protect the possibility of revising or rejecting their vision of the good life. In that way, freedom of conscience, including the right to freedom of speech and the press as well as free exercise of religion, secures for all the opportunity to deliberate about their life's course and fulfill their nature as free and independent persons and would clearly be among their most basic concerns in framing a constitution.

Besides freedoms of religion and speech, free and independent equals would also seek constitutional protections of their freedom of action, or what the Supreme Court has termed the right to "privacy."[41] It would be essential for them to secure a sphere in which they could pursue their lives independent of governmental interference. Thus, it would be expected that the Constitution should seek effective ways to protect the right of people not just to speak, assemble, and publish concerning their vision of the good, but also that there be put in place basic protections allowing them to *act* on that conception. These limits on governmental power would protect people's choice of a sexual partner, whether or not to have a family, and whom to marry, along with freedom of association in a multiplicity of private organizations representing different values and ways of life.

Another broad area of concern to democratic contractualists is criminal procedures. Aware that governmental powers to search people's homes and other private areas, conduct trials, and administer punishment have often been abused, free and independent citizens concerned to secure their good would seek, on the one hand, limits on those governmental activities. But, on the other hand, the social contractors also know that if the society is to function and win the ongoing support of its citizens, it must prevent some people from taking advantage of others' willingness to abide by the law; otherwise few may be willing to live in accord with the terms of the social contract. Thus, the contractors would seek to assure a reasonable compromise between the need to prevent crime, on one hand, and the dangers to basic liberties posed by authorities exercising police powers, on the other, leading them to seek constitutional assurances that government follow reasonable procedures in its enforcement of the law and its prosecution of those accused of violating it. So free and independent equals deliberating in a temperate moment about the terms of the social contract would also have good reason to protect basic due process rights.[42]

As was noted, however, in addition to securing the blessing of liberty the Preamble also speaks of promoting the general welfare. In contractualist terms, this phrase can be taken to mean that in addition to wanting to secure basic rights of religion, speech, privacy, and due process, contractors also know they will need economic wealth and opportunities if they are to have the opportunity to realize their conception of the good. They must be able to get food, health care, shelter, transportation, and whatever else they value. Indeed, without these, their other liberties would be useless to them.

So in that vein, persons reasoning in a Madisonian "temperate moment" would try to secure provision for them to develop their natural talents and skills, including public education and job training. But because of the potential for background social prejudices, they also know that mere equality of educational and other opportunities is not enough and so, I assume, would also protect despised minorities against workplace discrimination, assuring that those who are most suited for a job get it.

Although they know they may turn out to be in the group that would wish to discriminate, the consequences of living as a despised racial or ethnic minority would far outweigh whatever benefits they could expect from living in a society where discrimination is allowed. In that way, this case is analogous to religious freedom where the risks of suffering religious persecution would also outweigh any advantages one might get from oppressing a religious minority. And, finally, since even these provisions may leave some without the ability to earn a living, the social contract would provide at least a satisfactory minimum income for those unable to provide for themselves, thereby assuring that if they are disadvantaged in the competition for economic wealth they will not suffer unduly.[43]

It is important to emphasize that I am not making the utilitarian argument that *total* welfare would be greater if freedom is protected; here the question involves the prospects of a single individual facing a decision about the society in which he or she will live. So even if the minority were small enough that a utilitarian might be tempted to argue against religious freedom, it would still be the case that from the perspective of any individual, the risks of being in the minority would not be worth the potential benefits.

These then comprise the first group of constitutional demands people can make on each other as free and independent citizens entering society as equals. People know they will desire to pursue their own vision of the good life and therefore would press the claim that the constitution should assure, in various ways, that they have a reasonable prospect of achieving it. None of the provisions I have outlined, however, can assure that anybody will in fact *realize* their ideals—indeed nothing could do that. People may fail to accomplish their important life's projects for any number of reasons, including ill health, lack of talent, economic misfortune, and accidents of birth. But because *no society* can give all citizens everything they could wish for, it is no sign of constitutional failure that some experience such limits. As long as basic liberties are respected, reasonable criminal procedures are provided that do not endanger other liberties, equality of opportunity is maintained, discrimination is prevented, and a satisfactory economic minimum secured for those who cannot provide for themselves, government has done what it can to meet each citizen's legitimate demand of an equal opportunity to realize his or her conception of the good.[44]

Some, of course, may find that their ideals of the good life are incompatible with the rights free and independent persons have secured for themselves. For example, those whose religious faith requires that the government force others to share their beliefs will not be able to see their objectives realized. Nor will government protect those whose ideals endanger the equal opportunities of others. But that should not be distressing since no constitution could accommodate such demands without failing to meet the contractualist's commitment to finding a constitutional structure that can be defended to all persons viewed as free and independent equals.

I have discussed two broad ways in which citizens would press their demand that government provide them an equal opportunity to realize their conception of the good: The constitution must secure basic liberties and, second, it should promote the "general welfare" in the various senses I have outlined. The second demand that free and independent persons entering society as equals can legitimately make on each other is an equal opportunity to participate in the political process.[45]

Unlike the rights to speech, religion, due process, and so on, this demand is political and does not rest primarily on people's interests in realizing their ideals about the good life.[46] But what interests do people have that would lead them to press that second claim? The answer is that the social contractors want more from their constitution than the individual rights and economic opportunities essential to realize their conception of the good: They would also want to secure a sense of their own worth and dignity; that is, to feel that their goals and ideals are worthy and that they have the talents, intelligence, motivation, and other characteristics needed to achieve them. Acquiring a sense of one's own worth and dignity is important because without them it is difficult to take advantage of the educational and other opportunities society provides. Though basic rights may be protected and educational or other opportunities assured, these will mean little to people whose lack of a sense of their own worth and dignity makes them unable or unwilling to work, learn, and otherwise do what is necessary to realize a meaningful life. I will assume, then, that free and independent persons entering society as equals would have an interest in promoting their sense of dignity and worth. They know it is an important part of their willingness to strive to achieve their goals and that without it a fulfilling life is scarcely possible.

It must be admitted, of course, that the sense of one's own worth and dignity comes from many sources and is not entirely within the power of political institutions to control; family members and friends can be important, as can one's sense of belonging to a particular religious or other tradition. But the constitutional structure also plays an important role in encouraging its citizens' sense of worth and dignity when it provides for equal citizenship. This is done, first, by securing the basic rights, opportunities, and other requirements of legitimate government that have already been described. Respecting every citizen's freedoms of speech, privacy, and religion, banning discrimination, and providing equality of opportunity and a satisfactory economic minimum all encourage citizens' sense of their own worth and dignity. Nobody's rights or opportunities are to be sacrificed to the larger good, as utilitarianism might require.

Although an important start, however, these rights cannot stand alone but instead must be supported by the political process, because government also encourages or discourages self-worth in the way it distributes political power. If a constitution excludes some from the political process, it proclaims clearly and publicly that members of the excluded group are less worthy and capable of self-government. Dignity and political equality go hand in hand, since the chance to participate as an equal in the political process affirms in an important, public arena, that nobody is born the natural ruler of another, nor is anybody born into a social status making him naturally subservient to another. Those denied the opportunity to participate are treated as constitutional and political nonentities, unworthy of self-government and incapable of deliberation about matters of public concern. People entering society as free and independent equals would therefore demand the opportunity to participate, as equals, in the political process.

Just what that means, specifically, has already been considered in the context of democratic proceduralism. There, I argued, democratic procedures provide for equal opportunity to participate in two different ways. First, they require that votes are equally weighted: If a group is either completely excluded from voting or its vote is worth less than another's, the system is not fully "democratic" and members of the group are denied their status as political equals. Viewed from the perspective of democratic contractualism, then, weighted voting and other provisions giving extra votes to some also deny people's legitimate demand, based on their interest in securing their own sense of self-worth and dignity, to be allowed to participate in the political process.[47] Similarly, laws preventing or discouraging some citizens from serving in office, whether based on race, gender, or other irrelevant characteristics, are also incompatible with a constitutional commitment to promote each citizen's sense of self-worth and would therefore be rejected.[48] Each of these anti-democratic forms—denying people the right to an equally weighted vote and limiting the opportunity to run for office based on characteristics irrelevant to job performance—carries the suggestion that some people are natural rulers while others are naturally ruled, that is, are inferior and deserving of less respect. As such, they would be rejected by persons framing a constitution as free and independent equals. Such anti-democratic provisions are not compatible with the demand that all be given the opportunity to participate as political equals, based on people's interest in securing the political conditions that promote their sense of their own dignity and self-worth.

Besides this political consequence, people's interest in securing the constitutional conditions necessary to promote a sense of their own worth would also rule out the establishment of an official religion. The government must not give its official approval or disapproval to any particular religious (or anti-religious) conception over any other. In placing that limit on the majority, the constitution again acknowledges and reaffirms the conviction that all citizens regardless of religious or other deeply held values are equally worthy.[49]

It is worth emphasizing, finally, that there is another important reason, not based on self-worth and dignity, for the democratic contractualist to insist on democratic procedures.[50] Such processes, it is often claimed, make it more likely that laws will in fact meet the fundamental contractualist test since the process of debating and then voting, whether for representatives to a legislature or for those deciding on matters of public policy directly, requires that participants defend their decisions to all in the competitive political process. By forcing office seekers and other political actors to justify their record and their proposals in the open and then allowing all members of society an equal vote, democratic procedures increase the likelihood that laws can be defended to all, viewed as free and independent equals.

Democratic contractualists thus not only take rights and the welfare of all citizens seriously, they also take democracy seriously. Democratic procedures allowing each person an equal opportunity to participate in the political process would be supported by people contemplating joining society as free and independent equals for two reasons: They help protect everybody's sense of self-worth, and they make it more likely (though not certain) that laws emerging from the structure created by the constitution could be defended to free and independent persons entering society as equals.

So although democratic contractualism rejects the proceduralist's claim that democratic processes are a form of pure procedural justice (in the sense that any result they produce must be accepted), it nevertheless sees democratic institutions as an essential component of a legitimate constitution. Free and independent persons joining society as equals would insist, for their own, contractualist reasons, on protecting the right to an equally weighted vote, the right of all to run for office, and freedom of (political) speech. But rather than attempting to bring all rights under the umbrella of self-justifying democratic procedures, contractualism is able to incorporate democracy's virtues within its larger account of constitutional government by showing that democratic procedures would be insisted on by free and independent persons joining society as equals.

Note also that there is no need to use the "strong" proceduralist formulation that I discussed earlier, which insists that everybody have the same opportunity to influence the outcome rather than merely the same opportunity to participate in the process. Once basic rights, an economic minimum, equal opportunity, and the principle of non-discrimination are secured, there seems to be no further need to protect minorities against the majority. Contractualism thus provides for the protection of minority rights naturally, as an expression of inherent limits on governmental power, instead of straining to understand such rights instrumentally, in purely procedural terms.[51]

It is also clear that free and independent equals would reject the utilitarian principle that secures rights only if they serve the larger good, since such an approach does not put rights on a sufficiently secure footing.[52] There is no need, in other words, for contractors to risk basic rights like speech, religion, and equality of opportunity to the vague contingencies of utility calculations when they could simply protect them directly.[53] Yet that is not to deny—as Justice Brandeis noted in *Whitney*—that freedom of speech and other rights are also socially useful in a variety of ways. The point, rather, is that even if they were not able to be defended on those instrumental grounds such rights instrumentally, still can be defended on other, contractualist ones.

I have argued in this section that those who, like former Justice Brennan, are committed to rights and the dignity of the individual would do well to think in terms of the social contract. Interpreting freely, I suggested that Madison's defense of religious freedom in "Memorial and Remonstrance" can best be taken to suggest that the choice of a constitution should be made by free and independent persons joining society as equals and desiring to find a constitution and laws that are acceptable to all. Given that initial commitment, then, citizens' shared interests in realizing their particular conception of the good and developing a sense of their worth and dignity would lead to the conclusion that as free and independent equals they are entitled to make two demands against other citizens. First, they would demand an equal opportunity to realize their ideals about the good life, which requires protection of basic liberties as well as assurance of equality of opportunity, nondiscrimination, and a satisfactory economic minimum. And, second, they would also demand to participate equally in the political process as an assurance that the constitution does all it can to promote citizens' sense of their self-worth and dignity.

This vision of the social contract therefore differs from the Hobbesian one. Instead of an agreement born entirely of self-interest and the need to reach a compromise among deeply competing interests, here the social contract represents, in addition to an awareness of conflicting social interests, a shared commitment to find a system that expresses the equal dignity of all in the sense that nobody can reasonably reject its terms.[54] That important difference within the social contract tradition, between Hobbes, on one hand, and Kant, Rawls and (I am arguing) Madison, on the other, should not be overlooked.

Democratic contractualism also reflects a commitment to respect natural rights, since the justifications of these limits on governmental power are non-instrumental. For the democratic contractualist, rights are defended intrinsically, not on the ground that they are an effective means of maximizing total welfare. Thus, according to the contractualist, basic rights reflect those limits on government that would be insisted on by free and independent persons joining society as equals. And that fact—that social contractors would be moved not only to secure democratic procedures but also to limit them—can be justified, I argued, on both practical and moral grounds. Not only is it a practical solution to the problems posed by a religiously and culturally diverse people but also an answer to the fact that a government subordinates one citizen to another when it limits a citizen's rights to think, speak, worship, pursue an ideal of the good life in personal matters, and establish an official religion or when it denies citizens equal opportunity to participate in the democratic political process.

The arguments for democratic contractualism, both practical and moral, seem strong. It should be emphasized, however, that we have been considering only matters of constitutional design and law—what Rawls terms the "basic structure" of society.[55] Once the terms of the social contract are agreed to and a constitution and laws securing basic rights, democratic procedures, and fair equality of opportunity and other welfare provisions are in place, people are free to pursue their own ends. Limited inequalities in income would no doubt emerge, in part because some would want to take more demanding jobs, would have greater desire for leisure time, or would be more talented. But assuming the basic structure is fair, in the sense described, those inequalities can be defended to everybody, in the way that contractualism requires.

Before I consider judicial review and constitutional interpretation in the light of these thoughts, however, one further comment is in order. I have often emphasized democratic contractualism's roots in the U.S. political tradition, including its commitment to consent and its place in the thinking of the framers—especially James Madison. It should be emphasized, however, that I am not suggesting, in the spirit of original intent, that we should adopt democratic contractualism simply because of its historical roots or even that Madison's contractualist tendencies are evidence for the merits of that theory. But then why, one may ask, *are* such historical connections important?

The answer is that historical continuity and compatibility with political traditions are important to democratic contractualism because political stability is important. It is a virtue of any (reasonably just) political system, I assume, that it possess the capacity to sustain itself; utopian political visions, however attractive in theory, are of little value if they are unsuitable for governing real human beings as they are.[56] (This assumption was in the background of the discussion of contractualism's practical advantages, for example.) But if this assumption is true and stability is a virtue, then (assuming contractualism offers a reasonably just regime) the fact it is rooted in U.S. constitutional history and thinking may itself encourage people to think of the government as "theirs" and, thereby, to win for it wider support. In other words, if the fact that the "father" of the U.S. Constitution was a contractualist makes that understanding of the government more attractive to those living under it, and furthermore if the ideas to which contractualism appeals are arguably those of this tradition rather than another, then that stability adds another attractive feature to the theory.

Much more needs to be said, however, before we can confidently assess democratic contractualism as a theory of judicial review and constitutional interpretation. In this section, I have offered only a very general and rather intuitive sketch of what a democratic contractualist would hope to achieve in designing a constitution and system of law, leaving what are for purposes of this book the most important questions unanswered. First, we need to know what role judicial review would play in the contractualist's theory. Then, in light of those reflections, we will ask how democratic contractualism instructs judges to interpret the Constitution.

Democratic Contractualism and Judicial Review

On its face, judicial review would seem problematic given the democratic contractualist's commitment to democratic procedures. Why should unelected and unaccountable judges, appointed for life, have the power to decide a law's constitutionality when elected representatives have decided it is both wise and consistent with the Constitution? It is possible, as we have seen, for the contractualist to go a long way in defending judicial review against that charge by following democratic proceduralism's path. But unlike the proceduralist, the democratic contractualist is not a skeptic about natural rights, so that conflicts may now arise between two competing political principles. One commitment, to democratic government, inclines the contractualist against judicial review except when necessary to promote democracy itself; but because, as I have argued, there is no guarantee that even a perfectly operating democratic system will respect individual rights, secure an economic minimum, and protect against discrimination, contractualists may also seek to limit democratic processes in ways that protect those other principles.

If that diagnosis is accurate, then the normal way of envisioning judicial review's anti-democratic character—what Alexander Bickel termed the "counter-majoritarian difficulty"—is in one sense correct but in another misleading.[57] It is correct in the sense just noted—that contractualists will seek a governmental structure that satisfies, insofar as possible, two potentially conflicting ideals of democratic government and individual rights. But the counter-majoritarian charge is also misleading since we can now see that we have on hand a single, coherent defense of both democratic procedures and individual rights. Rather than resting on conflicting political theories, both flow from the same theoretical commitment to ensure that the Constitution and laws can be defended to all citizens, viewed as free and independent persons entering society as equals. In that sense, *both* democratic procedures and individual rights are part of the democratic contractualist's philosophical account of constitutional democracy, so that the real problem of constitutional design is to find the best balance between these two ideals. The CLS charge that law rests on contradictory political ideologies can therefore be met, at least in this context, by pointing out that instead of serving conflicting ends, democratic procedures and individual rights against the majority give expression to the same (contractualist) understanding of government.

The next question to be asked is whether the contractualist picture describes reasonably well the U.S. Constitution. We are concerned, after all, to discover the best theory of the U.S. Constitution, including especially judicial review and constitutional interpretation, which means we seek more than an attractive political theory; democratic contractualism must be able to be applied to this particular document in a way that would, if followed, present it as a reasonable effort to achieve worthy objectives.

Recall that democratic proceduralism seemed incompatible with various of the Constitution's structural features such as checks and balances (especially an independently elected executive with veto power) and a bicameral legislature including senators who represent widely divergent numbers of people in their states. Proceduralism does not describe the U.S. Constitution closely enough to allow the proceduralist to avoid calling into question some of its most basic features. How, then, does democratic contractualism fare in that respect? Could a constitutional convention committed to implementing the contractualist's ideal of government have reasonably adopted the U.S. Constitution?[58]

From the democratic contractualist's perspective, federalism, separation of powers, and judicial review are political structures available to help achieve the correct balance between contractualism's various ideals. Unlike a proceduralist convention, the objective of a contractualist convention would be to design a government that protects the various basic rights and opportunities described above while at the same time securing for people the chance to participate as equals in the political processes. Since these ideals may come in conflict, compromises among them are virtually inevitable, and democratic contractualism does not tell those who would frame a constitution how best to achieve that balance; it does, however, offer a broad, theoretical perspective from which to consider such questions. In that sense, then, the question for contractualists of whether to provide for judicial review is a practical, political one similar to choices between a unicameral and bicameral legislature, between an independently elected president or a prime minister chosen by the majority party, or between a directly elected president or one chosen by an electoral college. The extent of the power of the judicial branch, compared with the executive and legislative branches, cannot be determined a priori, by philosophical reflection, any more than can those other questions of constitutional design.

Viewed in that contractualist light, *The Federalist Papers* can be seen as an attempt to defend each provision of the U.S. Constitution as a workable balance between democratic participation and individual rights. Madison, Hamilton, and Jay argued that although electoral processes must play a role in government, it was also necessary that the proposed constitution insulate the people from political power in various ways. As Madison explained in "Federalist Number 10," too much democracy may lead to factionalism and eventually to tyranny since no democratic system can guarantee that "enlightened statesmen" will always be at the helm. But at the same time, argued the Federalists, the people and their representatives must play a role in the shaping of the government, so that there must be regular elections, established term limits, and so on. From the contractualist's perspective, therefore, those establishing a constitution must rely on the experience of history to construct a system that balances the needs to respect individual rights, promotes economic prosperity, provides for equality of opportunity, and prevents discrimination while also securing the opportunity for all citizens to participate in the political process as equals.

Turning specifically to the question of judicial review, there are three different possibilities that delegates to a constitutional convention who are committed to democratic contractualism might consider in order to realize their ideals:

1. A structure without either a bill of rights specifying the limits on governmental power or judicial review (the most "democratic" approach);
2. Judicial review, but again without a bill of rights, so that in exercising judicial review the courts are required to enforce the most reasonable understanding of the social contract (the approach giving the most power to judges);
3. A compromise between these in which judges exercising judicial review interpret a written constitution whose provisions include specific limits on government's power in a bill of rights that can be amended by a difficult, complex process.

It seems clear that contractualist framers of a constitution might reasonably believe the third option offers the best chance of achieving the various contractualist objectives we have been discussing. Judicial review could help protect democratic institutions, in the way proceduralists argued, as well as secure individual rights *against* the majority. But a *written* constitution and bill of rights could also cabin judicial authority and make the resulting system more predictable and less susceptible to judicial abuse than one in which judges were able to overturn laws on the basis of their own, unconstrained understanding of the terms of the social contract that free and independent equals would adopt. The fact that judicial review allows judges sometimes to thwart the will of the people's elected representatives in the name of individual rights, equality of opportunity, and non-discrimination is a compromise meant to achieve a reasonable balance among contractualism's political ideals.

Having decided on judicial review and a written guarantee of individual rights against legislative violations, contractualists would still need to decide which governmental responsibilities, including promoting economic prosperity; protecting rights to speech, religious exercise, privacy, and due process; securing equality of opportunity; preventing discrimination; and so on, should be incorporated into the constitution and which may better be left to legislation. Economic regulation, for example, might be left to legislative oversight except insofar as it infringes on the contractualist's understanding of individual rights.[59] Thus it might be the case that a contractualist convention would put in place constitutional provisions protecting citizens against government taking their property without compensation. Or it might be decided that the difficult questions of educational policy involved in deciding what constitutes genuine equality of educational opportunity should be left to elected officials with little constitutional oversight.[60] Other issues, however, may be thought more suitable for judicial oversight, so that courts would be charged with securing basic freedoms like religion, speech, criminal due process, and privacy, protecting the right to participate equally in the democratic process, and eliminating governmentally enforced discrimination.

None of this means, of course, that elected branches cannot also play a role in protecting individual rights. At some times and on some questions, it may be the federal legislature that should act to protect individual rights against incursions by states; other times the courts may also step in. A Supreme Court exercising judicial review is not the only institution capable of moving the government toward the contractualist's ideals.

One final point that has been in the background is also worth emphasizing here. Democratic contractualists might choose not to specify, in advance, the specific meanings of the limits they impose on the majority, refusing to write the constitution as if it were a tax code or a criminal statute. Aware that later generations will face situations the framers of the document cannot envision, they would hesitate to specify the extent and limits of freedom of religion, speech, and due process as well as the precise meaning of the document's general commitment to equality. For in addition to the fact that these and other concepts will have to be applied to unforeseen issues in the distant future, framers would also be aware of their own fallibility. Though they would surely have their own ideas about what constitutes cruel punishment, the establishment of religion, freedom of speech, equality, and criminal due process, they would not want to foreclose the possibility that others might someday come to a deeper understanding of what those require. In that way, the framers would intend the Bill of Rights to command that law not abridge these fundamental principles, as *correctly* understood, rather than that government not abridge the principles as they (mistakenly) interpreted them at the time of the framing.[61]

Suppose we assume then, that the contractualist framers have adopted a written constitution providing for both regular elections of the legislature, a bill of rights limiting legislative power, and courts charged with enforcing those limits through judicial review. What more, we may now ask, can be said from the contractualist's perspective about judicial review and constitutional interpretation? And how, more specifically, does the democratic contractualist instruct those charged with exercising judicial review to interpret the constitution?

Constitutional Interpretation and Neutral Public Discourse

For the contractualist, the U.S. Constitution is to be understood, insofar as possible, as the result of an agreement among free and independent equals establishing the governing institutions and laws under which they are all to live. The rights that it protects are to be understood as limits free and independent persons joining society as equals would impose on their government.[62] There will be limits on this, however, since both text and precedent pose important interpretive constraints. As I have already noted, the task of constitutional interpretation must always be distinguished from that of political philosophy and free moral inquiry: Its concerns are with discovering the meaning of the text, not describing the ideal constitution. In addition, although the Constitution itself does not specifically define the boundaries of the rights it protects, it also does not ask simply that judges enforce the terms of the social contract as they envision it. For the democratic contractualist, then, the best interpretation of the Constitution is not necessarily the particular one envisioned by the framers. Yet the fact that current interpreters are not bound by the framers' erroneous interpretations in no way requires that their views be ignored; the framers' ideas are always a good place to begin thinking about the document's purposes and how it is best interpreted. But a good beginning is not necessarily the last, or best, ending.

Democratic contractualists also part ways with utilitarian interpreters. Contractualists believe governments are bound to respect natural rights since constitutional protections of free speech, religion, equal protection, and so on reflect the equal dignity and worth of each person, expressed in the fashion of a social contract chosen in a temperate moment, rather than as instruments designed to maximize expected welfare. So although such matters as economic prosperity are important concerns of contractualist legislators, the general welfare is not the foundation of political authority or the ultimate standard by which to interpret the Constitution. But how, then, is the democratic proceduralist to make such interpretive judgments?

First, it is important to recall that although the contractualist denies the proceduralist's claim that democratic processes are a version of pure procedural justice, democratic processes are important to contractualists. Such procedures promote citizens' sense of self-worth and dignity by assuring that all have the same opportunity to participate in the political process and increasing the prospect that laws can be justified to all. These two important points establish the presumption that any law passed by a *truly* democratic legislature should be allowed to stand unless it violates basic constitutional principle.[63]

Precedent will also weigh in the contractualist's thinking about interpretation. The need to assure legal predictability and consistency in treatment of citizens as well as to protect the Court's political authority both mean that justices should not overturn past decisions without substantial justification. But stare decisis will not *always* outweigh the other considerations judges must consider, especially their own understanding of the document's meaning in light of the reasonable terms of the social contract, so that judges exercising judicial review will also at times feel bound to overturn their own precedents.

The proceduralist must acknowledge, therefore, that interpretive judgments often require weighing the importance of another right,[64] the general interest,[65] the democratic process, or precedent. Clearly, then, contractualists must weigh various values or ideals without any sort of formula that can be mechanically applied. Decisions will be based on the particulars of each case, of course, but more can be said about constitutional interpretation from the contractualist's perspective.

Most important, according to the contractualist, is the fact that political argument must be "channeled" or constrained in different ways. Certain subjects and methods of arguing must be placed beyond the bounds of legitimate political debate if the social contract is to secure the willing agreement of all persons, viewed as free and independent equals. Central to contractualism, in other words, is the claim that interpretation must proceed in terms that reflect everybody's perspective rather than from the viewpoint of any individual or group. Religious arguments are the paradigm of unacceptable forms of political discussion. Such limits fall into two categories: Some restrict the *content* of the arguments that can be made; others restrict the *methods* of argument that are acceptable in a constitutional democracy.[66] I will term political debate carried on within these constraints "*neutral public* discourse" and will discuss each of the two limitations in turn.[67]

It is helpful first to note that such limits on public deliberation are not unique to constitutional interpretation. In courts of law, for example, in order to guarantee a fair trial, evidence is often either excluded from the jury or jurors are instructed to ignore what they have heard.[68] Jurors are not to base their decision on *all* relevant evidence but instead only on evidence that should be considered given the various purposes trials serve, including protecting the rights of this and future defendants. Or consider the very different case of a religious group that frames its discourse by limiting itself to certain texts, which it takes as central to its faith, while ignoring others. The universe of discourse is constrained in each of these examples in service of the underlying purpose of the discourse, whether it is a legal procedure or religious association. Similarly, in the case of neutral public discourse the thought is that limits imposed on the method and the content of political discussions are justified because they serve the larger contractualist political understanding of a democratic political association.

The requirement of neutral public discourse thus imposes a (moral) obligation on both officials and citizens to channel political discussion in various ways, including how they decide to vote as well as how officials explain and defend their positions. Campaign speeches, debates in Congress, and votes are political, not private acts, so that they must be able to be defended to others in terms that are compatible with the contractualist's political principles. Thus, if I run for office on an anti-abortion platform that rejects abortion on grounds it is contrary to fundamental Christian values, or if I vote for a pro-choice candidate because Reform Judaism has adopted freedom of choice, I have not acted in accord with the requirements of neutral public discourse. For the democratic contractualist, political activities are not mere expressions of personal interest (as some utilitarians have suggested[69]) but instead constitute a political *judgment* that must not only be defended but must be defended in accord with the limits of neutral public discourse.[70]

Turning first to neutrality, the idea here is that the *content* of political discourse cannot be based either on the fact that a law or interpretation of the Constitution will *benefit me* or *benefit my group* (broadly construed to include family, religious groups, economic groups, and political groups) or, second, that it will promote or inhibit a religious or other *conception of the good life*.[71] In these ways, democratic contractualism demands that political discourse be neutral: Its content is restricted with an eye toward justifying laws to all persons seen as free and equal.[72] I will discuss each of them in turn.

The first requirement, that political argument excludes appeals to individual[73] and group interest, means that the justification of law and legal interpretation should set aside appeals to private interest in favor of claims about the common good, rights, and fairness.[74] The requirement does not deny that farmers may lobby for price supports, military leaders for tanks, scientists for public support, poor people for higher taxes, and the wealthy for lower ones; such appeals are common in constitutional democracies, and rightly so. It does mean, however, that those making such arguments must appeal either to the common good or else to principles of fairness and rights that all can accept. Price supports for agriculture, money for military defense and science, and different tax rates might be defended on the ground that the country needs strong family farms, good science benefits the economy, national defense is essential to protect the government, tax increases provide fair equality of opportunity, or tax cuts will increase investment and produce more jobs. Such policies could also be defended on neutral grounds of need: School lunches for the poor do more good for them than tax breaks do for the rich, for instance. Or they might be defended on the ground that other groups have been given such advantages before and fairness demands that it is now this group's turn. The point, however, is that in each case the appeal is not to the interests of the individuals or groups by themselves; the terms of public discourse channel discussion away from appeals to private interest into matters of the *public* good and political *principle*. What is excluded, then, is the bare assertion that ignoring whether it is in the public interest, a law should be accepted or rejected based solely on its impact on a particular group. Representatives of particular districts pressing their arguments should not defend a new law or project on the ground that although it is contrary to the national interest it should still be passed because it benefits their own districts.[75]

Though sometimes controversial, especially among those who see democratic government through the lens of interest group pluralism,[76] this requirement of *neutral* public discourse has in fact been a staple of constitutional interpretation since early in the century. When there is no fundamental right at stake, modern courts generally show wide deference to legislative decisions—typically on questions of economic regulation and taxation. But even in these cases the courts do not defer completely, insisting instead that the law have at least a "rational basis." In that way, the court enforces the requirement of neutral public discourse. If a law serves only a narrow interest group and so lacks any plausible foundation in the common good, fairness, or other broadly public values, then the law lacks a "rational basis" and is therefore constitutionally suspect.[77] In his well-known treatise on constitutional law Lawrence Tribe put it this way: "Supreme Court decisions since the 1930s demonstrate that the Court has wisely resisted the ... pluralist approach [which assumes that no public interest exists beyond the logrolling result of the legislative process], one that has been criticized as giving undeserved weight to highly organized, wealthy interest groups."[78] The Supreme Court itself expressed the underlying rationale of the rational basis test along with the corresponding commitment to neutral public discourse in a 1976 decision. Legislation, it said, must be an "exercise of judgment" rather than a "display of arbitrary power."[79]

I come, then, to the second constraint that neutrality imposes on public discourse—that laws must be defended and interpreted independent of any particular religious or other conception of the good life.[80] Following Madison's discussion in his "Memorial and Remonstrance Against Religious Assessments," I have already argued that people deliberating as free and independent equals would ignore their religious convictions; it would be neither practical nor fair to construct the social contract on any other basis than religious neutrality. But although that argument was correct and important as far as it went, there is no reasonable ground for excluding *only* religious beliefs from political discourse when many non-religious ideas occupy the same position in the lives of those who are not religious.

What is really at stake, then, is a distinction, sometimes overlooked, between two aspects of morality. One, which has been the focus of much that has gone on in this book, involves the regulations on behavior that are necessary if people are to successfully live together in society. The other set of norms, however, deal with what H.L.A. Hart termed "moral ideals" and includes, in addition to religious beliefs, a variety of non-religious ideas about the moral virtues, personal character, and the purposes of human life.[81] "Lives," Hart wrote, "may be ruled by dedication to the pursuit of heroic, romantic, aesthetic, or scholarly ideals, or, less agreeably, to mortification of the flesh."[82] Hart might also have added, besides these, religious faithfulness, acquisition of wealth or power, personal relationships among family and friends, and artistic creativity. So although religious beliefs occupy part of this terrain, they do not occupy it all: Non-religious people will also pursue their own vision of the good life in whatever terms they understand it.

It seems clear, given this wide and intractable diversity of opinion about moral ideals and the good life, that free and independent persons joining society as equals would insist that government remain neutral not only on religious issues but also on all questions of the meaning and goals of human life. Reasoning under the restraints of Madison's "temperate moment," people cannot know if their moral ideal would be shared by the majority or whether it would be regarded as mistaken, heretical, or simply evil. So given that they might find themselves in such a minority, social contractors would reject not only an official religion but any other officially established moral ideal and insist instead that they be allowed to make up their own mind about the purposes and value of human life.

It is also important to emphasize, in addition, that laws privileging one moral ideal would not only pose a threat to the realization of other ideals but would also constitute what Justice Brennan termed an affront to the "equal status" of all citizens. Such laws would be a public statement that some people's deepest values are officially disfavored and less than worthy and thereby challenge their self-worth.

A number of qualifying and explanatory remarks must be made about this second aspect of neutrality, however. First, channeling political discourse in this way obviously does not require government to be morally neutral in the full sense; neutrality is required only with respect to moral ideals about the best way of life. Laws preventing theft and murder, though not morally neutral, do not depend for their justification on the idea that one way of life is inherently superior to another. Neutral public discourse does demand, however, that the legislation not rest on simple moral disapproval of some religious or other ideal of the good. Without more, the state cannot tax or ban behavior, whether it be praying, smoking tobacco, drinking alcohol, or engaging in prostitution, unless doing so can be defended in terms of neutral public discourse. If the tax or ban is justified on public grounds, such as the need to protect public health and safety or prevent exploitation of women, then the law would not be incompatible with the requirements of neutral public discourse.

Second, although the *justification* of the law cannot rest on a particular moral ideal, the effects of laws need not be neutral among competing views of the good life. Any other standard would, from the contractualist's perspective, be neither possible nor desirable. No constitutional regime can avoid making it impossible for some citizens to fully achieve their moral ideal. For instance, theocrats and other religious fundamentalists may have an ideal of the good that requires replacement of constitutional democracy with a religious state. It is no argument against democratic contractualism, however, that it cannot always and in all circumstances remain neutral among all moral ideals, since no constitutional regime seeking to govern over diversity could meet the contradictory demands of Islamic fundamentalists, Christian fundamentalists, and atheists.

It is also important to keep in mind, however, that this insistence on governmental neutrality does *not* reflect contempt for the fundamentalists' moral ideal. In insisting on neutrality, the government is not saying that theocrats who wish to impose their ideals on others through law are somehow less worthy than other citizens or that their religious views are in some way erroneous. Rather, these limits on public discourse reflect the most practical and morally defensible constitutional structure for diverse citizens seeking to live together as equals under a single constitutional structure. The government's position, therefore, is that free and independent equals would not adopt a constitution that allowed religious establishment, not that those who believe otherwise are committed to an unworthy or false vision of the good life. From the *government's* perspective, the theocrat's religious view may be true or false, sound or unsound; the point is that to force religious or other moral ideals on an unwilling citizenry would be both impractical and, from the perspective of a social contract among free and independent persons joining society as equals, wrong.

Democratic contractualism thus does not reject all laws that adversely affect a particular moral ideal—even ones that are less extreme than the theocrat's. Suppose, for example, that the legislature required public schools to teach basic biology, including evolution, and further that such teaching tends to undermine the beliefs of religious fundamentalists. Neutral public discourse would not preclude teaching evolution unless the *motivation behind* the requirement is disdain for that religious view or desire to undermine it. If the law is justified on other grounds, such as the economic and educational value of scientific training, then the law and its justification do not violate the constraints of neutral public discourse.

A recent case involving the question of teaching evolution nicely illustrates these problems. In it, the courts were asked if a school district's adoption of textbooks that teach evolution and other tenets of "secular humanism" was unconstitutional. Holding that it was not, the judges explained that the state did not have as its "purpose" the establishment of religion—a position that reflects the contractualist's commitment to neutral public discourse—but rather the teaching of science. Furthermore, said the judges, the state is not required to eschew teaching all values; everything depends on what the values are. These specific books are acceptable, said the judges, because they "instill in Alabama public school children such values as independent thought, tolerance of diverse views, self-respect, maturity, self-reliance and logical decision-making. This is an entirely appropriate secular effect."[83]

So inherent in this contractualist position is another important distinction, paralleling Hart's, between two sorts of virtues: "private" ones that the government may not undertake to promote and "public" values that government may legitimately encourage and enforce. Rather than resting, as private values do, on a particular religious or other vision of the ideal life, public values such as tolerance and freedom of inquiry are what Hart terms "mandatory," that is, grounded in the practical requirements of maintaining a stable, democratic government that can be justified to every citizen. So far from rejecting such public values, free and independent persons joining society as equals would want government to promote them; the stability and even the existence of democratic government itself, they know, may depend on the degree to which citizens are motivated by them. Without values like (political) toleration, self-respect, and the capacity for informed and logical thinking, neither self-government nor the economic prosperity on which it relies could succeed. To insist that government refuse to encourage such values would be to refuse to secure the conditions for the furtherance of the government itself—hardly a choice rational persons reasoning in a "temperate moment" would make.

It is often difficult, of course, for courts to determine with certainty what were the real motives of a legislature. Evidence of legislators' motives is not itself mysterious; it is the same evidence we use to discover motives in other contexts. Statements by sponsors of the legislation are one part of the picture, of course, although other actions taken by the legislature, such as rejection or passage of an amendment, may also be relevant. Thus, in the example mentioned above, whether a school text was chosen for acceptable, public reasons or based on forbidden, private reasons such as disdain for a religious group's ideals would depend entirely on the facts of the case. How likely is it that this group would be the subject of such disdain? What did the legislators actually say and do? What were their alternatives, and why did they reject some in favor of the one they actually chose? Only from that perspective--from inside, so to speak—can a court hope to determine if the law is suitably neutral.

Besides these two substantive constraints demanded by *neutral* public discourse, a second limitation must also be met if political decisions are to be justified to each person viewed as a free and independent equal: Political discourse must also be *public.* This means that the *methods* of political discussion and argument employed by members of a constitutional democracy must be widely shared and their validity must not be in serious doubt.[84] That this methodological limitation is distinct from the substantive limitations on interests and moral ideals that were already discussed can be seen from the fact that religions include more than a picture of the ideal or best way of life.[85] Consider, for example, a person who believes, based on Biblical teachings, that God has commanded people never to debase, in private or in public, the one true church or the one almighty God. Such a belief, I assume, is not based on publicly accessible forms of argument such as science or common sense; but neither, it is clear, does it directly involve a moral ideal. The question, then, is whether such a person should act, politically, on such a belief and work for censorship laws, as well as whether the constitutional regime should *allow* such a political argument to gain the force of law.

It is important, then, that even though a citizen believes she has special access to the truth through scripture, that access is not available to all. Unlike revelation and other essentially individual or group-centered sources of belief, *public* discourse is broad-based and shared by all. This includes scientific and mathematical reasoning as well as common-sense appeals to economic, political, and other aspects of different issues. What the publicity requirement rules out, therefore, are special and controversial forms of moral and political persuasion such as appeals to religious texts and to personal religious or mystical experience accessible only to some—normally members of a select group.

This methodological constraint, like the earlier content-based limitations, flows from the contractualist's philosophical commitments. If the constitution and laws are to be justifiable to each person, viewed as a free and independent equal, then there can be no appeals to methods of argument or sources of evidence that have credence only to particular individuals or groups. Political debate about the laws to govern a diverse, pluralistic community must take place in a common arena, using shared methods of argument and discussion, or else the results will not meet the standards imposed by contractualism.[86]

I therefore disagree with Kent Greenawalt's claim that there should be various "exceptions" made for religious people who may want to use religious premises to defend important matters of general political concern to all members of society.[87]

Insofar, for example, as the Catholic bishop's pronouncements on nuclear war, birth control, and so on are (1) aimed at influencing the political process rather than merely instructing their religious followers and (2) not based on public methods of argument, the bishops are not acting in accord with reasonable restraints on political argument. That is not to say, however, that the bishops cannot address matters of public policy using the methods of neutral public discourse, let alone that they cannot preach whatever moral lessons they think appropriate to their religious charges using whatever religious arguments they choose. It is also open to Catholics, Orthodox Jews, and fundamentalist Protestants to offer arguments on topics that overlap with religious convictions; abortion is one such example. But here, as elsewhere, the political argument proceeds using public methods. Questions involving when "life" begins, the status of the pre-born, and the rights of a prospective mother are all relevant; but the fact that the church opposes abortion or the *Bible* condemns it is not.

It may also be the case, however, that the ideal of neutral public discourse cannot be fully realized. As I have noted, methodological neutrality imposes limits on both political institutions and citizens. It demands that legislators and judges make and interpret laws in accord with the constraints of neutral public discourse and that citizens vote on similar grounds.[88] They may *also* have religious reasons for what they do, of course, but those cannot be the basis of their (public) deliberation or the basis of their political decisions. Clearly, then, people may fail to live up to this democratic ideal. Citizens may vote out of religious conviction rather than acting as responsible public citizens, and legislatures and judges may either be unwilling or unable to decide an issue while setting aside religious and other considerations having no relationship to the common good or political principle. In that sense, then, the contractualist obligations of citizenship in a constitutional democracy are strict—stricter, perhaps than is often thought—though they are not, I think, unreasonable.

It is most important, of course, that matters involving what Rawls terms "constitutional essentials" and "basic justice" be decided in this way.[89] Fundamental rights and provisions for equality of opportunity, an economic minimum, and non-discrimination are most important and must be decided without violating either the content or methodological constraints of neutral public discourse. Other times, however, it may not be possible to resolve disputes without violating democratic contractualism's basic commitments.[90] Nonetheless, says the contractualist, we must realize that insofar as this does occur the liberal political regime has failed to live up to its own ideals. Perhaps, for example, there is no way to defend public expenditures on "high" culture such as symphonies and opera without assuming the moral ideal that enjoying the arts is better than watching sports and popular television.[91] But even assuming that such an assumption is necessary and further that it is important to continue the subsidies, it does not follow that this failure of neutrality is to be welcomed. Necessary evils are still evil.

Judicial review is thus important to contractualism because it demands that the *limits* imposed on popular rule by the Constitution be defended in the arena of neutral public discourse. It forces electoral majorities (by the terms of legal argument and institutional practices) to defend their decisions not on the basis of power and political interest but on the basis of right. Whether the issue involves legally segregated schools, a publicly financed creche, a law banning abortion, censorship of obscenity and hate speech, or affirmative action, legal practice demands that justices explain and defend their interpretive judgments in accord with neutral public discourse. If limits are to be imposed on the majority, precedents overturned, or distinctions made among apparently similar cases, the reasons must be explained in terms that all can accept, without benefit of raw appeals to group or individual interest, to moral ideals, or to special, private methods of argument. Dissenting Court opinions as well as law review articles and political debate all contribute to public discourse on the meaning of the Constitution's broad limitations on legislative power.[92]

Illustrations

To develop further the discussion of democratic contractualism, I want next to illustrate the contractualist's vision by returning briefly to two issues I discussed earlier: capital punishment and the right to privacy. Along the way, I will consider some of the objections that might be raised against the contractualist position, turning in the next section to some important feminist charges along with possible contractualist responses.

As we have already seen, Justice Brennan rejected executions on the ground that they are incompatible with "human dignity." But how might a contractualist understand the connection between dignity and the meaning of the Eighth Amendment's ban on "cruel and unusual punishment"? To answer that, we must first make some assumptions. Suppose a judge believes that no justification for executions is compatible with neutral public discourse: It offers no added deterrence of crime, it does not offer significant savings to society, and it cannot be defended on retributivist grounds.[93] Under those circumstances, it seems clear that free and independent citizens entering society as equals would reject capital punishment. It would be irrational for them to accept a practice that inflicts pointless, gratuitous harm on any group of citizens.[94] Some familiar arguments made on behalf of the practice (for example, appeals to the Biblical injunction of an eye for an eye) are ruled out, as is the claim that executions might somehow encourage religious faithfulness or other private moral ideals. In *that* sense, capital punishment violates human dignity. It is a form of punishment that cannot be defended to everybody, viewed as free and independent equals.

The situation looks different, however, if executions deter crime or are justified on retributivist grounds. Since it would then not be "excessive" or merely gratuitous harm, the majority would not be prevented from using it by the terms of the social contract.

But these philosophical reflections, although important to the contractualist's overall assessment of the Eighth Amendment's meaning for capital punishment, are not the whole story. Perhaps earlier judges have already ruled on the constitutionality of executions, so that the issue must now be addressed in light of those precedents. But if the earlier Court's decision on the subject is now seen to be mistaken, then the interpreter must consider the range of possible consequences, both theoretical and practical, of overturning that precedent. What would be the effect, for example, on other areas of law were this precedent to be rejected? How important is it for the Court to be consistent as well as to appear to remain consistent?

So whether a law permitting executions should be overturned on constitutional grounds depends, for the democratic contractualist, on various empirical, political, and historical considerations, including the purposes of punishment, the potential benefits and risks of executions, and the importance of following legal precedent. Contractualists cannot simply ask what the framers thought about executions or even whether they would somehow foster democracy or would promote social welfare. Contractualism cannot answer this or other important constitutional questions without weighing a range of relevant factors, many of which are unique to the specific issue of executions. Nevertheless, a philosophical commitment to this interpretive theory will shape and channel a judge's thinking, directing her toward the areas I have outlined.

The second example I will discuss is the right to privacy. Since there is no explicit textual basis on which to rest the claim that a law infringing the right to privacy is unconstitutional, interpreters must first ask whether such a constitutional right exists. From the contractualist's perspective, the philosophical basis of the right to privacy is freedom of action; free and independent persons joining society as equals would secure for themselves a private sphere in which to pursue their conceptions of the good life free of governmental interference. But assuming a contractualist government would respect the right to privacy, the question remains whether the text of the U.S. Constitution can reasonably be interpreted to include it among the limits imposed on the majority. Supreme Court justices do not have a blank check to enforce whatever they take to be the most reasonable terms of the social contract; their responsibility, rather, is to find the best interpretation of the limits the *U.S. Constitution* imposes, when read in reasonable, contractualist terms. On what grounds, then, might a contractualist respond to those who charge that judges who overturn laws enacted by the majority's representatives without such a textual basis misunderstand the constitutional limits imposed on elected branches?[95]

The contractualist's defense of "unenumerated" rights, such as privacy, can take at least two forms. First, it is possible to rely on the various open-ended provisions contained in the Constitution that at least suggest judges should also consider unenumerated rights. The Ninth Amendment, for instance, states: "The enumeration in the Constitution, of certain rights, shall not be construed to deny or disparage others retained by the people," clearly suggesting that there are unenumerated rights the Supreme Court should protect.[96] And the Fourteenth Amendment provides, in part, that the states shall not deprive any citizen of "equal protection" of the law, abridge the "privileges and immunities" of citizens of the United States, or deprive any person of "life, liberty or property" without due process of law. As with the Ninth Amendment's mention of rights "reserved" to the people, the Fourteenth also does not define "equal protection," "privileges and immunities of citizens," or "liberty," leaving open the possibility that privacy should be included among such rights.[97]

Unenumerated rights can also be defended on the ground that the best interpretation of explicit texts and past decisions *presupposes* such rights exist, even though they are not mentioned explicitly in either the Constitution or in earlier legal cases. This approach is a familiar idea in U.S. law: The rights to travel and freedom of association, though not specifically mentioned in the Constitution, have received constitutional protection because without them the (explicitly enumerated) rights of speech and assembly would be insufficiently protected.[98] In a similar vein, Samuel Warren and Louis Brandeis argued more than a century ago that a right to privacy (in the sense of control over information about oneself) exists even though no court or legislature had explicitly recognized it.[99] Such an unenumerated right exists, they claimed, because it is a necessary extension of the *principles* on which other established rights depend. Settled law would be rendered incoherent, they thought, if the right to privacy were not included among property and other rights explicitly recognized in the law. The underlying principles, embedded in explicitly recognized rights, require that privacy also be protected. Without the power to acknowledge unenumerated rights, embedded in principles underlying other explicit rights, the law would not develop in the coherent, consistent manner demanded by the rule of law itself. "Political, social and economic changes entail the recognition of new rights," they wrote, "and the common law, in its eternal youth, grows to meet the demands of society."[100] Many years later, while serving on the Supreme Court, Justice Brandeis defended the general "right to be let alone" in much the same way, claiming it was inherent in the Constitution's other, explicitly protected rights.[101] In more recent times, Justice William O. Douglas also defended the constitutional right to privacy (including control over certain personal choices) in similar terms. Douglas claimed that, taken together, the existence of constitutionally enumerated rights such as the right to be secure in persons, houses, papers, and effects, against unreasonable searches and seizures and self-incrimination, and the prohibition against quartering troops "in any house" have "penumbras" establishing a "zone of privacy" that government may not enter. Such a zone, he said, includes the right of married couples to use contraceptives.[102]

Suppose, then, that we assume the constitutional right to privacy exists, either in the Ninth and Fourteenth Amendments or else in the "penumbra" of other rights, along the lines suggested by Warren, Brandeis, and Douglas.[103] As with other rights, however, determining the extent and limits of the right requires careful legal and philosophical argument. Obviously, for example, the right to privacy must be restricted when it conflicts with other, more important rights: It cannot include the right to commit murder in the privacy of one's bedroom. It does seem clear, however, that the Court was on firm contractualist footing when it over-turned state laws banning the sale and use of contraceptives. Such laws could not be justified to free and independent persons joining society as equals, since anti-contraceptive laws reflect an intention to impose a religiously inspired vision of virtuous sexual behavior.

Laws criminalizing homosexual sodomy are similarly flawed from the contractualist's perspective. Assuming it could not be shown that such laws are justified as a reasonable public health measure aimed at preventing AIDS, the only other likely justification would be the forbidden one that the majority disap-proves of homosexuality as a way of life. Indeed, Georgia used that erroneous ar-gument to defend its law against homosexual sodomy. Defending the state's ban on homosexual sodomy, the Georgia attorney general wrote in his brief that it "demotes these sacred institutions [of marriage and family] to merely other alter-native lifestyles."[104]

Abortion provides a final illustration of the contractualist approach to privacy. First, contractualists would reject claims that it should be illegal because the Ro-man Catholic Church disapproves of it; neutral public discourse precludes that sort of reliance on religious or other moral ideals. Similarly, pro-life arguments that women's lives are best led if they are mothers rather than if they work outside the home and pro-choice arguments based on the idea that women's lives are best lived in the public world rather than in more traditional family roles[105] violate the requirement that political contestants not rely on assertions about the ideal or best way of life.

None of this means, however, that the contractualist will be silent about the in-clusion of abortion rights in the right to privacy, for plainly abortion raises a wide range of political and constitutional questions that lie within the boundaries of neutral public discourse. Does the anti-abortion law reflect prejudice against women, in violation of the Equal Protection Clause? Are fetuses constitutional "persons" and therefore deserve protection against being killed without due pro-cess of law? These are the terms in which the issue must be debated, in both legis-latures and courts. Other arguments that are based on private interest or religious and other moral ideals or that rely on methods of argument that are not publicly recognized and accepted must be excluded.

It is clear from the preceding reflections on the Eighth Amendment and the right to privacy that contractualism does not dictate answers to constitutional questions. Democratic contractualism demands that judges consider difficult philosophical and legal questions about which there is wide disagreement, some-times taking positions at odds with the views of a majority. Like other interpretive theories, however, it shapes and gives direction to the interpreter's task in ways that the theory considers reasonable. It provides an account of judicial review and constitutional interpretation, rooted in U.S. legal history and traditions, that weaves into a coherent and attractive whole the ideals of universal consent, major-ity rule, and individual rights.

Is Contractualism Male?
Some Feminist Objections

Philosophical theories, including interpretive ones, must be judged globally, so that the case for contractualism rests largely on these positive arguments as well as on the weaknesses of its competitors that have been described in this and earlier chapters. I want to conclude the discussion of democratic contractualism by looking at the theory from another angle, focusing on some of the objections that might be brought against it, especially ones that have been pressed by legal feminists.[106]

One oft-heard criticism leveled against law and legal practices by feminists points to the repeated failures of legislators and judges to appreciate the degree to which law often reflects gender bias, though at the same time they identify the "neutral" position with the familiar, male viewpoint. Thus, for example, Martha Minow argues that what may appear objective from one perspective may look anything but that from another. Rules governing the workplace, for instance, often assume the worker is cared for in *his* personal life by someone who does not work outside the home and that pregnancy is a medical option not unlike cosmetic surgery and so should not require a leave of absence. Typical of the "assumptions" made in law, she argues, is that other perspectives are irrelevant, that the status quo is "natural, uncoerced, and good," that differences are "intrinsic," and that there is an "unstated norm."[107] These problems can be overcome, she concludes, only after "judges admit the limitations of their own viewpoints, when judges reach beyond those limits by trying to see from contrasting perspectives, and when people seek to exercise power to nurture differences, not to assign and control them."[108] To accomplish this, she writes, judges must seek out "unfamiliar perspectives and analogies" as well as consider the "human consequences" of their decisions.

None of that, however, is at odds with the ideals of democratic contractualism; to the contrary, in expressing the hope for a perspective that no longer expresses biases of gender, race, religion, or culture, Minow describes an ideal that is arguably the centerpiece of democratic contractualism—the search for a moral perspective from which to judge law that *truly is* fair rather than one that gives only lip service to impartiality while in fact reflecting the perspective, position and interests of white males.[109]

Another feminist criticism, which does attack contractualism directly, is that the theory assumes, erroneously, the existence of a neutral, impartial moral or political perspective allowing people to set aside their cultural and social differences. Martha Minow seems to suggest that when she writes "We often forget how to take the perspective of another. We forget even that our point of view is not reality and that our conceptual schemes are simplifications, serving some interests and uses rather than others. We forget because our minds—and probably our hearts—cannot contain the whole world. ... We do not see that [our perspectives] embody our early experiences of discovering how we are the same as and different from our parents. We forget how we learned from them to encode the world into the same classifications they used to serve their own needs."[110] Complete impartiality, she is suggesting, is impossible given the important role experiences and background play in how we understand and relate to the world. Assuming Minow is correct, it could then be argued that this (mistaken) assumption of impartiality infects contractualism at two points: first, with its claim that the Constitution should be understood as the result of an agreement reached from an impartial, morally neutral standpoint (the perspective of free and independent persons joining society as equals) and, second, with the claim that politics should proceed in the manner prescribed by neutral public discourse. It is naive, according to this criticism, to think that people who must inevitably view things from diverse gender, cultural, religious, and ethnic perspectives could ever find common ground on the terms of the social contract, as contractualism assumes.

The contractualist response to this claim, that the moral ideal of impartiality is impossible because people could not be persuaded to accept similar terms of a social contract, is to point out that the objector has so far done nothing more than raise the question; it has not been shown that such agreement is in fact impossible. And why, the contractualist may ask, should we prejudge the success or failure of the contractualist's project? Perhaps as a result of feminist argument the contractualist's theory would need to be modified in some way in order to win universal support, or maybe there is some ambiguity in the argument that could be clarified. Or maybe some particular assumption the contractualist has made along the way would need to be revised because it betrays a distinctively male (or some other) perspective. But the charge that agreement is impossible cannot simply be assumed, any more than it should be assumed that everybody *will* be persuaded by the contractualist argument. The critical conclusion must be earned, just as the contractualist must show that agreement, in fact, *could* be reached under the proper circumstances. Simply noting the important fact of diversity of values and perspectives, the problems such diversity creates, and the theoretical possibility of a better theory is very different from having such a theory on hand, and defenders of democratic contractualism are on firm ground in insisting that their position has not been weakened until their critics can present and defend a better alternative.

There remains, however, an important truth behind the critic's emphasis on the degree to which people differ morally, religiously, sexually, and culturally. In the end, however, I believe this is less an objection to contractualism than a question about the possibility of democratic government itself. Recent experience in Eastern Europe and Africa eloquently testify to the necessity of at least some shared commitment to democratic values if diverse groups are to coexist in an environment that respects democracy and freedom. It is easy to imagine various economic, religious, or ethnic groups, determined to impose their will on others, finding the practical and moral arguments offered in defense of democratic contractualism without weight. But what follows from the fact that this state of affairs can never be ruled out? Democratic institutions and argument *are* culturally dependent and cannot flourish without a broad commitment to toleration, a willingness to set aside individual and cultural differences, and the felt need to seek common ground with others. But democratic contractualism is not alone in requiring such a public culture; the project of limited, democratic government can never flourish if differences among people are so great that the arguments I have been testing cannot take hold. The alternative, however, should not be welcomed.

Besides questioning whether there exists an impartial, objective ground on which to rest legal institutions and practices, other feminists have pressed an "objectivity" attack on liberalism for the precisely opposite reason. Instead of charging liberal theories like democratic contractualism with assuming that there exists an "objective" moral stance, these critics charge that liberal theories like contractualism wrongly assume law can proceed *independent* of moral and political argument. So instead of charging that it mistakenly assumes law can be based on objective moral standards, here the thought is that liberalism wrongly assumes law can be neutral in the sense that it exists independent of morality. Thus, Catharine A. MacKinnon writes: "In Anglo-American jurisprudence, morals (value judgments) are deemed separable and separated from politics (power contests), and both from adjudication (interpretation). Neutrality, including judicial decision making that is dispassionate, impersonal, disinterested, and precedential, is considered desirable and descriptive. ... Government of laws, not of men, limits partiality with written constraints and tempers force with reasonable rule-following. ... Formally, the state is male in that objectivity is its norm. Objectivity is liberal legalism's conception of itself."[111] In making this charge, MacKinnon seems particularly to have in mind the Lochner Era and the conservative, free-market economic and philosophical views that accompanied it. And it is of course true that the Supreme Court sometimes argued that progressive labor regulations such as maximum hour and minimum wage provisions were illegitimate intrusions of "politics" into neutral "law."[112] Minimum wage laws, for instance, were described as "labor legislation" with the implication that the legislature had gone beyond the bounds of legitimate political debate and entered into the forbidden realm of economics. Yet it is wrong, the contractualist would insist, to equate all of "Anglo-American jurisprudence" with such positions, and especially democratic contractualism. Rather than denying the connections between politics and law, as originalism and democratic proceduralism tried to do by requiring judicial neutrality,[113] contractualism (along with utilitarianism) actually affirms, *with MacKinnon,* the impossibility of such judicial "neutrality." So not only does contractualism reject the substantive, political assumptions of free-market libertarianism, it also rejects the attempt to rest interpretive theory in general on a neutral, non-political foundation. It also rejects both original intent and democratic proceduralism, which claimed judges should themselves be neutral. Democratic contractualism thus agrees that law and political morality cannot be separated; but it denies that this separation excludes the female perspective. Indeed, in searching for laws that can be defended to all persons, regardless of gender, the contractualist both expresses the political character of law and at the same time attempts to insulate law from gender and other biases. That commitment to find a basis on which all can reasonably agree was one of the important reasons for the contractualist's insistence that the Constitution and laws be chosen under conditions in which people are unaware of morally irrelevant factors and thereby are forced to deliberate as free and independent equals in a Madisonian "temperate moment."

Another charge that may be brought by feminists is that contractualism is not gender-neutral since the idea of a universally accepted social contract and the notion of a shared political discourse both reflect the perspective of liberal, Western, and predominantly male culture and politics.[114] Far from being politically neutral, democratic contractualism depends instead on a commitment to familiar Western ideals like consent, democratic rule, and individual rights. To this charge, the contractualist must plead guilty. Though it does not rest on any particular moral ideal or vision of the good life, democratic contractualism is nonetheless a political theory, and it does indeed include consent, democracy, and rights among its ideals. Yet it should also be recalled that in considering different interpretive theories, we began with a practical problem of governing a widely diverse people whose visions of the good, religious ideals, and basic values often conflict—a problem that is not, presumably, going to solve itself. And assuming, further, that the Constitution is to include judicial review, conscientious judges must inevitably consider how they can best do their job, which means the interpretive questions we have been addressing cannot be avoided. The burden, it seems to me, has then shifted to the critic to provide a more attractive account of constitutional interpretation.

Having noted contractualism's political character, however, the critic might now seem to be on firmer ground in charging it with male bias. Relying on a theme that is familiar from the earlier discussion of CLS, it might now be argued that because of its roots in the social contract tradition, democratic contractualism assumes an "individualistic" and therefore unrealistic picture of human nature and social life.[115] In adopting that political vision, contractualism assumes that people are rational, self-interested, and wholly independent entities seeking agreement on the terms of a social contract. But, the argument concludes, this picture—of people disconnected from others and without the bonds of family and community—ignores just those features of human life and personality that many feminists argue is central to personal identity.[116]

Now in one sense, of course, the objector is correct: Democratic contractualism does hold that *for purposes of political debate and constitutional interpretation* we do well to think of ourselves as separate individuals with rights that can be pressed against others when interests and needs conflict. Questions of constitutional design and interpretation are best approached, says the contractualist, without assuming the same level of concern for fellow citizens as is expected among family members or even good friends. The contractualist does not claim, however, that this is an accurate picture of how persons understand themselves in their private lives, let alone that it is the correct picture of the person from a psychological or philosophical perspective.[117] Democratic contractualism offers a way to understand constitutional politics in a pluralistic democracy; it does not offer a conception of human nature.[118] The contractualist's claim is that when we reflect on political relationships among citizens, we can reasonably think of ourselves *for that purpose only* as separate individuals entitled to press various claims against each other but also sharing a commitment to identify a constitution and laws that all can reasonably accept.

Perhaps, however, instead of claiming that the contractualist's metaphysical conception of the self is mistakenly individualistic, the critic could argue that the last paragraph illustrates why the contractualist's vision of a *citizen* and of the bonds of citizenship is mistaken. By distinguishing the bonds of citizenship from familial and other ties, according to this criticism, the contractualist assumes it is reasonable to envision fellow citizens in these individualistic terms. Perhaps, however, that abstract picture of fellow citizens and of politics is mistaken or at least not universally correct.[119] Robin West, for example, claims that it is a distinctively male way of thinking of fellow citizens and the problem of politics.[120] Traditional "liberal legalism," she argues, reflects distinctively male political attitudes toward others by seeing them in Hobbesian terms, as threatening the freedom and lives of their fellows. Law therefore emphasizes individual rights *against* such interference of others from whom (males) are "essentially separated," as she puts it, and who are seen primarily as threats to each other. The charge would then be that contractualism reflects those same attitudes by envisioning others as potentially threatening and the social contract as a means for addressing that threat rather than seeing others in society as persons to whom we are essentially connected.

The contractualist has two responses to this. First, and most obviously, it is important to point out that being threatened by others or needing the law's protection is not a particularly male plight. Feminists do not condone assault and rape, for example, nor are they inclined to underestimate their impact on the lives of women.[121] All persons, regardless of gender, need protection of themselves and their property.

Second, democratic contractualism is not in fact Hobbesian: It does not see politics and the choice of a constitution as simply an agreement among individuals based on their private interests. The social contract is made in a temperate moment among political equals and in that way must be justified from everybody's perspective—including the weakest, most unfortunate, or least popular. It represents a constitutional commitment to governing a diverse citizenry based on principles that transcend differences and focus instead on shared interests and common moral ideals. In that sense, then, contractualism is far from individualistic and assumes instead strong bonds of community.[122] It demands of all citizens that they set aside information about their social class, race, gender, and natural talents in choosing the constitution and laws that are to govern their common society. Its picture of society is not the Hobbesian one of self-interested individuals accepting law based on mutual advantage but instead demands impartiality in the sense I have already described.[123] The terms of the social contract do not consist of the minimum price that each citizen must pay for others' willing cooperation but instead are motivated by the desire to find reasonable terms that can be defended to everybody viewed as free and independent equals. In that way, the contractualist seeks a middle ground between those who conceive of the bonds of citizenship on the model of the family and those who see government merely as a mutually beneficial agreement among individuals concerned to advance their own interests.[124]

Constitutional interpretation, I have argued, is inevitably a *political* act and is therefore always open to challenge and debate. Even originalist and proceduralist defenders of judicial neutrality and restraint cannot avoid the deeper political and moral commitments on which their theories rest. Conscientious judges must confront the political and moral questions embedded in constitutional interpretation. Democratic contractualism, I have argued, offers the most attractive conception of judicial review and constitutional interpretation now in the field.

Conclusion

The Preamble speaks of the Constitution as the creation of "we the people," but instead of the literal, originalist understanding of that phrase, democratic contractualism seeks willing social cooperation on reasonable terms. The Preamble expresses three other major commitments: to establish justice, to promote the general welfare, and to secure the blessings of liberty, while the Fourteenth Amendment added what we now see as perhaps the Constitution's deepest ideal: equality. Democratic contractualism attempts to weave these into a coherent whole, claiming that nobody is born the natural inferior of any other and that both the Constitution and the law must be defensible from the perspective of everybody, viewed as free and independent equals. Yet the specific terms of that social contract have not been, and indeed can never be, finally set; they are open to continuing debate and revision. Viewed that way, the Constitution is less a recipe for government than an aspiration. It set the nation on a course of unknown duration and undefined direction, leaving it for later generations to reform and, we may hope, to improve its institutions and practices.

Judicial review protects that constitutional vision by injecting a strikingly philosophical tenor into the political process. It is never enough, under the U.S. Constitution, to know the majority supports a law; laws must also be compatible with the limits imposed by the terms of the social contract. What those limits are is controversial, of course; it is an open and often disputed question just which rights should be respected as well as how they should be defined and shaped. But by raising these philosophical issues in the context of constitutional interpretation, judicial review helps realize the contractualist's ideal that those limits can be defended to all citizens viewed as free and independent equals.

We conclude, then, where we began—with a nation comprising diverse cultures, races, religions, and languages yet bound together under a common Constitution. Echoing Frederick Douglass's remarks I quoted at the beginning of the book, Abraham Lincoln described well the democratic contractualist's vision of a Constitution that doubly binds, uniting the nation under the ideal of equality as well as constraining legislative power in order to respect basic rights. Speaking on the eve of the Civil War, he expressed the hope that the Constitution—if it survived—might be viewed as a "maxim for free society," which, he went on, "should be familiar to all, and revered by all; constantly looked up to, constantly labored for, and even though never perfectly attained, constantly approximated, and thereby constantly spreading and deepening its influence and augmenting the happiness and value of life to all people of all colors everywhere."[125]

Notes

Introduction

1. For an excellent study of the historical and cultural roots of American constitutional thought and attitudes, see Michael Kammen, *A Machine That Would Go of Itself* (New York: Alfred A. Knopf, 1986).

2. William Manning, quoted in Kammen, *A Machine That Would Go of Itself* (1986) at xxiii.

3. For a discussion of the issue whether slavery was incompatible with the Constitution, see William M. Wiecek, *The Sources of Antislavery Constitutionalism in America, 1760–1848* (Ithaca: Cornell University Press, 1977).

4. Carl Bode, *The American Lyceum: Town Meeting of the Mind* (New York: Oxford University Press, 1956).

5. CBS Reports, "Mr. Justice Douglas," September 6, 1972.

6. Frederick Douglass, "The Constitution of the United States: Is It Pro-Slavery or Anti-Slavery?" (1860), in Philip Foner, ed., *The Life and Writings of Frederick Douglass* (New York: International Publishers Co., 1950) at 467.

7. Such controversies are at least a century old. James Bradley Thayer famously argued in 1893, for example, that federal courts should reject congressional enactments only if the law's unconstitutionality cannot reasonably be doubted. See James Bradley Thayer, "The Origin and Scope of the American Doctrine of Constitutional Law," 7 *Harvard Law Review* (1893).

8. Indeed, given the picture of constitutional theory I will defend, it would be quite surprising if the most attractive views were *not* familiar to the legal and political tradition.

Chapter 1

1. Judicial review of state law had been exercised prior to *Marbury v. Madison*. See, for example, *Ware v. Hylton*, 3 U.S. (3 Dall.) 199 (1796) along with the Judiciary Act of 1789 giving the Supreme Court appellate jurisdiction over federal issues decided initially in state courts. But federal judicial protection against state violation of individual rights such as religion, speech, and criminal due process did not become accepted political practice until this century and was based on the Fourteenth Amendment.

2. The Constitution does explicitly provide for the federal court to hear cases involving ambassadors, admiralty and maritime law, controversies between states, controversies between a state and a citizen of another state, and disputes between citizens of different states.

3. This impact has been felt largely in state law; the Court's exercise of judicial review has been more limited in the case of Congress.

4. In addition to *The Federalist Papers,* many other federalist writings supported adoption.

5. For a helpful discussion of the role of the anti-federalists, whose objections ranged far beyond the potential power of the judiciary, see Paul Finkelman, "Antifederalists: The Loyal Opposition and the American Constitution," 70 *Cornell Law Review* 182 (1984), and, of course, Herbert J. Storing, *What the Anti-Federalists Were For,* vol. I of *The Complete Anti-Federalist* (Chicago: University of Chicago Press, 1981).

6. Brutus, "Essays," in Herbert J. Storing, ed., *The Anti-Federalist: Writing by the Opponents of the Constitution* (Chicago: University of Chicago Press, 1985) at 163.

7. Brutus, "Essays," in Storing, ed., *The Anti-Federalist: Writing by the Opponents of the Constitution* (1985) at 165.

8. Max Farrand, ed., *Records of the Federal Convention of 1787,* vol. 1 (New Haven: Yale University Press, 1966) at 21.

9. Robert A. Rutland et al., eds., *Papers of James Madison,* vol. 11 (Charlottesville: University of Virginia Press, 1977) at 212.

10. Rutland et al., eds., *Papers of James Madison,* vol. 11 at 297.

11. Rutland et al., eds., *Papers of James Madison,* vol. 11 at 293.

12. Alexander Hamilton, "Federalist Number 78," in Clinton Rossiter, ed., *The Federalist Papers* (New York: New American Library, 1961) at 467.

13. Alexander Hamilton, "Federalist Number 78," in Rossiter, ed., *The Federalist Papers* (1961) at 467.

14. Gerald Gunther, *Constitutional Law,* 12th ed. (Westbury NY: The Foundation Press, 1985) at 15.

15. Edwin Corwin, Testimony before Congress on the 1937 Court-packing plan. Quoted in Leonard Levy, *Judicial Review and the Supreme Court* (New York: Harper & Row, 1967) at 8.

16. In fact, the commission at issue involved the position of justice of the peace for the District of Columbia.

17. Interestingly, the person who did not deliver it was John Marshall, who then was serving as secretary of state under President Adams.

18. *Marbury v. Madison,* 5 U.S. 137 (1803) at 163.

19. The relevant section of Section 13 of the Judiciary Act of 1789 reads as follows: "The Supreme Court shall ... have power to issue ... writs of mandamus, in cases warranted by the principles and usages of law, to any courts appointed, or persons holding office, under the authority of the United States."

20. In fact, after the ruling Marbury chose not to pursue his case in lower courts, where Marshall said he should have gone in the first place.

21. Judicial review of state legislation infringing the Bill of Rights came later, well after passage of the Fourteenth Amendment.

22. *Marbury v. Madison*, 5 U.S. 137 (1803) at 177.

23. *Marbury v. Madison*, 5 U.S. 137 (1803) at 177.

24. *Marbury v. Madison*, 5 U.S. 137 (1803) at 178.

25. *Marbury v. Madison*, 5 U.S. 137 (1803) at 180.

26. *Marbury v. Madison*, 5 U.S. 137 (1803) at 178.

27. *Marbury v. Madison*, 5 U.S. 137 (1803) at 177.

28. H.L.A. Hart makes a similar distinction the foundation of his conception of law. See H.L.A. Hart, "Law as the Union of Primary and Secondary Rules," in *The Concept of Law* (London: Oxford University Press, 1961).

29. *Eaken v. Raub*, 12 Sergeant & Rawle (PA.) 330 (1825).

30. *Eakin v. Raub*, 12 Sergeant & Rawle (PA.) 330 (1825) at 346–347.

31. *Eakin v. Raub*, 12 Sergeant & Rawle (PA.) 330 (1825) at 350–351.

32. That important claim—that constitutional interpreters should aim to read the document so that it is a reasonable attempt to achieve worthy objectives—is elaborated and defended later in this chapter.

33. I discuss the rule of law in greater detail in Chapter 3.

34. Richard S. Kay, "Adherence to the Original Intentions in Constitutional Adjudication: Three Objections and Responses," 82 *Northwestern University Law Review* 2 (1988), defends originalism on different grounds, claiming that it provides both clarity and stability. But those cannot constitute the philosophical grounding of originalism. If stability and clarity really were the only values on which the choice of an interpretive theory relies, as he suggests, then originalism would not be chosen since it is likely that the historians' understanding of the framers' intentions will change with the discovery of new documents or better understanding of those already known. Clarity and stability would recommend simply remaining with whatever interpretation has been provided in the past, whether consistent with the framers' intentions or not.

35. James Madison, "Federalist Number 39," in Rossiter, ed., *The Federalist Papers* (1961) at 240.

36. Originalism has been defended by various authors and judges, including Robert Bork, "Neutral Principles and Some First Amendment Problems," 47 *Indiana Law Journal* 1 (Fall 1971); William Rehnquist, "The Notion of a Living Constitution," 54 *Texas Law Review* 692 (1976); Raoul Berger, *Government by Judiciary: The Transformation of the Fourteenth Amendment* (Cambridge: Harvard University Press, 1977); Richard S. Kay, "Adherence to the Original Intentions in Constitutional Adjudication: Three Objections and Responses," 82 *Northwestern University Law Review* (1988) at 226; Edwin Meese III, "Construing the Constitution," 19 *University of California, Davis Law Review* 22 (1985); Gregory Bassham, *Original Intent and the Constitution: A Philosophical Study* (Lanham MA: Rowman and Littlefield, 1992).

37. Bork, "Neutral Principles and Some First Amendment Problems" at 10. Bork has reiterated essentially the same position described in his account of the confirmation hearing where he was rejected for the U.S. Supreme Court. See Robert H. Bork, *The Tempting of America: The Political Seduction of the Law* (New York: Free Press, 1990).

38. Rehnquist, "The Notion of a Living Constitution" (1976) at 704.

39. Rehnquist, "The Notion of a Living Constitution" (1976) at 704.

40. Rehnquist, "The Notion of a Living Constitution" (1976) at 705, quoting Oliver Wendell Holmes.

41. Rehnquist, "The Notion of a Living Constitution" (1976) at 705.

42. In later chapters I will consider other ways consent may be thought to lend legitimacy to the Constitution.

43. Alexander Hamilton, "Federalist Number 78," in Rossiter, ed., *The Federalist Papers* (1961) at 467.

44. *Rutherford v. M'Faddon,* Ohio Unreported Judicial Decisions (1807) at 71 and 73.

45. *Rutherford v. M'Faddon,* Ohio Unreported Judicial Decisions (1807) at 71.

46. J. Bayard, *Brief Exposition of the Constitution of the United States,* 2nd ed. (Philadelphia: Hogan-Thomson, 1834) at 123.

47. James Bradley Thayer, "The Origin and Scope of the American Doctrine of Constitutional Law" 7 *Harvard Law Review* (1893) at 549.

48. Thayer, "The Origin and Scope of the American Doctrine of Constitutional Law" (1893) at 550.

49. Bork, "Neutral Principles and Some First Amendment Problems" (1971) at 2.

50. Bork, "Neutral Principles and Some First Amendment Problems" (1971) at 3 (emphasis added).

51. Rehnquist, "The Notion of a Living Constitution" (1976) at 698.

52. Rehnquist, "The Notion of a Living Constitution" (1976) at 698 (emphasis added).

53. Bork, "Neutral Principles and Some First Amendment Problems" (1971) at 6 and 8.

54. For a helpful discussion of this distinction in the context of constitutional government, see Stephen Holmes, "Precommitment and the Paradox of Democracy," in Jon Elster and Rune Slagstad, eds., *Constitutionalism and Democracy* (Cambridge: Cambridge University Press, 1988) at 195.

55. Jon Elster, *Ulysses and the Sirens* (Cambridge: Cambridge University Press, 1984), discusses these issues in detail.

56. Alexander Hamilton, "Federalist Number 6," in Rossiter, ed., *The Federalist Papers* (1961) at 54–58.

57. For a discussion of the distinction between normal and constitutional politics, both theoretical and historical, see Bruce Ackerman, "The Storrs Lectures: Discovering the Constitution," 93 *Yale Law Journal* 1013 (1984).

58. Emphasis added; these contractualist origins of the U.S. Constitution can be interpreted in a different, non-originalist fashion as well, as I argue in Chapter 5.

59. Rehnquist, "The Notion of a Living Constitution" (1976) at 698.

60. Bork, "Neutral Principles and Some First Amendment Problems" (1971) at 8.

61. For a discussion of this view of contract law, see Charles Fried, *Contract as Promise* (Cambridge: Harvard University Press, 1981).

62. Letter from Thomas Jefferson to James Madison, September 6, 1789, *Writings of Thomas Jefferson,* vol. VII at 454–455.

63. Letter from Thomas Jefferson to James Madison, September 6, 1789, *Writings of Thomas Jefferson,* vol. VII at 459.

64. See for example James Madison's letter to Thomas Jefferson, February 4, 1790, in Gaillard Hunt, ed., *The Writings of James Madison* (New York: Putnam's Sons, 1904) at 437.

65. This example is from A. John Simmons, *Moral Principles and Political Obligations* (Princeton: Princeton University Press, 1979) at 79–83. What follows is indebted to his helpful discussion of these issues.

66. Henry Campbell Black, *Black's Law Dictionary,* 4th ed. (St. Paul MN: West Publishing Company, 1951) at 632, citing *Marshall v. Wilson,* Or., 154 P.2d 547, 551. Two types of estoppel are equitable, where *justice* forbids the assertion of rights, and legal, where *public policy* forbids the assertion of rights.

67. See Black, *Black's Law Dictionary* (1951) at 1039.

68. I leave aside here the further complication that it is not the people themselves but their elected representatives who must adopt any amendment and I thereby ignore the possibility that an amendment may fail despite having overwhelming popular support.

69. John Locke, *Second Treatise of Government,* ed. C. B. Macpherson (1689; reprint Indianapolis IN: Hackett Publishing Co., 1980) at Section 119 (emphasis added).

70. One of the most important exponents of this view is John Rawls, "Legal Obligation and the Duty of Fair Play," in Sidney Hook, ed., *Law and Philosophy* (New York: New York University Press, 1964).

71. Simmons seems to confuse these when he argues consent is "intentional," suggesting that an insincere person cannot actually consent to X while intending to do not-X. See Simmons, "Locke and the Failure of Tacit Consent," in *Moral Principles and Political Obligations* (1979) at 83–95.

72. Obligations grounded on "objective" tacit consent are not, however, absolute. Suppose, for example, that the card players discover in the rulebook a provision that blacks cannot play with whites and that one of the original players demands that the newcomer, who is black, relinquish her winnings based on *that* rule. It would be ludicrous to say she consented to that rule, just as slaves who participated actively in the legal system (to the extent they were allowed) can hardly be said to be obligated to obey the rules merely because they led others,

reasonably, to the erroneous conclusion that they would do so. Tacit consent therefore must assume that the system is not grossly unfair or unjust.

73. David Hume, "Of the Original Contract," in Alasdair MacIntyre, ed., *Hume's Ethical Writings* (London: Collier Macmillan, 1965) at 263.

74. For a valuable discussion of whether coercion should be understood as a psychological or as a moral idea, together with a defense of the moral account, see Alan Wertheimer, *Coercion* (Princeton NJ: Princeton University Press, 1987).

75. There are many discussions of these problems, and my discussion is especially indebted to the following: Paul Brest, "The Misconceived Quest for the Original Understanding," 60 *Boston University Law Review* 234 (1980); Ronald Dworkin, *A Matter of Principle* (Cambridge: Harvard University Press, 1985), chapter 2; Gregory Bassham, *Original Intent and the Constitution: A Philosophical Study* (1992); and Paul Finkelman, "The Constitution and the Intentions of the Framers: The Limits of Historical Analysis," 50 *University of Pittsburgh Law Review* 2 (1989).

76. See, for example, *Katz v. United States,* 389 U.S. 347 (1967).

77. Kay, "Adherence to Original Intentions in Constitutional Adjudication" (1988) at 246–247.

78. In fact, assuming (implausibly) that the ratifying body had the same intentions as people as a whole, the framers would presumably be limited first to those members of the body who actually voted to ratify, so that the intended meaning would then be found in the majority of that majority.

79. This distinction is discussed by Dworkin, *A Matter of Principle* (1985) at 44–45.

80. Originalists might deny the distinction, of course, claiming that all interpretations are equally reasonable. I discuss that skeptical claim in detail in Chapter 3.

81. See Leonard Levy, *The Legacy of Suppression: Freedom of Speech and the Press in Early American History* (New York: Harper Torchbook, 1963), and, more recently, Anthony Lewis, *Make No Law: The Sullivan Case and the First Amendment* (New York: Random House, 1991).

82. Berger, *Government by Judiciary: The Transformation of the Fourteenth Amendment* (1977), argues that members of Congress proposing the Fourteenth did not intend that it be used to abolish segregation.

83. Two especially helpful discussions of the framers' interpretive views, on which the following comments rely, are H. Jefferson Powell, "The Original Understanding of Original Intent," 98 *Harvard Law Review* 885 (1985) and Paul Finkelman, "The Constitution and the Intentions of the Framers: The Limits of Historical Analysis" (1989).

84. It might be argued, however, that the framers thought of these as technical terms and so felt it unnecessary to be more specific. That view is plausible, if at all, in only those cases, such as "due process of law," where reasonably wide legal agreement existed as to what the phrase meant. It is implausible, however, to make such a claim for other concepts where no settled body of legal opinion had

yet developed such as "freedom of speech," "establishment" and "free exercise" of religion, or "equal protection."

85. The following comments are not meant to prove that the framers were clear or unanimous in intending that later judges not follow originalism's recommendations, for plainly they were not. Kay, "Adherence to the Original Intentions" (1988) disputes these historical claims, as does Berger, *Government by Judiciary* (1977). The point, rather, is that some of the important framers who attended the convention took this position. Whether the majority of the ratifying body, let alone "the people" as a whole, felt that way seems an impossible question to answer since, as the following remarks suggest, framers differed among themselves and some even took a different position at different times.

86. H.C. Lodge, *The Works of Alexander Hamilton,* vol. 3 (New York: Putnam and Sons, 1882) at 463.

87. Letter to Thomas Ritchie in Hunt, ed., *The Writings of James Madison,* vol. 9 at 219. Madison did say, however, that "the only authoritative intentions were those of the people of the States, as expressed through the conventions which ratified the constitution" (Powell, "The Original Understanding of Original Intent" [1985] at 938–939, quoting 1830 letter of Madison). Just how the intentions of the people as a whole were to be determined, while ignoring those who attended the convention that wrote the Constitution, is unclear.

88. 2 *Annals of Congress* 1986 (1791), quoted in Finkelman, "The Constitution and the Intentions of the Framers: The Limits of Historical Analysis" (1989) at 362.

89. *McCulloch v. Maryland,* 17 U.S. 306 (1819) at 407.

90. *McCulloch v. Maryland,* 17 U.S. 306 (1819) at 433.

91. *Cong. Globe,* 39th Cong., 1st Sess., 2765 (1886) (emphasis added).

92. It is possible, of course, for the originalist to maintain at this point that the only intentions that are binding on current interpreters are ones concerning the meaning of the text and that their "meta-intentions" about how later generations should interpret it can be ignored. But then the originalist owes an explanation *why* we should follow those specific intentions while ignoring their interpretive ones.

93. The following argument is developed in detail by John Hart Ely, *Democracy and Distrust* (Cambridge: Harvard University Press, 1980) at 34–41.

94. See for example Hunt, ed., *The Writings of James Madison,* vol. 5 at 271–272.

95. This argument has not gone uncriticized, however. Kay, for example, argues that the fact the Ninth Amendment speaks only of rights that are "retained" by the people is incompatible with the view that it was originally meant to "create" ones that were not specifically intended. Kay does admit, however, that the framers may have thought of "natural rights" as among those that already existed and so deserved protection under the Ninth Amendment (Kay, "Adherence to the Original Intentions" [1988] at 270). How that can be made compatible with original intent is unexplained.

96. The view of legal interpretation that I now describe, traced to Madison, Marshall, and Wilson, is also similar to Dworkin's. That should not be surprising since, as Dworkin himself emphasizes, his project is in part to describe the practice of common law interpretation. See, especially, "How Law Is Like Literature," in *A Matter of Principle* (1985) and *Law's Empire* (Cambridge: Harvard University Press, 1986).

97. See for example Justice Brandeis's concurring opinion in *Whitney v. California*, 274 U.S. 357 (1927).

98. See for example Justice Holmes's dissenting opinion in *Abrams v. United States*, 250 U.S. 616 (1919).

99. James Madison, "Federalist Number 40," in Rossiter, ed., *The Federalist Papers* (1961) at 248.

100. *McCulloch v. Maryland*, 17 U.S. 306 (1819) at 415 (emphasis added).

101. *McCulloch v. Maryland*, 17 U.S. 306 (1819) at 415.

102. *McCulloch v. Maryland*, 17 U.S. 306 (1819) at 408.

103. *McCulloch v. Maryland*, 17 U.S. 306 (1819) at 433 (emphasis added).

104. Robert Green McCloskey, ed., *The Works of James Wilson*, vol. 1 (Cambridge: Harvard University Press, 1967) at 183.

Chapter 2

1. Robert Bork, "Neutral Principles and Some First Amendment Problems" 47 *Indiana Law Review* 1 (Fall 1971) at 6.

2. Prominent among these authors are Joseph A. Schumpeter, *Capitalism, Socialism, and Democracy*, 3rd ed. (New York: Harper and Row, 1950), and Robert Dahl, *A Preface to Democratic Theory* (Chicago: University of Chicago Press, 1956).

3. *Kramer v. Union Free School District*, 395 U.S. 621 (1969), holding that the vote on school district elections cannot be limited to property owners and parents.

4. *Lassiter v. Northhampton County Board of Election*, 360 U.S. 45 (1959), holding that literacy requirements are compatible with the Fourteenth Amendment's equal protection clause. The Voting Rights Act of 1965, however, requires that nobody who has completed the sixth grade may be denied the right to vote.

5. *Reynolds v. Sims*, 377 U.S. 533 (1964), holding that the Fourteenth Amendment requires that seats in both houses of state legislatures be apportioned on the basis of population with all votes equally weighted.

6. *City of Mobile v. Bolden*, 446 U.S. 55 (1980), holding that at large city elections do not unconstitutionally dilute the voting power of blacks.

7. *Buckley v. Valeo*, 424 U.S. 1 (1976), holding that freedom of speech means Congress may limit the contributions made to candidates but may not limit a candidate's expenditures.

8. *United States v. Carolene Products*, 304 U.S. 144 (1938).

9. *Lochner v. New York*, 198 U.S. 45 (1905).

10. *Adkins v. Children's Hospital*, 261 U.S. 525 (1923).

11. *Coppage v. Kansas*, 236 U.S. 1 (1915).

12. 304 U.S. 144 (1938) at 152–153 (emphasis added).

13. In Footnote 4 Justice Stone described prejudice as a second defect in the democratic process. That issue is addressed in the next section.

14. The most important book defending this approach, to which my discussion is indebted, is John Hart Ely, *Democracy and Distrust* (Cambridge: Harvard University Press, 1980).

15. *Carrington v. Rash*, 380 U.S. 89 (1965).

16. *Dunn v. Blumstein*, 405 U.S. 330 (1972).

17. *Kramer v. Union Free School District*, 395 U.S. 621 (1969).

18. *Kramer v. Union Free School District*, 395 U.S. 621 (1969) at 647–648.

19. *Gomillon v. Lightfoot*, 364 U.S. 339 (1960).

20. *Wesberry v. Sanders*, 376 U.S. 1 (1964) at 8.

21. *Wesberry v. Sanders*, 376 U.S. 1 (1964) at 17.

22. *Reynolds v. Simms*, 377 U.S. 533 (1964).

23. *Sailors v. Board of Education*, 387 U.S. 105 (1967).

24. *Dusch v. Davis*, 387 U.S. 112 (1967).

25. *Avery v. Midland County*, 390 U.S. 474 (1968) at 486.

26. *Brandenburg v. Ohio*, 395 U.S. 444 (1969).

27. New York Times *v. Sullivan*, 376 U.S. 254 (1964).

28. Of all the cases heard before his Court, Chief Justice Earl Warren regarded voting apportionment as most important.

29. These distinctions are taken from John Rawls, *A Theory of Justice* (Cambridge: Harvard University Press, 1971) at 85–86.

30. It could be argued that a competitive market, and perhaps also democratic processes modeled on competitive markets, exemplifies *perfect* procedural justice. There is an independent test of justice—laws that mirror the will of the people— and properly functioning democratic processes assure that this outcome is achieved. I discuss these and related issues in Chapter 4, when weighing utilitarianism and its relationship with economics.

31. See for example John Stuart Mill, *Considerations on Representative Government* (Indianapolis: Bobbs-Merrill, 1958) at 15 and 24–26.

32. Rawls, *A Theory of Justice* (1971) at 356–362.

33. Schumpeter, *Capitalism, Socialism and Democracy* (1950).

34. Carole Pateman, *Participation and Democratic Theory* (Cambridge: Cambridge University Press, 1970).

35. John Stuart Mill, "Of the Extension of the Suffrage," in *Considerations on Representative Government* (1861).

36. Democratic proceduralism's main defender, John Ely, further confirms this by arguing against any form of judicial activism that would allow judges to appeal to "moral reasoning" or to "natural rights." See Ely, *Democracy and Distrust* (1980) at 48–54 and 56–60.

37. For a similar point, see Peter Singer, *Democracy and Disobedience* (Oxford: Oxford University Press, 1973).

38. See for example Carl Cohen, "The Justification of Democracy," in *The Monist*, vol. 55, no. 1 (January 1971).

39. The institution of slavery clearly illustrates how failing to allow people the opportunity to participate in the lawmaking process is incompatible with the ideal of equality. It is sometimes said that slavery was wrong because it failed to treat slaves as "persons." In fact, however, American slavery explicitly *acknowledged* the humanity of slaves. The three-fifths compromise (Article I, Section 2), for instance, sets the size of congressional districts based on the number of free persons plus "three-fifths of all other *persons*." But although slavery did not assume slaves were only "three-fifths persons," it *did* put them in the status of being non-citizens, denying them what the Warren Court later termed, in *Wesberry v. Sanders,* 376 U.S. 1 (1964), the "most precious" of all rights.

40. I discuss this important Lockean suggestion and its relationship to constitutional interpretation in the last chapter.

41. John Locke, *Second Treatise of Government,* ed. C. B. Macpherson (1689; reprint Indianapolis IN: Hackett Publishing Co., 1980) at section 375 (emphasis in original).

42. An especially good discussion of these issues is Brian Barry, "Is Democracy Special?" in Peter Laslett and James Fishkin, eds., *Philosophy, Politics and Society,* 5th series (New Haven: Yale University Press, 1979).

43. James Madison, "Remarks on Mr. Jefferson's Draught of a Constitution" sent to J. Brown (ca. October 15, 1788) in Gaillard Hunt, ed., *The Writings of James Madison* (New York: Putnam's Sons, 1904), vol. V at 286.

44. Letter from James Madison to Thomas Jefferson, October 17, 1788, in Hunt, ed., *The Writings of James Madison,* (1904) vol. V at 272.

45. James Madison, "Federalist Number 48," in Clinton Rossiter, ed. *The Federalist Papers* (New York: New American Library, 1961) at 310–311, quoting Jefferson with approval (emphasis in original).

46. James Madison, "Federalist Number 51," in Rossiter, ed., *The Federalist Papers* (1961) at 321.

47. For a more extended discussion of the philosophical assumptions behind the original constitution, see John Arthur, *The Unfinished Constitution* (Belmont CA: Wadsworth Publishing Co., 1989).

48. John Hart Ely makes this argument. See Ely, *Democracy and Distrust* (1980), chapter 4.

49. It might be argued that political battles over which religion to establish could ultimately endanger the democratic process itself by distracting it from its more important work, or perhaps even lead to dangerous conflict. Neither of those, however, seems important enough standing alone to explain the primacy of freedom of religion. For an insightful discussion of these questions, see Stephen Holmes, "Gag Rules or the Politics of Omission," in Jon Elster and Rune Slagstad, eds., *Constitutionalism and Democracy* (Cambridge: Cambridge University Press, 1988) at 19.

50. Important amendments protecting those accused of crimes are "procedural" in the judicial sense of the term, though they have little to do with *democratic* procedures.

51. One of proceduralism's most ardent defenders, John Ely, rejects the political interpretation of the First Amendment in favor of an approach that protects all forms of speech except those that fall within a few, selected categories. But in doing so he opens himself up to the charge that he has abandoned proceduralism's commitment that judges avoid substantive value commitments, for there seems to be no basis other than the value of the speech (or lack of it) on which judges can rest the decision that obscenity, for example, is unprotected though art and science are protected. See Ely, *Democracy and Distrust* (1980) at 105–116.

52. The most systematic discussion of these issues is Ronald Dworkin, *Law's Empire* (Cambridge: Harvard University Press, 1986).

53. See for example Herbert Wechsler, "Toward Neutral Principles in Constitutional Law," 73 *Harvard Law Review* 1 (1959).

54. *U.S. v. Carolene Products,* 304 U.S. 144 (1938) at footnote 4.

55. *Plessy v. Ferguson,* 163 U.S. 537 (1896).

56. *United States v. Reese,* 92 U.S. 214 (1875).

57. *Korematsu v. United States,* 323 U.S. 214 (1944).

58. *Brown v. Board of Education,* 347 U.S. 483 (1954).

59. *Loving v. Virginia,* 388 U.S. 1 (1967).

60. *Reed v. Reed,* 404 U.S. 71 (1971) was the first Supreme Court decision overturning a gender-based classification on equal protection grounds.

61. *City of Cleburne v. Cleburne Living Center,* 473 U.S. 432 (1985).

62. *Levy v. Louisiana,* 391 U.S. 68 (1968).

63. *Nyquist v. Mauclet,* 432 U.S. 1 (1977).

64. As John Ely argues. See *Democracy and Distrust* (1980), Chapter 6.

65. For an extended discussion of these questions, on which my own partly rests, see Bruce Ackerman, "Beyond Carolene Products," 98 *Harvard Law Review* 713 (1985).

66. Although the famous case upholding Georgia's prohibition of sodomy, *Bowers v. Hardwick,* 478 U.S. 186 (1986), was argued and decided on the basis of the right to privacy, there is no reason it cannot be analyzed in terms of equal protection. Indeed, I have argued, the argument is at least as strong that Georgia's law was unconstitutional if placed in that latter context. See John Arthur, "Privacy and the Constitution," in John Arthur and William H. Shaw, eds., *Social and Political Philosophy* (Englewood Cliffs NJ: Prentice-Hall, 1992).

67. I assume here there is no good public health argument for banning it. For a defense of that claim, see Arthur, *The Unfinished Constitution* (1989) at 186–191.

68. This argument is suggested in Ely, *Democracy and Distrust* (1980), footnote 92 at 255–256. See also John Hart Ely, "The Wages of Crying Wolf: A Comment on *Roe v. Wade,*" 82 *Yale Law Journal* 920 (1973).

69. See for example Lani Guinier, "Keeping the Faith: Black Voters in the Post-Reagan Era," 24 *Harvard Civil Rights/Civil Liberties Law Review* 393 (1989), and

"No Two Seats: The Elusive Quest for Political Equality," 77 *Virginia Law Review* 8, 1413 (November 1991).

70. It is important to note that it is only the *opportunity* to influence political outcomes that strong proceduralism demands. If people choose not to exercise that opportunity and refuse to vote or attend political meetings because they take no interest in democratic politics, it would not mean the process is unfair or the political process is defective.

71. In *San Antonio School District v. Rodriguez*, 411 U.S. 1 (1973), the Supreme Court considered but rejected this argument.

72. *Brown v. Board of Education of Topeka*, 347 U.S. 483 (1954). Though *Brown* rejected segregated educational facilities on grounds that they are inherently unequal, rather than on the political grounds I am envisioning here, the Court did stress the impact of segregation on black children's self-esteem.

73. I will argue in the last chapter, however, that important insights of proceduralism can be incorporated into a contractualist understanding of democratic government, thereby providing a more attractive conception of judicial review and constitutional interpretation than either the strong or standard versions of proceduralism provides alone.

74. Just what those grounds might be will be considered in the following chapters. I will discuss further the twin ideals of fairness and equality, arguing that if properly understood they lead beyond democratic proceduralism to a different conception of constitutional democracy and constitutional interpretation. Democratic procedures are important, I will argue, though for different reasons than the ones advanced here, so that we can accommodate the virtues of democratic government while avoiding the problems faced by proceduralism.

Chapter 3

1. I will speak interchangeably of "human" or "moral" rights throughout, in order to distinguish that type from both legal and conventional rights. Sometimes human rights are described as "pre-political" in order to emphasize the fact that if they exist it is not merely because they are recognized in law or in society's social moral code. It is therefore an interesting and complex question, to be taken up shortly, whether human rights exist.

2. In fact, of course, CLS goes beyond this general, theoretical point and offers a more specific, leftist political program. As we will see, however, there is nothing in CLS's interpretive theory that requires its specific political conclusions. Those on the political right, although rejecting the CLS political program, might nonetheless agree with its rights skepticism, its skepticism about the power of legal argument, and its emphasis on judicial pragmatism.

3. It is important that philosophers not be misled by the term "realism" here, for its meaning in this context is opposed in many ways to standard philosophical usage. Legal realists were not realists in the philosophical sense of believing in the existence of scientific and other theoretical entities, or in the truth of scientific

and moral propositions. The idea here is closer to the effort to be "realistic" about how the law actually works by looking past the rhetoric of judges to describe the wide power judges are in fact able to exercise when interpreting both statutes and the Constitution.

4. For reasons that will become apparent, the disputes between formalists and realists were in the background of Franklin Roosevelt's frustration with Supreme Court justices who protected liberty of contract by overturning many of the economic regulations proposed by the New Deal. The case that has come to symbolize this formalistic, pro-market vision of law is a case decided in 1905, *Lochner v. New York*, 198 U.S. 45. Roosevelt's threat to pack the Court, combined with the opportunity to replace many of the older justices, meant that the Court by the end of his terms included many judges sympathetic to the legal realists.

5. Whether or not anybody ever actually held this formalist position is questionable. Those typically cited are Christopher Columbus Langdell, *Cases on Law and Contracts* (Boston: Little, Brown & Co., 1871), preface to 1st ed.; David Dudley Field, "Magnitude and Importance of Legal Science," in Sprague, ed., *Speeches, Arguments and Miscellaneous Papers of David Dudley Field* (New York: Titus, Manson Co., 1884) at 515; and Joseph H. Beale, *A Treatise on the Conflict of Laws* (New York: Baker Voorhis, 1935), sections 3 and 4.

6. Among the most unqualified defenders of legal realism is Jerome Frank, *Law and the Modern Mind* (1930; reprint, New York: Doubleday & Co., 1963). See also Karl Llewellyn, "Some Realism About Realism," 44 *Harvard Law Review* (June 1931); Felix Cohen, "Transcendental Nonsense and the Functional Approach," 25 *Columbia Law Review* (June 1935); and Lon Fuller, "American Legal Realism" 82 *University of Pennsylvania Law Review* (1934).

7. Frank, *Law and the Modern Mind* (1930) at 135.

8. Not all legal realists took Frank's extreme position. Karl Llewellyn, for example, wrote somewhat obscurely that although laws do not have "absolutely binding" force they nonetheless do "guide" judges even if they cannot "control" them. Karl Llewellyn, "Law and the Modern Mind: A Symposium," 31 *Columbia Law Review* (1931) at 90.

9. Bruce A. Ackerman, *Reconstructing American Law* (Cambridge: Harvard University Press, 1984) at 19.

10. David Kairys, "Legal Reasoning," in David Kairys, ed., *The Politics of Law* (New York: Pantheon Books, 1982) at 15.

11. Clare Dalton, "An Essay in the Deconstruction of Contract Doctrine," 94 *Yale Law Journal* (1985) at 1002.

12. Mark Tushnet, *Red, White and Blue: A Critical Analysis of Constitutional Law* (Cambridge: Harvard University Press, 1988) at 191–192.

13. Stanley Fish, "Almost Pragmatism," in Michael Brint and William Weaver, eds., *Pragmatism in Law and Society* (Boulder CO: Westview Press, 1991) at 76.

14. Fish, "Almost Pragmatism," in Brint and Weaver, *Pragmatism in Law and Society* (1991) at 77.

15. Joseph Hutcheson, "The Judgment Intuitive: The Function of the 'Hunch' in Judicial Decision," 14 *Cornell Law Quarterly* 274 (1929) at 285.

16. Frank, *Law and the Modern Mind* (1930) at 121.

17. For a helpful collection of articles exploring both sides of the dispute about pragmatism, see Brint and Weaver, *Pragmatism in Law and Society* (1991).

18. So we see people firmly anchored on the political right, like Richard Posner, declaring himself a pragmatist as well as the much more leftist members of CLS. See especially Chapter 12 of Richard A. Posner, *The Problems of Jurisprudence* (Cambridge: Harvard University Press, 1990), where the author explicitly identifies himself as a pragmatist as well as Chapter 6 in which he argues that law's inevitably ideological content precludes the possibility of a right or best legal answer.

19. Tushnet, *Red, White and Blue: A Critical Analysis of Constitutional Law* (1988) Chapters 4, 7, and conclusion.

20. It is important, however, not to confuse the anti-theoretical, pragmatic position of CLS with the utilitarian theory discussed in the next chapter. Although both are forward-looking and consequentialist, utilitarians are not skeptical about the possibility of interpretation and do not deny the possibility of constitutional theory based on an account of moral rights. Instead, as we will see, utilitarians offer their own conception of how the Constitution can be understood and extended in order to make it internally coherent and politically attractive.

21. Joseph Singer, "The Player and the Cards: Nihilism and Legal Theory," 94 *Yale Law Journal* (1984) at 13.

22. Duncan Kennedy, "Form and Substance in Private Law Adjudication," 89 *Harvard Law Review* 1685 (1976).

23. Roberto Unger, "The Critical Legal Studies Movement," 96 *Harvard Law Review* (1983) at 571.

24. The same claim is made in a recent book on constitutional law by two scholars not normally associated with CLS. The error of "hyper-integration," according to Lawrence H. Tribe and Michael C. Dorf, occurs when interpreters ignore the fact that the document contains "distinct parts" that were added at different times, favored and opposed by "greatly disparate groups" and so "reflect quite distinct, and often radically incompatible, premises." Lawrence H. Tribe and Michael C. Dorf, *On Reading the Constitution* (Cambridge: Harvard University Press, 1991) at 20.

25. David Kairys, "Introduction," in Kairys, ed., *The Politics of Law* (1982) at 6.

26. See Ronald Dworkin, "Integrity in Law" in *Law's Empire* (Cambridge: Harvard University Press, 1986).

27. The possibility of legal coherence might be increased further if we could show not just that legal incoherence is *thought* to be a political defect but also that it in fact *is* a defect. I take up that question shortly, asking whether the rule of law really is a worthy political ideal.

28. John Locke, *Second Treatise of Government*, ed. C. B. Macpherson (1689; reprint Indianapolis IN: Hackett Publishing Co., 1980) at 15.

29. Friedrich Hayek, *The Road to Serfdom* (Chicago: University of Chicago Press, 1944) at 72.

30. John Rawls, *A Theory of Justice* (Cambridge: Harvard University Press, 1971) at 235.

31. By saying laws are rules or principles that are addressed to citizens, I mean to avoid familiar disputes about whether they include principles that cannot be equated with rules, as well as whether they are commands of the sovereign as Hobbes and others have argued.

32. As described below, no legal system can overcome all indeterminacy; but neither, I am suggesting, can it fall too far short of the rule of law without losing its character as a system of *law*.

33. For a helpful discussion of these and other ways a system may fail to achieve the status of law, see Lon Fuller, *The Morality of Law* (New Haven: Yale University Press, 1964) at 33–41. Fuller's list is best seen, I think, as a slightly longer and more precise conception of the rule of law.

34. One of the most explicit, detailed discussions of the CLS critique of rights is found in Mark Tushnet, "An Essay on Rights," 62 *Texas Law Review* 1393 (1984).

35. 410 U.S. 113 (1973).

36. *Planned Parenthood of Southeastern Pennsylvania v. Casey*, 112 S.Ct. 2791 (1992).

37. Mark Kelman, *A Guide to Critical Legal Studies* (Cambridge: Harvard University Press, 1987) at 289.

38. See Wesley Newcomb Hohfeld, *Fundamental Legal Conceptions* (1919; reprint New Haven: Yale University Press, 1964).

39. Although rights imply duties, the converse may not be true; one may have a duty without it being the case that another has a corresponding right. Thus, for example, we may have a duty to give to charity without it being true that any particular individual has the *right* to receive the help. Similarly, it might be claimed, we have moral duties to avoid cruelty to animals that, although genuine, do not imply the animals have moral rights.

40. Notice an interesting difference between legal rights and conventional moral rights: Legal rights impose duties on officials as well as individuals, while conventional moral rights do not necessarily impose duties on third parties, such as to get involved to see that people are not lied to.

41. Moral rights thus presuppose, if not that there is a moral "fact of the matter," at least that not all moral views are equally well justified. I take it that, at least before people come in contact with much philosophy, we assume that is true. I will, however, take up these issues in the last section of this chapter.

42. The fact that a person has a moral right provides a reason for convention and law to impose the appropriate duties, though in the case of law there may be overriding reasons not to do so. The practical and other costs of legally enforcing people's moral right not to be lied to, for example, may be sufficiently great to outweigh whatever benefits could be gotten by using the law's power in that way.

43. This should be understood with the caveat that there are no practical or other reasons that outweigh the officials' duties in this case. Such exceptions occur, as described above, when the right is relatively weak and unimportant and the practical or moral costs of enforcement are significant.

44. Just what those grounds might be must await the next two chapters, though it should at least be clear that this conception of moral rights leaves open how such an argument should go. That there is a substantive moral basis for claiming law should respect a right is central to the thinking of those who defend moral rights; the nature of that justification, however, is controversial.

45. Strictly speaking, of course, all we can say is that having the moral right involves being *justified,* which is not the same as being right. Nevertheless, presumably being justified is at least related to truth, so that although it is not certain she is right it is at least more likely she is by virtue of the fact she rather than law and convention has the sounder position.

46. *Scott v. Sanford,* 60 U.S. 393 (1857).

47. In fact, there is a lively debate within CLS about rights discourse. See, for example, Frances Olsen, "Statutory Rape: A Feminist Critique of Rights Analysis," 63 *Texas Law Review* 387 (1984); A. Vallimore, "The Left's Problem With Rights," 9 *Legal Studies Forum* 39 (1985); and Patricia Williams, "Alchemical Notes: Reconstructed Ideals from Deconstructed Rights," 22 *Harvard Civil Rights/Civil Liberties Law Review* 401 (1987).

48. Many people have taken this position, both within CLS as well as outside it. See, for example, Kelman, *A Guide to Critical Legal Studies* (1987) at 284, suggesting that "rights consciousness itself is suspect" rather than simply the "reactionary content" of particular rights.

49. Peter Gabel, "The Phenomenology of Rights-Consciousness and the Pact of the Withdrawn Selves," 62 *Texas Law Review* 1563 (1984) at 1577. See also Frances Olsen, "Statutory Rape: A Feminist Critique of Rights Analyses," 94 *Texas Law Review* 387 (1984).

50. Locke's view is that God has given mankind the power of reason, and with it the power to see what reason dictates and thereby what God wills. Indeed, Locke stressed, the dictates of reason and the commands of God are identical. See for example Locke, *Second Treatise of Government,* section 6 at 311 and section 56 at 347.

51. Rehnquist, "The Notion of a Living Constitution" (1976) at 705 (quoting Oliver Wendell Holmes).

52. It has been argued, most notably by John Mackie, that people suffer from widespread, deep confusion about morality. John Mackie, *Morality: Inventing Right and Wrong* (New York: Penguin Books, 1977). Absent persuasive arguments on its behalf, however, this sort of deep error theory seems unpersuasive. Aware of that burden, Mackie argues that the vast amount of disagreement noted among different societies and the "queerness" of moral properties both support his error thesis. For a response to Mackie, see David O. Brink, "A Critique of Ethical Skepticism," 62 *Australasian Journal of Philosophy* 2 (1984) at 111–125.

53. It is also worth noting that scientists, too, sometimes hold to theories out of personal conviction, personal commitment, or personal interest. In that vein, see Thomas Kuhn, "The Response to Crisis," in *The Structure of Scientific Revolutions*, 2nd ed. (Chicago: University of Chicago Press, 1970).

54. It is easy, however, to overlook the difficulties facing those who assume the objective character of common sense or science. The claim that "the book in front of me is red" may be thought an objectively true statement, if ever there was one. But viewed as a swirl of subatomic particles the book's redness seems to have more to do with "subjective" experience than scientific fact. So what does the "objective" statement "The book is red" finally amount to? That "normal" humans who are not colorblind have the "subjective" experience of redness when looking at it under "normal" light? And what about subatomic particles themselves? Are statements that they exist also true? Such claims make sense within certain forms of discourse—in this case the theories of modern physics—just as the statement that the book exists belongs in another, very different discourse. The language of physics is not unchanging, after all, and whether one looks for witches or epilepsy has much to do with the theory one starts out with. And of course there is a well-known dispute within philosophy of science between realists who see scientific theories as at least potentially discovering what actually constitutes the basic "furniture of the universe" and instrumentalists who claim scientific theories are nothing more than useful devices for making important predictions and accomplishing other useful tasks.

55. David Hume, "Enquiry Concerning the Principles of Morals" (1751) in P. Nidditch, ed., *Hume's Enquiries* (Oxford: Oxford University Press, 1975) at 272.

56. See, for example, Roderick Firth, "Ethical Absolutism and the Ideal Observer," 12 *Philosophy and Phenomenological Research* (1952) at 317–345. I am also indebted to Richard Brandt, "The Justification of Ethical Beliefs," in *Ethical Theory* (Englewood Cliffs NJ: Prentice-Hall, 1959).

57. I will explore these questions in more detail in the final chapter, where I consider how notions of impartiality and rationality can be brought to bear on constitutional theory via the Madisonian notion of a social contract that would be agreed upon by free and equal persons deliberating in a "temperate moment."

58. Firth, "Ethical Absolutism and the Ideal Observer" (1952).

59. The exact nature of the connection between attitudes of a completely impartial, rational, and well-informed observer, on one hand, and moral truth, on the other, is not clear. "Torture is wrong" and "Torture would be disapproved of by an impartial, rational, well-informed person" seem not to mean exactly the same thing, since people who utter the former statement may know nothing of the ideal observer theory. (It does seem to me, however, that the two expressions are at least reasonably close in meaning.) An alternative to the claim that the two expressions mean the same could be that being wrong and being disapproved of by an ideally informed, rational, and impartial observer is analogous to the relationship between something being water and its being H_2O molecules. I do not

believe, however, that anything I have said or will say in the following chapters hangs on this question.

60. Though I do not make it here, the implicit distinction between primary and secondary qualities is controversial, of course; however, I do not think anything I have said relies on it. It has seemed to some that colors, understood as dispositions to cause certain phenomenological experiences in people with certain kinds of brains and other attributes, are no less properties of the object than weight or shape (which also can be thought of as dispositions to cause other sorts of experiences). Despite that, however, it does seem to be the case that secondary properties are mediated by processes such as light reflection in ways that the sensations of shape or weight are not mediated. But whatever the problems the distinction faces if pressed to the end, thinking of colors this way may help explain the ideal observer theory.

61. Much more, of course, would need to be said to fill in the ideal observer account in ways that help our understanding of judicial review and constitutional interpretation. I will discuss how that might be done in the following chapters.

Chapter 4

1. I will use the terms "welfare," general or common "good," and "utility" interchangeably, leaving discussion of different accounts of what is involved for a later section.

2. I thus focus here only on utilitarianism viewed as a *legal* theory, not as a complete account of the moral. Most utilitarians, of course, have extended their utilitarianism beyond the legal and political, but whether that can be successfully accomplished is beyond the scope of this book.

3. In that sense utilitarianism resembles pragmatism, though as I have argued it offers itself as a constitutional theory in competition with the others (albeit it is one that grounds politics in the future) rather than rejecting the possibility of theory altogether as pragmatism does.

4. Another defense of utilitarianism, which I will not discuss, argues that the logic of moral language and argument requires somebody who makes a moral judgment to "prescribe" that action "universally" as the correct decision for all persons in similar circumstances. But then, it is argued, we are led to utilitarianism since universal prescriptions demand we give equal weight to the happiness of all. For an extended discussion of this version of utilitarianism, see R.M. Hare, *Freedom and Reason* (Oxford: Oxford University Press, 1963).

5. See for example James Rachels, *Created from Animals* (New York: Oxford University Press, 1990) at 158–159.

6. See Richard Brandt, *A Theory of the Good and the Right* (Oxford: Oxford University Press, 1979) at 138–148.

7. See for example J.J.C. Smart, "An Outline of a System of Utilitarian Ethics," in J.J.C. Smart and Bernard Williams, *Utilitarianism For and Against* (Cambridge: Cambridge University Press, 1963).

8. T.M. Scanlon, "Contractualism and Utilitarianism," in Amartya Sen and Bernard Williams, eds., *Utilitarianism and Beyond* (New York: Cambridge University Press, 1982).

9. Other accounts of the foundation of utilitarianism have much in common with the contractualist position described in the next chapter. That mixed view, though interesting, seems to me to overlook what has historically been the driving force behind utilitarianism—the thought that individual well being and sympathy are at the foundation of morality rather than the social contract.

10. Scanlon, "Contractualism and Utilitarianism" (1982) at 115–116.

11. I discuss in the next chapter the possibility that people should be assumed to be ignorant of who they are. Though this is not the same as mistakenly believing they are somebody else, that approach is still contrary to the assumption of full information usually associated with the ideal observer. *Why* it makes sense to alter traditional ideal observer theory in that way will be considered in detail.

12. Richard Brandt makes this point; see *A Theory of the Good and the Right* (1979) at 226–228.

13. So because I understand utilitarianism to rest at its most fundamental level on sympathy rather than equality, it is committed to the view that the morally right is to be understood in terms of natural states of affairs in the world. Realization of those states is therefore the ultimate standard, not equality or equal consideration. Others, however, take the second, equality based, approach. Prominent among these is Peter Singer, *Practical Ethics* (Cambridge: Cambridge University Press, 1979) at 12–23; and John Harsanyi, *Essays on Ethics, Social Behavior and Scientific Explanation* (Dordrecht: Reidel Pub. Co., 1976) at 13–20. That latter view, however, is based on a deeper commitment to equality and is not, I think, the position associated with classical utilitarians. For a discussion of these issues, see John Rawls, *A Theory of Justice* (Cambridge: Harvard University Press, 1971) at 24–27; and Bernard Williams, *Moral Luck* (Cambridge: Cambridge University Press, 1981) at 4.

14. The example is suggested by Robert Nozick's discussion of an "experience machine" in *Anarchy, State, and Utopia* (New York: Basic Books, 1974). I differ with Nozick, however, because as I indicate once the distinction between pleasant experiences and enjoyable ones is kept in mind the experience theorist has a response that addresses his objection.

15. In fact, what the scientist being interviewed described were two such suits, one on a business man traveling away from home and the other available for his wife to wear. Then, he suggested, the two could simulate, via a phone line linking themselves to a common computer, whatever experiences they wished to have together even though they are miles apart. It would be as if they were together in the same room; nothing about the experience in the virtual reality machine would be distinguishable from experiences they could actually have.

16. I address the economic theory in the context of utilitarianism for two reasons. First, it is a matter of historical fact that Adam Smith and other important figures in the study of markets and their advantages were philosophical utilitari-

ans. I also believe that the best defense of markets rests on their ability to increase society's wealth and, thereby, increase social welfare. Others, however, would defend the free market on the basis of individual liberty. In the next chapter I take up social contract theory and with it the limits on free exchange.

17. This also assumes, of course, that people are rational. This means really two things: that people want to promote their own welfare and that they are effective in doing so. If one of the traders is a young child, for example, then all utility bets are off.

18. See Nicholas Kaldor, "Welfare Propositions of Economics and Interpersonal Comparisons of Utility," 49 *Economic Journal* (1939).

19. *United States v. Carroll Towing Company*, 159 F.2d 169 (2nd Cir. 1949).

20. These points were first developed in an important article on law and economics by R.H. Coase, "The Problem of Social Cost," 3 *The Journal of Law and Economics* (October 1960).

21. Richard Posner, *The Economic Analysis of Law* (Boston: Little, Brown and Company, 1973), develops these ideas in detail.

22. There would be other options, of course, including running at a moderate speed or adding more pollution control systems. But although complicating the case, these would not affect the basic approach taken by defenders of law and economics.

23. It is instructive that one of the leading exponents of this approach originally defended law and economics in explicitly utilitarian terms, but has since tried to defend it on contractualist and then pragmatic grounds as well. See Richard A. Posner, "Utilitarianism, Economics and Legal Theory," 8 *Journal of Legal Studies* 103 (1979) (defending utilitarianism as the basis of law and economics); "The Ethical and Political Basis of the Efficiency Norm in Common Law Adjudication," 8 *Hofstra Law Review* (1980) (defending social contract as the basis of law and economics); and *The Problems of Jurisprudence*, Chapter 12 (Cambridge: Harvard University Press, 1990) (defending pragmatism as the basis of law and economics).

24. Brandt, *A Theory of the Good and the Right* (1979) discusses these issues in detail and with great ingenuity.

25. The desire utilitarian may wish to discount or even ignore addictive desires because they will lead to illness and other situations that are not desired. My point here, however, is a different one, viz. that the bare fact that a desire is caused by chemical addiction calls into question whether fulfilling it increases the addict's over-all welfare. The fact that not giving the addict the drug causes the addict pain also seems relevant here, though that would be of interest to the experience theorist rather than the desire theorist.

26. For a useful discussion of the legal implications of preference adaptability, see Cass R. Sunstein, "Preferences and Politics," 20 *Philosophy and Public Affairs* 1 (Winter 1991).

27. The opposite can also happen, as people come to desire something more because they believe it is beyond their reach.

28. This illustration is from Derek Parfit, *Reasons and Persons* (Oxford: Oxford University Press, 1984), Appendix I.

29. I leave open the question whether or not this view would exclude the pleasant experiences of the sadist, drug addict, or adaptive person.

30. For an especially helpful discussion of these and the related issue of hedonism, see Shelly Kagan, "The Limits of Well-Being," 9 *Social Philosophy and Policy* 2 (Summer 1992).

31. I speak for convenience here of consequences flowing from actions, though I will argue shortly that it is the expected consequences of rules, not actions, that should finally be the focus of a utilitarian judge's concern.

32. I am not arguing here that such welfare calculations are the only factors people (especially judges) should consider in deciding what to do. In later sections, for example, we take up the question how following rules may also fit into the utilitarian's theory.

33. Amartya Sen proposed a kind of compromise between the desire and experience views, which he terms a "vector" theory. Welfare, he thinks, has *many different components* including pleasant experiences, fulfilled desires, and possibly others as well, and utilitarians should calculate the weighted sum of all those components (Amartya Sen, "Plural Utility," in *Proceedings of the Aristotelian Society* [1980–1981]). Though this might meet some of the objections I raised, it also brings its own problems, especially how these different, valuable components of welfare could be compared and combined with each other so that the utilitarian's goal of "maximizing" expected welfare could be achieved. It is also unclear, as I have said, that a sympathetic, benevolent person concerned to maximize welfare would care about fulfilling desires unless experiences are also at stake.

34. No regime is perfect, of course, so this should be seen to function as an ideal. Legitimate regimes will more closely approach the ideal than others.

35. 183 F.2d 201 (2d Cir. 1950).

36. *Dennis v. United States*, 183 F.2d 201, 206 (2d Cir. 1950).

37. It could be argued that a third stage is needed where a judge *evaluates* the quality of the different forms of desires or experiences she has identified and discounted. John Stuart Mill, for instance, thought some experiences were intrinsically less valuable than others. Pleasures derived from looking at obscene books or from insulting Jews by marching in Nazi costumes are good candidates for low evaluations. Others, however, would disagree with Mill and claim any enjoyment or fulfilled desire, considered by itself, is valuable.

38. Except in the sentencing phase of the trial, but that is because the *law* explicitly gives judges discretion to weigh the consequences of a long jail term on the defendant as well as on the rest of society.

39. We will look shortly at another important distinction the utilitarian judge must also make—between direct and indirect utilitarianism.

40. Richard B. Brandt, "The Real and Alleged Problems of Utilitarianism," in *The Hastings Center Report* (April 1983) at 38.

41. Rule utilitarians are therefore not rights skeptics, as I have understood the term, since they believe that legal rights are justified or not on substantive grounds of utility rather than historical intentions or democratic procedures.

42. In the next chapter I consider another, contractualist conception of moral rights—a view that belongs in the "natural rights" tradition of Locke, Rousseau, and Kant rather than the utilitarian tradition of Bentham and Mill.

43. Democratic government has often been defended by utilitarians and on a variety of different grounds. Prominent among the classical utilitarian defenders are of course: Jeremy Bentham, *Fragment of Government* (London: Payne, 1776); James Mill, "Essay on Government" (1820), in James Lively and Rush Rees, eds., *Utilitarian Logic and Politics* (Oxford: Oxford University Press, 1978); and John Stuart Mill, *Considerations on Representative Government* (1861), in J. Robson, ed., *Collected Works of J.S. Mill* (Toronto: University of Toronto Press and London: Routledge & Kegan Paul, 1977) vols. 18 and 19. For a helpful recent discussion of that topic, to which some of my remarks are indebted, see Jonathan Riley, "Utilitarian Ethics and Democratic Government," 100 *Ethics* (January 1990).

44. James Mill, "Essay on Government" (1820).

45. Alexis de Tocqueville, *Democracy in America*, P. Bradley, ed. (1835; reprint, New York: Vintage Books, 1945), vol. 1 at 247.

46. This utilitarian defense of democracy is suggested by John Hart Ely in *Democracy and Distrust* (Cambridge: Harvard University Press, 1980) at 157. A law is motivated by prejudice, he says, whenever the welfare of a particular group is not given "equal consideration."

47. See, for example, Peter Railton, "Alienation, Consequentialism and the Demands of Morality," 13 *Philosophy and Public Affairs* (Spring 1984); and David Brink, "Utilitarian Morality and the Personal Point of View," 83 *Journal of Philosophy* (1986).

48. We consider shortly whether the framers' intentions with respect to the Eighth Amendment would be important for the utilitarian.

49. For a clear illustration of this approach, see Justice Stewart's opinion for the majority upholding the death penalty in *Gregg v. Georgia*, 428 U.S. 153 (1976).

50. It does not matter to the utilitarian, of course, whether the framers thought executions were "cruel and unusual" punishment. The task is to find the best interpretation of the Eighth Amendment, not the one the framers thought best. In fact the framers plainly thought executions were *not* unconstitutional, for they envisioned their use in the due process clauses of both the Fifth and Fourteenth Amendments. These clauses forbid government from taking "*life*, liberty or property without due process of law" (emphasis added).

51. Isaac Erlich, "The Deterrence Effect of Capital Punishment: A Question of Life and Death," 65 *American Economic Review* 397 (June 1975).

52. David A. Conway, "Capital Punishment and Deterrence: Some Considerations In Dialogue Form," 3 *Philosophy and Public Affairs* (Summer 1974).

53. This was so called because it was first submitted by Louis Brandeis in *Muller v. Oregon*, 208 U.S. 412 (1908).

54. As will be discussed shortly, however, there may be other reasons that a utilitarian judge would heed the historical record.

55. Richard Posner argues in that way that much of the common law is compatible with the economic theory even though no central decision was made that it must evolve that way. See, for example, Richard Posner, *The Problems of Jurisprudence* (Cambridge: Harvard University Press, 1990), Chapter 12.

56. One especially striking recent example occurred when three conservative justices, one of whom had previously indicated an intention to overturn *Roe v. Wade,* refused to do so in large part based on concern for the political stature and integrity of the Court. *Planned Parenthood of Southeastern Pennsylvania v. Casey,* 112 S.Ct. 2791 (1992), opinion by Justices O'Connor, Kennedy, and Souter.

57. That same judge might, however, adopt the familiar maxim that she has more latitude in constitutional interpretation to ignore the original intent of the framers than in interpreting a statute. This could be because people will more readily accept (in the case of constitutional interpretation) the notion that the world is a very different place than it was two hundred years ago and that therefore the framers' views should be ignored or at least discounted.

58. Dworkin, "The Model of Rules," in *Taking Rights Seriously* (1978).

59. *Gregg v. Georgia,* 428 U.S. 153 (1976).

60. Jeremy Bentham, *An Introduction to the Principles of Morals and Legislation* (1789), chapter 10, part 4, section 40.

61. Thus, Justice Marshall argues in that same case that executions are unconstitutional because recent studies cast doubt on claims that they actually deter. See *Gregg v. Georgia* 428 U.S. 153 (1976), Justice Marshall, dissenting.

62. Whether Justice Brennan meant to defend the strong or moderate version is left open, as is the question of which is finally the best way to understand individual dignity.

Chapter 5

1. The social contract tradition, especially in Kant, Rousseau, and Locke, has of course been reinterpreted and extended by John Rawls. Though I differ from Rawls in important ways, and my primary concern is constitutional interpretation—an issue he largely ignored—his influence on this chapter will be made apparent as we proceed.

2. John Locke, *Two Treatises of Government* (Indianapolis IN: Hackett Publishing Co., 1983).

3. *Engel v. Vitale,* 370 U.S. 421 (1962).

4. *Pierce v. Society of Sisters,* 268 U.S. 510 (1925).

5. *Sherbert v. Verner,* 374 U.S. 368 (1963).

6. James Madison, "Memorial and Remonstrance Against Religious Assessments," in Gaillard Hunt, ed., *The Writings of James Madison* (New York: Putnam's Sons, 1904), vol. II at 188 (emphasis added).

7. *Lynch v. Donnelly,* 465 U.S. 668 (1984).

8. *Grand Rapids School District v. Ball,* 105 S.Ct. 3216 (1985).

9. *Lee v. Weisman,* 112 S.Ct. 2649 (1992).

10. *Collin v. Smith,* 578 F.2d 1197 (1978), holding that Nazis cannot be prevented from marching based on the offensiveness of their ideas or the possibility of violence.

11. *Hoffman Estates v. Flipside,* 455 U.S. 489 (1982), holding that government may require a license and detailed record keeping of sales of items for use with drugs.

12. *United States v. O'Brian,* 391 U.S. 367 (1968), holding that burning a draft card is not constitutionally protected speech.

13. *Texas v. Johnson,* 109 S.Ct. 2533 (1989), holding that burning the U.S. flag is a constitutionally protected expression under the First Amendment.

14. *Metromedia v. San Diego,* 453 U.S. 490 (1981), holding that a ban on virtually all outdoor advertising is unconstitutional. Some justices thought the ban was not content-neutral; others that the city had not demonstrated a serious commitment to "aesthetic concerns" necessary to justify such a restriction.

15. John Stuart Mill, *On Liberty,* ed. Elizabeth Rapaport (1859; reprint Indianapolis IN: Hackett Publishing Co., 1978) chapter II.

16. For example *Hudnut v. American Booksellers Association, Inc.,* 475 U.S. 1001 (1985).

17. *Whitney v. California,* 274 U.S. 357 (1927).

18. Joel Feinberg, "The Nature and Value of Rights," 4 *Journal of Value Inquiry* (1970) at 252.

19. James Madison, "Federalist Number 49," in Clinton Rossiter, ed., *The Federalist Papers* (New York: New American Library, 1961) at 313.

20. Letter from Thomas Jefferson to James Madison, Paris, September 6, 1789, in Andrew Lipscomb and Albert Bergh, eds., *The Writings of Thomas Jefferson* (Washington DC: Thomas Jefferson Memorial Association, 1903–1904), vol. VII at 454.

21. James Madison, "Federalist Number 49" in Rossiter, ed., *The Federalist Papers* (1961) at 316.

22. James Madison, letter to Thomas Jefferson, February 4, 1790, in Hunt, ed., *The Writings of James Madison* (1904) vol. V at 446 (emphasis in original).

23. In addition to the following, Madison also suggests in the letter to Jefferson that there may be no alternative but to suppose people give their "tacit" consent to acts of the majority. Given the vagueness of that notorious idea, along with his other thoughts on government that I describe below, it seems best to explore his understanding of consent in these hypothetical terms rather than in the literalist fashion I outlined in discussing original intent.

24. James Madison, "Memorial and Remonstrance Against Religious Assessments," in Hunt, ed., *The Writings of James Madison* (1904), vol. II at 185.

25. James Madison, "Memorial and Remonstrance Against Religious Assessments," in Hunt, ed., *The Writings of James Madison* (1904) Section 4 (references in original).

26. Max Farrand, ed., *Records of the Federal Convention of 1787*, vol. 1 (New Haven: Yale University Press, 1966) at 421 (emphasis added).

27. I leave aside, for historians, the question of the extent to which the U.S. Constitution, as some have argued, was not in fact the outcome of an impartial deliberative process but favored instead the interests of propertied white men. See, e.g., Charles A. Beard, *An Economic Interpretation of the Constitution of the United States* (New York: Free Press, 1913). That view has not gone uncriticized, however. Most notably, see Forest McDonald, *We the People: The Economic Origins of the Constitution* (Chicago: University of Chicago Press, 1958). My interest, rather, is in Madison's vision of the ideal process of constitutional choice and how that might inform our understanding of judicial review and constitutional interpretation.

28. Recalling Madison's concern that consent to the basic terms of the social contract must be "unanimous" if it is to do its work.

29. Immanuel Kant, "On the Proverb: That May Be True In Theory, But Is Of No Practical Use (1793)," in Ted Humphrey, trans., *Perpetual Peace and Other Essays* (1789; reprint Indianapolis IN: Hackett Publishing Co., 1983) at 77.

30. The discussion that follows is indebted to the work of T.M. Scanlon and especially John Rawls, though the account I give of the social contract and the motivating interests people have in choosing the terms of the social contract, including the Constitution, differs importantly from Rawls's well-known description of the original position. See especially John Rawls, "The Basic Liberties and Their Priority," in Sterling M. McMurring, ed., *The Tanner Lectures on Moral Philosophy: Liberty, Equality and Law* (Salt Lake City: University of Utah Press, 1987); John Rawls, "Social Unity and Primary Goods," in Amartya Sen and Bernard Williams, eds., *Utilitarianism and Beyond* (Cambridge: Cambridge University Press, 1982); John Rawls, "Kantian Constructivism in Moral Theory," 77 *Journal of Philosophy* (September 1980); John Rawls, "The Idea of an Overlapping Consensus," 7 *Oxford Journal of Legal Studies* 1 (Spring 1987); and especially John Rawls, *A Theory of Justice* (Cambridge: Harvard University Press, 1971). Rawls's writings since *A Theory of Justice* are revised and collected in *Political Liberalism* (New York: Columbia University Press, 1993). See also T.M. Scanlon, "Contractualism and Utilitarianism," in Amartya Sen and Bernard Williams, eds., *Utilitarianism and Beyond* (New York: Cambridge University Press, 1982).

31. Since it is likely there are different constitutional arrangements (e.g., the number of senators) that would be acceptable, the most accurate formulation is in terms of an agreement that nobody can reasonably reject instead of the one that everybody must accept. For ease of expression, however, I will sometimes speak of "the" contract rather than of a range of acceptable alternatives.

32. Rawls largely ignored questions of gender in his description of the social contractors' situation. For a very helpful discussion of the question of gender and its implications for the approach Rawls takes, including its importance to the family, justice, and relations between men and women, see Susan Moller Okin, *Justice, Gender and the Family* (New York: Basic Books, 1992).

33. For an extended discussion and defense of this view of contract law, see Charles Fried, *Contract as Promise* (Cambridge: Harvard University Press, 1981).

34. James Madison, "Memorial and Remonstrance Against Religious Assessments," in Hunt, ed., *The Writings of James Madison* (1904), vol. II at 189.

35. Rawls takes this view. See Rawls, "Kantian Constructivism in Moral Theory" (1980) and *Political Liberalism* (1993), Lecture III.

36. Allan Gibbard distinguishes impartiality from both reciprocity and mutual advantage. Although mutual advantage appeals to self-interest as the basis of contract and impartiality demands that the agreement be able to be defended to everybody, reciprocity requires that agreements be defended to others on grounds that participants *gain* from the social order. See Allan Gibbard, "Constructing Justice," 20 *Philosophy and Public Affairs* 3 (Summer 1991). Rawls agrees with Gibbard that his view expresses reciprocity; see Rawls, *Political Liberalism* (1993) at 17. One way to defend the contract to everybody, as impartiality requires, would be to show that everybody benefits from it, which would then require some benchmark against which to compare their current situation that Rawls envisioned as the absence of any agreement whatsoever. I will continue, however, to use the more familiar notion of impartiality. See also Scanlon, "Contractualism and Utilitarianism" (1982).

37. Rawls, *A Theory of Justice* (1971) at 104.

38. I owe this way of describing the motivation behind contractualism to T.M. Scanlon. See especially Scanlon, "Contractualism and Utilitarianism" (1982). See also in this connection Samuel Freeman, "Contractualism, Moral Motivation, and Practical Reason," LXXXVII *The Journal of Philosophy* 6 (June 1991).

39. In that way, democratic contractualism as I understand it differs importantly from John Rawls's account of the original position.

40. Rawls argues, of course, that there are three "special features" of this decision that make it rational for persons to "maximin," i.e., select the least bad outcome (Rawls, *A Theory of Justice* [1971] Section 26). For purposes of defending constitutional rights, however, this machinery is unnecessary since the intuitive argument for protecting them is strong as it stands.

41. This right has been developed by the Court under the general heading of privacy, though that is a somewhat misleading way to characterize what is at stake. As the Court has developed it, privacy includes both control of information and freedom to make certain critical choices about how one is to lead one's life.

42. Though religion, speech, privacy, and due process are the four major categories, other rights such as travel would also presumably be protected as well. In *Shapiro v. Thomson,* 394 U.S. 618 (1969), the Supreme Court upheld the right to travel despite the absence of explicit constitutional language supporting the right.

43. I here avoid the question whether they would go beyond providing a satisfactory minimum and adopt Rawls's "difference principle," viz., that economic inequalities are justified only if they benefit the least advantaged. Although important in considering taxation and related policies, that question is of less inter-

est, I will argue shortly, in weighing basic matters of constitutional design and fundamental rights.

44. I leave aside here the question of contractors wanting also to build into their constitutional structure the requirement that private harms like negligence and products liability also be compensated for. That there should be such requirements seems clear, though it is not obvious if it must be dealt with in the Constitution or left to legislatures. I discuss in a later section how a contractualist would approach these and other questions of constitutional design.

45. Rawls pays little attention to the distribution of political power in general and democratic processes in particular. It is an important advantage of the approach I am taking that it allows these important topics to be brought within a generally contractualist framework.

46. I say "primarily" here because, as I argue later, there *is* a sense in which democratic procedures can be defended on these grounds as well as those emphasized in the next paragraphs.

47. Though here, as elsewhere, there will be room for argument about many issues, including limits on voting rights such as youth, criminal record, or literacy, caps on campaign expenditures and contributions, and strategies to assure minority group representation, such controversies do not take anything away from the underlying connection between political participation and self-worth. More will be said about these questions in the next section.

48. Again, however, there is some room for disagreement about which characteristics are relevant. Should naturalized citizens be prevented from holding certain offices, for example?

49. But as I discuss below, this ideal cannot always be achieved in practice and must sometimes be compromised to secure other, more important goals. That fact, however, does not show that government may ignore its responsibility to promote citizens' sense of self-worth and dignity.

50. The following point relies on William Nelson's excellent discussion of democratic government in *On Justifying Democracy* (Boston: Routledge and Kegan Paul, 1980). See especially Chapter VI.

51. As will be discussed in the next section, contractualism also has the advantage over proceduralism that it can comfortably explain such anti-democratic features of the U.S. Constitution as separation of powers, federalism, and the executive veto as well as the non-proceduralist features of the judicial review.

52. John C. Harsanyi famously disputes this, arguing that the contractualist approach leads to utilitarianism. See "Cardinal Utility in Welfare Economics and in the Theory of Risk-Taking," 61 *Journal of Political Economy* 1553.

53. This point—that the utilitarian principle would not emerge from the contractualist approach—should not be confused with the different point that interpreters would do well to understand the constitution in contractualist terms and reject the (different) utilitarian vision based on sympathetic concern.

54. Samuel Freeman makes a similar point. See "Constitutional Democracy and the Legitimacy of Judicial Review" 9 *Law and Philosophy* (1990–91) at 356.

55. See John Rawls, "The Basic Structure as Subject," in 14 *American Philosophical Quarterly* (April 1977).

56. Note, however, that I am not claiming stability is a virtue of *all* political systems—only those that are reasonably just. A stable slave regime, for instance, is no more attractive than an unstable one merely because it is structured in a way that allows it to continue in the face of those who seek to change or undermine it.

57. Alexander Bickel, *The Least Dangerous Branch* (New Haven: Yale University Press, 1986). First published in 1962, Bickel's book set the stage for a generation of debate about constitutional interpretation.

58. Samuel Freeman discusses the possibility of defending judicial review in similar terms. Though this chapter was originally written before I saw his article, I have benefitted from his very thoughtful discussion of the issues. See Freeman, "Constitutional Democracy and the Legitimacy of Judicial Review" (1990–91).

59. As the U.S. Supreme Court's efforts to protect the right to contract during the turn-of-the-century Lochner Era illustrate, questions of property rights and freedom of contract once played a far larger role than they do today. Nothing in the contractualist's general approach, however, precludes the Court exercising judicial review in the way the Lochner Court did. To do so, however, would require a different understanding of the terms of the social contract than I have described—one that puts the right to property and freedom of contract beyond government regulation.

60. But as the dissenters argued in *San Antonio Independent School District v. Rodriguez*, 411 U.S. 1 (1973), and as I also argued in discussing strong democratic proceduralism, a powerful case can be made that equal educational opportunity *should* be given constitutional protection.

61. Those who, like Robert Bork, think that rights merely express preferences would deny the distinction between the right or best understanding of these principles and the one that the framers (or anybody else) happen to have. But because contractualists view natural rights differently, they would affirm rather than reject the distinction.

62. I describe in the paragraphs that follow in much more detail how these ideas would be filled out.

63. It is important to emphasize, however, that this depends crucially on the assumption that the legislation emerged from a genuinely free and open democratic process. To the extent that this is not the case and some citizens are denied the opportunity to participate as equals in the process, the presumption that legislation should be let stand is weakened.

64. See for example *Wisconsin v. Yoder*, 406 U.S. 205 (1972), holding that the state cannot force fourteen- and fifteen-year-old Amish children to attend public school. One of the issues in this case involved the conflicting rights of the children (to get an education) and of parents (to pass on their religious beliefs to their children).

65. Thus, the Court has insisted that government show a "compelling state interest" that cannot be protected in a way that is less restrictive of religious free-

dom if a law is to pass the test of the free exercise clause. See, for example, *Sherbert v. Verner,* 374 U.S. 398 (1963), holding that government cannot deny unemployment benefits to a person who was dismissed for refusing to work on Saturday.

66. Andrew Altman usefully terms such limits "epistemological neutrality" in that they "demarcate the boundaries of permissible politics." Andrew Altman, *Critical Legal Studies* (Cambridge: Cambridge University Press, 1990) at 73.

67. The term "neutral public discourse" has its roots in Kant, who speaks of "public reason." Immanuel Kant, "What is Enlightenment?" in Ted Humphrey, trans., *Perpetual Peace and Other Essays* (1784; reprint Indianapolis IN: Hackett Publishing Co., 1983). My discussion here is especially indebted to Rawls's discussion of public reason. See Rawls, "The Idea of an Overlapping Consensus" (1987) and, most recently, in *Political Liberalism* (1993) Lecture VI. Though I have benefitted greatly from these discussions, my understanding of neutral public discourse varies in many respects from Rawls's notion of public reason.

68. I owe this comparison to Rawls. See *Political Liberalism* (1993) at 218.

69. See for example William C. Mitchell, "Efficiency, Responsibility and Democratic Politics," in J. Roland Pennock and John W. Chapman, eds., *Liberal Democracy, Nomos XXV* (New York: New York University Press, 1983) at 343.

70. For a helpful discussion of these two ways of understanding democratic politics together with a criticism of the private or "market" model, see Jon Elster, "The Market and the Forum: Three Varieties of Political Theory," in Jon Elster and Aanund Hylland, eds., *Foundations in Social Choice Theory* (Cambridge: Cambridge University Press, 1986) at 103.

71. This is again similar to what Andrew Altman terms "epistemological neutrality." Altman, *Critical Legal Studies* (1990) at 73.

72. The reference to "discourse" should not therefore be taken to refer only to what can be *said*. It also limits what government may *do* by insisting that the justifications for what is done be of a certain sort. In that way, the purpose or intent of the legislation, and therefore the legislation itself, may be rejected based on its failure to meet the requirements of neutral public discourse.

73. The idea that officials such as legislators and judges should ignore their own, personal interests is hardly controversial; political corruption is the term normally used to describe decisions made in light of such considerations. It is less obvious, however, that voters and others attempting to influence officials should respect such limits.

74. Cass Sunstein argues, for instance, that an important function of judicial review is to ensure that "something other than a naked preference for one person or group over another" lies behind legislation ("Naked Preferences and the Constitution," 84 *Columbia Law Review* 1689 [1984] at 1713).

75. Whether the argument actually meets, or is even seriously meant to meet, the standards of neutral public discourse is another question, of course. But as I discuss in the following paragraphs, the fact that a limit is not always followed is no evidence the norm does not exist, much less that it is unjustified.

76. Many have of course seen democratic politics in that way, though the classic statement (in modern times, at least) comes from Joseph Schumpeter, *Capitalism, Socialism and Democracy*, 3rd. ed. (New York: Harper and Row, 1950). Schumpeter assimilates democratic politics into a market in which leaders compete for votes among people who, though largely uninformed, are also assumed in voting to express their interests rather than considered judgments.

77. See for example Lawrence H. Tribe, *American Constitutional Law*, 2nd ed. (Mineola NY: The Foundation Press, 1988) at 581–584.

78. Tribe, *American Constitutional Law* (1988) at 583.

79. *Mathews v. DeCastro*, 429 U.S. 181 (1976) at 185, quoting *Helvering v. Davis*, 301 U.S. 619 (1937) at 640.

80. Ronald Dworkin and Bruce Ackerman defend positions similar to this. See Ronald Dworkin, *A Matter of Principle* (Cambridge: Harvard University Press, 1985), Chapter 8; and Bruce Ackerman, *Social Justice and the Liberal State* (New Haven: Yale University Press, 1980), Chapter 1.

81. H.L.A. Hart, *The Concept of Law* (Oxford: Oxford University Press, 1961) at 177–180.

82. Hart, *The Concept of Law* (1961) at 178.

83. *Smith v. Board of School Commissioners of Mobile County*, 827 F. 2d. (11th Cir. 1987).

84. What I am terming methodological neutrality is discussed by John Rawls in "The Idea of an Overlapping Consensus" (1987) and, especially, in *Political Liberalism* (1993), Lecture VI. Bruce Ackerman also mentions it in speaking of the liberal state as being "deprived of divine revelation" (*Justice and the Liberal State* [1980] at 103), though he does not distinguish clearly, as I do, between the requirement that politics avoid moral ideals and the demand that it rely only on public methods of argument.

85. Kent Greenawalt, *Religious Convictions and Political Choice* (New York: Oxford University Press, 1988), discusses this distinction at 54–55.

86. Bruce Ackerman argued ("Why Dialogue?" LXXXVI *The Journal of Philosophy* 1 [January 1989]) that we should rely only on "premises" or "propositions" that are commonly shared. But I find his suggestion mysterious since he does not distinguish, as I do here, between the limits based on content and on method. If, as he suggests, we can only use "propositions" that are common, then it is unclear that there would be any disagreements at all, much less how we could talk about them. But if he is thinking of common "premises" then perhaps he means common methods of reasoning, as I described.

87. Greenawalt, *Religious Convictions and Political Choice* (1988), Chapter 12.

88. Rawls thinks that neutrality applies only when people "engage in political advocacy in the public forum" and not to their "personal deliberations and reflections about political questions" (Rawls, *Political Liberalism* [1993] at 215). The reason for this, he says, is that otherwise political discussion runs the risk of being "hypocritical." He is of course right about that risk, as I have noted. But the alternative view Rawls adopts only increases the hypocrisy since people's public pro-

nouncements could be at odds with the private reasons that actually provide the basis of their judgments. It seems to me better in both the theoretical and practical sense for people to come to see the limits on democratic politics as not just constraining what they can utter in public but also how they should think about politics. In that sense, I agree with Robert Audi that the secular reasons should actually be the reasons people have and that those who speak or vote for other (religious, in his case) reasons violate an important moral obligation. See Robert Audi, "The Separation of Church and State," 18 *Philosophy and Public Affairs* 3 (Summer 1989) at 279.

89. Rawls, *Political Liberalism* (1993) at 223–230.

90. Kent Greenawalt argues this in areas of animal rights, environmental policy, and abortion. See Greenawalt, *Religious Convictions and Political Choice* (1988), Chapters 6 and 7.

91. It might be argued, however, that such expenditures in fact benefit everybody, including those who find little of direct value in opera, symphonies, and poetry. Musical comedies and popular music, for example, often owe much to opera and the great composers. Or it might be argued that public financing is necessary to secure these as options, while popular culture can survive on its own. Insofar as that is true, however, public expenditures on the arts need not depend on the assumption that those who watch only television lead less valuable lives but instead that these expenditures are necessary to a flourishing, diverse artistic tradition that benefits everybody.

92. Ronald Dworkin argues that because judicial review is vital to the U.S. system, those who disobey laws out of conscience perform the important political role of testing a law's constitutionality and, therefore, that it is a mistake to think they must be prosecuted on grounds that their behavior is no different from an ordinary criminal's. See Ronald Dworkin, "Civil Disobedience," in *Taking Rights Seriously* (Cambridge: Harvard University Press, 1977).

93. I assume here that there would be no reason for a democratic contractualist to object to criminal laws as long as they are enforced without violating basic rights and other contractualist principles.

94. And, as we have seen, that is just how the Court approached the question. It held that the critical constitutional question is whether such punishment is "excessive" and concluded, controversially, that legislatures may reasonably believe executions serve a legitimate purpose. See *Gregg v. Georgia*, 428 U.S. 153 (1976); opinion by Justice Stewart, who argued that it is not excessive, and dissent by Justice Marshall, who argued that it is excessive.

95. As Robert Bork, among others, aggressively argues. See Robert Bork, "Judicial Moral Philosophy and the Right of Privacy," in *The Tempting of America: The Political Seduction of Law* (New York: The Free Press, 1990).

96. As we noted in Chapter 2, it is sometimes suggested that the Ninth Amendment's purpose is only to emphasize that powers of Congress are enumerated and therefore that the existence of specific rights in the document does not mean Congress has power to do *everything but* what is explicitly prevented. But the

Tenth Amendment says exactly that, only less ambiguously: "The powers not delegated to the United States by the Constitution, nor prohibited by it to the States,
are reserved to the States respectively, or to the people." Why, then, would the
Constitution repeat itself, as it would do if this narrow reading of the Ninth were
adopted? Nevertheless, the Ninth Amendment also does not say that it is the Supreme Court's responsibility to protect these rights that are "retained" by the
people, although it seems odd that such a provision would be included in the
Constitution without any provision for meeting the commitment. Essays taking
various sides of these issues are collected in Randy E. Barnett, ed., *The Rights Retained by the People: The History and Meaning of the Ninth Amendment* (Fairfax
VA: George Mason University Press, 1989).

97. In one well-known constitutional law text, the authors list thirteen rights,
all unenumerated, that are currently recognized by the courts. These include, in
addition to the right to privacy, the right to vote, the right to the presumption of
innocence and requirement of proof beyond a reasonable doubt in criminal cases,
the right to equal protection from the federal government as well as states, the
right to associate with others, to travel, to marry or not to marry, to have children
and to educate them (both within reasonable limits), and to pursue a profession.
See Walter Murphy, James Fleming, and William Harris, *American Constitutional
Interpretation* (Mineola NY: The Foundation Press, 1986) at 1084.

98. *NAACP v. Alabama,* 357 U.S. 449 (1958).

99. For Warren and Brandeis, the right to privacy was different and more narrow than it has now become. It involved the right to protect one's thoughts and
emotions against public view, not freedom of action in personal matters such as
the home, family, and reproduction as the Supreme Court has more recently held.

100. Samuel Warren and Louis Brandeis, "The Right to Privacy," 4 *Harvard Law
Review* 193 (1890).

101. *Olmstead v. United States,* 277 U.S. 438 (1928). Interestingly, Brandeis and
Warren used the same phrase in their article on privacy, attributing it to Thomas
Cooley, *Cooley on Torts,* 2nd ed. (Chicago: Callaghan, 1880) at 29.

102. *Griswold v. Connecticut,* 381 U.S. 479 (1965).

103. I am not arguing by these brief remarks that privacy is, in fact, included
among the unenumerated rights but only suggesting the general form of argument a contractualist might use to establish such a claim.

104. Brief of Attorney General Michael Bowers in *Bowers v. Hardwick,* 478 U.S.
186 (1986) at 37. In an opinion by Justice White, the Supreme Court upheld the
constitutionality of the law, largely on grounds that privacy protects traditional
values like home and family and not homosexuality. Legislatures, he said, may legitimately impose that moral judgment. The dissenting opinion by Justice
Blackmun, however, reflected a clearly contractualist approach.

105. Both of these illegitimate premises have played a role, however, in arguments of conservative defenders of the pro-life position and feminist proponents
of pro-choice. For a discussion, see "Abortion," in John Arthur, *The Unfinished
Constitution* (Belmont CA: Wadsworth Publishing Co., 1989).

106. Among the works most directly relevant to the problems I discuss here are: Catharine A. MacKinnon, *Feminism Unmodified* (Cambridge: Harvard University Press, 1987); Catharine A. MacKinnon, *Toward a Feminist Theory of the State* (Cambridge: Harvard University Press, 1989); Robin West, "Jurisprudence and Gender," 55 *University of Chicago Law Review* (1988); Martha Minow, "Justice Engendered," 101 *Harvard Law Review* 10 (1987); and Wendy W. Williams, "The Equality Crisis: Some Reflections on Culture, Courts, and Feminism," 7 *Women's Rights Law Reporter* 175 (1982).

107. Minow, "Justice Engendered" (1987) at 32–33. Minow also sometimes expresses skepticism about claims that any single position or viewpoint is "neutral" rather than merely "a perspective." Yet at the same time she praises judges and others who succeed at understanding the perspective of others, suggesting again that her ideals may not be as impractical as some of her remarks may suggest. So although she does not explicitly say so, Minow may share the concerns I discuss shortly about the impossibility of ever achieving true impartiality.

108. Minow, "Justice Engendered" (1987) at 95.

109. It should also be emphasized that there is nothing in the contractualist's position requiring its defender to take lightly the problems of economic inequality, racial prejudice, and gender discrimination its critics sometimes emphasize. Indeed, it is clear that contractualism provides a vantage point from which to attack such problems. For an especially good discussion of these implications of contractualism, see Thomas W. Pogge, *Realizing Rawls* (Ithaca: Cornell University Press, 1989).

110. Minow, "Justice Engendered" (1987) at 72–73.

111. MacKinnon, *Toward a Feminist Theory of the State* (1989) at 162.

112. Most notoriously, perhaps, in *Lochner v. New York*, 198 U.S. 45 (1905) (overturning state law establishing minimum hours for bakers on the ground that this infringes the liberty of contract) and *Coppage v. Kansas*, 236 U.S. 1 (1915) (overturning state law banning "yellow dog" contracts that require employees to agree not to join a union as a condition of employment on the same ground). In each case, the justices appear to assume that such legislative regulations constitute unacceptable "political" interference into the neutral objective working of the market.

113. Despite their emphasis on neutrality at the interpretive level, originalists and democratic proceduralists rest, ultimately, on the deeper and decidedly nonneutral premise that their account of judicial review and constitutional democracy is sounder, morally and politically, than the alternatives.

114. Robin West argues this forcefully in "Jurisprudence and Gender" (1988).

115. This is a familiar theme in much recent feminist writing, and it owes much to Carol Gilligan's well-known studies of the moral development of girls. See Carol Gilligan, *In a Different Voice* (Cambridge: Harvard University Press, 1982). Elizabeth Wolgast was an early exponent of this thought. In 1980, two years before Gilligan's book, she wrote, "We [feminists] need a model that acknowledges ... other kinds of interest than self-interest" (Elizabeth Wolgast, *Equality and the*

Rights of Women [Ithaca: Cornell University Press, 1980] at 156). For more recent, legally oriented discussions of these issues see especially Joan C. Williams, "Deconstructing Gender," 87 *Michigan Law Review* 797 (1989).

116. This is a point that has been pressed not only by feminists but also by many men who argue that the model of "possessive individualism" is an inaccurate account of the person generally and not just of women. For a helpful discussion of these and other issues I have been addressing here from the feminist perspective, see Iris Marion Young, *Justice and the Politics of Difference* (Princeton: Princeton University Press, 1990), especially Chapter 4; and West, "Jurisprudence and Gender" (1988). Chief among the "communitarian" critics of liberalism is Michael J. Sandel, *Liberalism and the Limits of Justice* (Cambridge: Cambridge University Press, 1982), and "The Procedural Republic and the Unencumbered Self," 12 *Political Theory* 1 (1984).

117. As Rawls himself often points out. See, for example, "The Basic Structure as Subject" (1978) and *Political Liberalism* (1993) at 27.

118. Recent work by communitarians often miss this important point. See for example Sandel, *Liberalism and the Limits of Justice* (1982), Chapter 1; Alasdair MacIntyre, "Is Patriotism a Virtue?" (The Lindley Lecture, University of Kansas, 1984), and *After Virtue* (South Bend IN: University of Notre Dame Press, 1981), Chapter 17.

119. Karl Marx stresses the distinction, which he finds inherent in liberalism, between the "abstract" vision of the person in the liberal vision of government and the other, fuller conception found in civil society. But while Marx takes the distinction to indicate a weakness of liberalism, I have argued that it is a source of liberalism's strength. See, for example, Karl Marx, "On the Jewish Question" (1843), in Robert C. Tucker, ed., *The Marx-Engels Reader* (New York: Norton Company, 1972) at 24.

120. West, "Jurisprudence and Gender" (1988).

121. MacKinnon famously argues, for example, that heterosexual intercourse is like rape and that pornography should be banned (legally) as part of a strategy to protect women against rape. See, for example, MacKinnon, "Rape: On Coercion and Consent," in *Toward a Feminist Theory of the State* (1989), and *Only Words* (Cambridge: Harvard University Press, 1993).

122. For an interesting account of community that I believe is consistent with the democratic contractualist model, see Ronald Dworkin, "Liberal Community," 77 *California Law Review* 3 (May 1989), and *Law's Empire* (Cambridge: Harvard University Press, 1986), chapter 6.

123. Gibbard, "Constructing Justice" (1991) at 264–267. As noted above, Gibbard distinguishes both impartiality and reciprocity from agreements made based only on the fact that the parties each gain (mutual advantage). Impartiality, he argues, requires that choices be able to be defended to others and does not demand, as reciprocity would, that everybody also gain from the agreement. I have spoken throughout of impartiality, rather than reciprocity, though as I indicated earlier (note 36) I do not think anything depends here on the distinction. But it is

important, as I have stressed, to understand that democratic contractualism is not founded simply on mutual advantage: The social contract is not justified egoistically, as it would be if it rested on that more Hobbesian picture. Instead it is based on the ideal that its terms can be defended to all, viewed as free and independent equals (impartiality) and that all share in the benefits of social cooperation (reciprocity).

124. Nor, as I have indicated, is contractualism committed to the libertarian, market-oriented vision of government sometimes associated with classical liberalism. Indeed, I have argued, the democratic contractualist would go far beyond the mere protection of rights against the interference of others to protect further rights including the provision for a satisfactory economic minimum, unemployment and other social welfare legislation, fair equality of educational opportunity, and an equal opportunity to participate in the democratic political process. To equate "liberalism" with libertarianism and the refusal to acknowledge such economic and other rights of recipience ignores much of importance in the philosophical tradition, including utilitarianism and democratic contractualism.

125. Abraham Lincoln, speaking in Springfield, Illinois, June 26, 1857. John G. Nicolay and John Hay, eds., *Abraham Lincoln, Complete Works* (New York: The Century Co., 1894) at 338.

About the Book and Author

The words of the U.S. Constitution limit the possibilities of political action: they bind us in certain ways. How they bind us, however, depends upon how these words are interpreted and upon the distinctively American practice of judicial review.

In *Words That Bind*, John Arthur examines conflicting theories of constitutional interpretation and judicial review, arguing that each of the dominant legal approaches—from original intent to law and economics, from legal pragmatism to Critical Legal Studies—rests on a distinct philosophical conception of democracy.

Turning to recent work in political philosophy, Arthur explores the important but oft-ignored implications of both utilitarianism and social contract theory for constitutional interpretation and judicial review. He addresses such important and contested issues as the justification of rights, the rule of law, popular consent, equality, and feminist constitutional theory. The book makes an especially significant contribution through the fruitful interaction of two traditions: constitutional jurisprudence and contemporary political theory.

Words That Bind presents a careful and nuanced treatment of a set of ideas and institutional forms absolutely central to U.S. democracy. Arguing that neither legal theory nor political philosophy can proceed independently of the other, Arthur illuminates both topics as no other recent author has.

John Arthur is professor of philosophy and director of the Program in Philosophy, Politics, and Law at Binghamton University. He is the author of *The Unfinished Constitution* (1989) as well as numerous articles in legal and political theory. He has also edited several books including, most recently, *Campus Wars: Multiculturalism and the Politics of Difference* (Westview, 1995, coedited with Amy Shapiro). In 1992 he was awarded the SUNY Chancellor's and Binghamton University awards for excellence in teaching.

Table of Cases

Index